Spring 79

IRISH CULTURE &
DEPTH PSYCHOLOGY

A JOURNAL OF
ARCHETYPE
AND
CULTURE

Spring 2008

SPRING JOURNAL
New Orleans, Louisiana

CONTENTS

ANCIENT IRELAND: MYTH AND MAGIC

MODERN IRELAND: WORDS AND MUSIC

CONTEMPORARY IRELAND: PRESENT-DAY BARDS, IRISH ART, AND THE CELTIC TIGER

IRISH AMERICANS: LONGING FOR HOME

JUNGIANA

FILM REVIEWS

BOOK REVIEWS

ANCIENT IRELAND:
MYTH AND MAGIC

THIN PLACES AND THIN TIMES

JERRY R. WRIGHT

ONCE UPON A TIME ... according to Irish and Celtic storytellers, the visible and invisible worlds were one. Matter and spirit were intertwined, and human beings and gods and goddesses cavorted together. However, this commingling was confusing to mortals who needed separation in order to know what was "real" and "unreal." Out of compassion for the human dilemma, the creative Powers hung a great curtain between the visible and invisible worlds.[1] Furthermore, to encourage the continuing dialogue and relationship between the parties, there were certain places where the curtain remained very thin and certain times when the traffic through the curtain was especially heavy. These highly-charged places and times came to be known as *thin places* and *thin times*.

The experience of the world as *thin*—where the visible and invisible tumble into each other and where a visitor from the otherworld may

Jerry R. Wright is a Jungian analyst in private practice in Decatur, Georgia and Flat Rock, North Carolina and a graduate of the Inter-Regional Society of Jungian Analysts. He is on the faculty of the Haden Institute for Training in Spiritual Direction and Dreamwork. In addition, he gives lectures and workshops on themes related to the integration of Jungian psychology and spirituality, and organizes and leads pilgrimages to sacred sites.

appear at any ordinary place or moment—has shaped Irish mythology, literature, and culture and continues to fertilize the Irish imagination. From this perspective, the Irish landscape and soul are very *thin*, which may account in large measure for the enduring fascination and love affair with all things Irish. In a similar vein, as this article will explore, the soul of analytical psychology can be imaged as *thin*, since its theory and clinical practice honor the continuous interplay between the visible and invisible, conscious and unconscious. Seen through the lens of this archetypal image, Jungian analysis involves the careful attention to the experiences of *thin places/times* within client and analyst, and between them, which facilitates the processes of transformation and individuation. Learning to move back and forth through the imaginal curtain between conscious and unconscious, thereby honoring the seamless connection between matter and spirit, constitutes a primary task of being a Jungian analyst. Widening the lens, it also describes the task of the modern religious person.

Thin Places/Times in Irish and Celtic Lore

Other Irish myths chronicle with greater detail how Ireland came to be regarded as *thin*. One account tells how the Tuatha De Danann, the original mythological inhabitants of Ireland, took up residence in the otherworld, that invisible domain which runs close to, and contiguous with, the visible. After an extended battle with the invading Milesians, who were Celts, a compromise was reached. It was decided that the Celts would rule the visible parts of Ireland while the Dananns would take possession of the invisible regions, sometimes imaged as being just below ground and other times just beyond the seas.[2] Contrary to the modern dualistic worldview which separates matter/spirit and physical/spiritual, however, the two domains were of one fabric. Their distinction had to do with what was seen or unseen.

The invisible otherworld was accessible through *thin places* in the natural landscape such as unusual stone formations, special trees, caves, wells, springs, and other portals such as the *sidhe*, or fairy-mounds, the countless prehistoric burial mounds dotting the Irish landscape. Other places of human construction such as Stonehenge and the tomb at Newgrange were portals to and from the otherworld, as well. Scattered throughout Ireland and the British Isles, these were places where one experienced "a very thin divide between past, present, and future," and encountered an ancient reality in the present moment.[3]

Not only did the Celts experience contact with the otherworld in highly-charged places, they were attuned to *thin times*, which were special seasons, festivals, and life events like birth and death, when the curtain between the two domains seemed especially transparent. Most notable was the festival of Samhain, the Celtic New Year (November 1), when the usually thin curtain all but disappeared resulting in an environment which was both festive and dangerous. The eve of Samhain was an in-between time, neither summer nor winter, neither light nor dark, and in this borderland time the supernatural had the greatest power to influence the lives of mortals.[4] Because the boundaries between time were lifted, Samhain was thought to be the occasion for divination to discover who might die in the coming year, or marry, and who might be one's bride or groom.[5] It was the night when the fairy-mounds opened and spirits appeared, often in disguise. This Celtic celebration survives to the present day as Halloween, the night when spooks and goblins roam around, and treats are given to appease the visitors from the otherworld who might otherwise provide an unsavory trick. The modern tradition of wearing masks or disguises (*guizing*) at Halloween is rooted in this ancient *thin time* festival.[6]

On a recent pilgrimage to Ireland which included several days on the Aran Islands off the rugged western coast, our group was intrigued listening to the locals talk about the continuing celebration of Samhain. All the homes and dwellings are opened that night and the islanders, disguised, are free to roam through the homes of their neighbors, usually without speaking. To us Americans who vigilantly guard our homes and belongings, and dismiss Halloween goblins at the door with treats of candy, hearing how our Aran hosts celebrate Samhain was spooky, indeed.

The Tuatha De Danann carried on their lives of feasting and merriment just out of sight of Celtic life but were always at liberty to interfere in human affairs if they so desired. They were thought to possess superior intelligence in certain arenas and had power over the fertility of the land. They were, therefore, in a position to make life easy or difficult for mere mortals. This gave rise to a plethora of rituals to honor or placate the invisible ones such as the "trick or treat" transaction mentioned above. In addition, the Celts regularly left offerings and sacrifices at *thin places* such as crossroads and holy wells and springs. To the present day, the trees and shrubs around Irish holy wells and springs are bedecked with colorful offerings of string, ribbon, and other gifts left by faithful pilgrims to honor the ancient spirits who continue to inhabit the sacred sites. Another interesting placatory ritual involved milking the first couple of strokes from the cow onto the ground, rather than into the bucket, as an offering to the fairies.[7]

It should be noted that the occupants of the otherworld in Irish lore have numerous appellations in addition to the Tuatha De Danann. In his masterful *Irish Fairy and Folk Tales*, William Butler Yeats notes that they are sometimes called banshees, the gentry, the gods of pagan Ireland, or "fallen angels who were not good enough to be saved, nor bad enough to be lost!" Do not think the fairies are always little, he cautions, for they seem to take whatever size or shape pleases them. Their chief occupations are feasting, fighting, making love, and playing the most beautiful music. Yeats concludes,

> They have only one industrious person among them, the *leprechaun*—the shoemaker. Perhaps they wear their shoes out with the dancing! Near the village of Ballisodare is a little woman who lived among them for seven years. When she came home she had no toes—she had danced them off.[8]

The inhabitants of the otherworld were also believed to have certain paths in the visible world along which they walked. Often referred to as fairy paths, or *trods,* they were barely visible to mortals, sometimes a deeper shade of green or circular or labyrinthine. People seeking relief from particular ailments could walk these *thin places*, but were warned to avoid them at times when the otherworldly beings were using them. Should a Celt meet a procession of fairies on the path and not move aside, it could prove fatal. Likewise, to build a dwelling on one of the paths could prove disastrous.[9] On the aforementioned pilgrimage to Ireland, we read with interest the newspaper account of a major squabble between a housing developer and local residents. At issue was a huge boulder long held to be a fairy dwelling, or *thin place*, a portal to the otherworld. The locals won the fight and the boulder was left undisturbed.

Modern Irish storytelling abounds with ordinary people who hear songs of merriment of the fairy folk and are taken into or slip into the twilight of the otherworld. In *The Celtic Twilight*, Yeats recalls such an encounter as he walked along the seashore, a notable *thin place*, with a young girl. She heard laughing, singing, and fairy music and saw the "good people" dancing at the mouth of a cave. Yeats and the young girl fell into a "kind of trance, in which what we call the unreal had begun to take upon itself a masterful reality."[10] While walking along on an ordinary day, both had found a threshold to the otherworld.

Living with a finely tuned *thin place/time* attitude, the Celts had a particular fondness for places and conditions that were "betwixt and between," such as twilight, dawn and dusk, mist, fogs and bogs. Crossroads, borderlands, and places or conditions marked by ambiguity, paradox, or fluidity, where the imaginal curtain was deemed particularly threadbare, were especially highly charged. This preference for "threshold consciousness" reveals itself in the love story of Diarmaid and Grainne. Diarmaid tells his bride-to-be that he will not accept her unless she comes to him under certain, nearly impossible, conditions. One version of his requirements was, "I will not take you either by day or by night, clothed or unclothed, on foot or on horseback, neither within nor without." Grainne seeks help from a fairy woman who gives the young girl clothing made from mountain flowers. She appears to her potential groom, then, at dusk riding a goat. When she is in the doorway, she announces herself, "I am not without nor within; I am not on foot nor horseback; I am not clothed nor unclothed; it is neither day nor night." She had answered the riddle, and won her husband.[11]

Finally, the experiences surrounding death, wakes, and funerals were considered to be especially *thin times*. On the occasion of death, not only did the deceased move through the curtain, but the spirits of deceased ancestors were free to revisit their old homesteads. Furthermore, the living and the dead could communicate at burial places and the deceased could intervene on behalf of the living, which later became part of the meaning of the communion of saints. In preparation for their final crossover at death, many Celts sought out *thin places* which they designated as "a place of resurrection," a particular portal back through the curtain through which they had been birthed years before.[12]

Thus, the circle of life and death was seamless, which preserved the perspective of the world as a unified whole with no distinction between matter and spirit, or between physical and spiritual, except for what was seen and unseen. Margo Adler, in *Drawing Down The Moon*, summarizes the Celtic perspective:

> The world is holy. Nature is holy. The body is holy. Sexuality is holy. The mind is holy. The imagination is holy. You are holy. Divinity is imminent in all nature. It is as much within you as without.[13]

Thin Experiences in Analytical Psychology

In his writings Carl Jung made frequent allusions to the archetypal image of the *thin place/time*. Describing himself, Jung said, "The difference between most people and myself is that for me the *dividing walls* are transparent. This is my peculiarity."[14] Referring to his near fatal illness when he was in his late sixties, Jung claims in one of his letters that it provided him with "the inestimable opportunity of a glimpse behind the veil." Again, referring to the protective walls which the modern ego erects out of fear of "mystical" experiences, he notes that the walls prove to be very *thin* against the energies of the deep unconscious.[15]

Echoing the Celtic concern to honor the inhabitants of the otherworld, and the potential consequences of neglecting them, Jung reminds us that when the unconscious powers are no longer mediated because of neglect or repression, they form an ever present and destructive shadow. Using a companion metaphor, he notes that when the powers are neglected "the gates of the psychic underworld are thrown open," resulting in all forms of dis-ease, personal neurosis, or collective disorientation, dissociation, violence, and war.[16]

Furthermore, Jung built his theoretical psychological house on the foundation of *thin* experiences called *numinous*, a descriptive word coined by Rudolph Otto in his 1923 book, *The Idea Of The Holy*.[17] From the Latin words *numen* (a god) and *neure* (to nod), a numinous experience is likened to "a nod from the gods," which is reminiscent of the encounters with the otherworld spoken of thus far. Otto's description of the *mysterium tremendum*, and the "holy dread" which often accompanies numinous experiences, provided Jung with a way to make meaning of his experiences of the otherworld which, of course, he called the unconscious. In *Memories, Dreams, Reflections*, Jung describes in great detail his strange and uncanny experiences throughout his childhood, as well as during his descent into the unconscious following his break with Freud. His discovery of Otto's work was, therefore, especially significant.

The experience of the numinous, or numinosum, became the foundation on which Jung built his psychological house, including his consideration of the interplay between psychology and religion, and his concern for loss of soul and its recovery. With an experiential grasp of the numinous, one can appreciate Jung's unique contribution to depth psychology and to religious experience. Without that, the uniqueness of his work may very well be lost.

In his Terry Lectures at Yale University in 1937, Jung spoke at length about the meaning of the word "religion," describing it as "a careful and scrupulous observation of what Rudolph Otto aptly termed the *numinosum*;" and religion "designates the attitude peculiar to a consciousness which has been changed by experience of the *numinosum*."[18] Giving even a greater nod to the centrality of numinous experiences, in his 1945 letter to Mr. P. W. Martin, Jung wrote,

> You are quite right, the main interest of my work is not concerned with the treatment of neurosis but rather with the approach to the numinous. But the fact is that the approach to the numinous is the real therapy and inasmuch as you attain to the numinous experiences you are released from the curse of pathology.[19]

Underlying Jung's psychological reflections was what he referred to as a "religious outlook" or "attitude." In his now-famous observation about patients in the second half of life, he identified the loss of a religious outlook as a key component of their illness, and then declared that "none of them has really been healed who did not regain his religious outlook."[20] Jung's own religious attitude grew out of his encounters with the numinous in the form of images, thoughts, and feelings which he felt were forced upon him by some mysterious other which his ego had not conjured, but to which his ego had to bow. The powerful experiences of the other came upon him unbidden, unexpected, unannounced, and often in unconventional ways. However they appeared, Jung knew that these encounters came from some source beyond or outside the ego, from some invisible dimension which had its own life, power, and autonomy. Recognizing, engaging, and honoring these encounters constituted Jung's religious attitude, an "attitude which meets a transcendent reality halfway."[21] That same attitude could be called a *thin place/time* attitude.

Numerous other *thin place/time* analogues are apparent in analytical psychology. Most obvious is the imaginal space between conscious and unconscious, that delightful and dangerous threshold which is so heavily traveled day and night. In his essay on synchronicity, Jung describes the archetypal affective conditions which produce a partial *abaissement du niveau mental*, a lowering of the threshold of consciousness. This in turn "gives the unconscious a favorable opportunity to slip into the *space vacated*."[22] In the language of this article, the *space vacated* is the psychological *thin place* where the numinous contents from the unconscious make their appearance. The *abaissement* produces an opening in the curtain which normally separates conscious and unconscious contents. In this imaginal space "unexpected or otherwise inhibited unconscious contents break though and find expression."[23] This dynamic is reminiscent of Samhain when the doors between the visible and invisible were opened wide and spirits and mortals intermingled.

One of the most powerful *thin places* in clinical practice is, of course, the interpersonal space between analyst and analysand which, again, can be delightful and/or dangerous. Into this space pour the energies of the unconscious, personal and archetypal, in all their guises and valences, and each, like the inhabitants of the Celtic otherworld, require attention and honor lest they pull an unsavory trick. In the transference and countertransference relationship, both analysand and analyst are affectively involved and, therefore, both are potentially transformed by the analytic *thin place/time*.

Jung addressed this powerful interpersonal, interactive field in *The Psychology of The Transference*. Furthermore, at times he even "placed" the unconscious psyche in the intermediate zone between analyst and analysand. For example, in replying to a letter from a colleague who asked why dreams of a certain patient seemed to be referring to the analyst, Jung replied, "In the deepest sense we all dream not *out of ourselves* but out of what lies *between us and the other*."[24]

Other depth psychologists and analysts have written extensively about the powerful encounters and psychological dynamics which occur at the imaginal threshold, including Donald Kalsched, James Hollis, Murray Stein, and D. W. Winnicott.[25] The soulful writings of John

O'Donohue and Philip Newell, both authorities on Celtic spirituality, also honor the transformative encounters at the threshold that connects the visible and invisible.[26]

A final consideration of *thin places/times* in analytical psychology and its clinical practice concerns the necessity of honoring these sacred encounters. Drawing from the wisdom of our Irish and Celtic ancestors, it is imperative that the invisible powers receive some kind of ritual acknowledgement or offering. Otherwise, we open ourselves to the possibility of a psychological inflation or deflation. While there are countless ways to acknowledge the numinous encounters at *thin places/times*, they may be summarized with one metaphor, the metaphor of "bowing." Furthermore, this ritual posture is implied in the meaning of the word *numinous* which we noted means "a nod from the gods." The appropriate human response seems to be a reciprocal nod or bow.

Bowing of this kind is first and foremost an "inner nod," an "attitude," whatever outward manifestation of word, gesture, or creative product may accompany the attitude. This is consistent with how Jung described the religious attitude as "the allegiance, surrender, or submission to a supraordinate factor or to a 'convincing' (overpowering) principle."[27] In terms of actual behavior, to bow may mean to submit, or to move away from, or to engage the energies of the unconscious. In all cases, it means to respect/reverence the numinosity of the archetype.

When one encounters the numinous, whether uplifting or disturbing, bowing is the best insulation from suffering a psychological inflation or deflation. The ego is inclined to value the numinous experience too much or too little. When encountering the benevolent gods who come through the curtain, the ego may be tempted to identify with them rather than relating to them. When this happens one becomes subject to inflation. If the encounter carries the more destructive side of the archetypal energies, the ego may be more susceptible to a deflation or depression. In either instance, bowing brings one back to earth, or to sea level, neither too high nor too low. Bowing promotes the dialectical relationship between conscious and unconscious so that the ego does not suffer too much *identification* with the Self or too much *alienation* from the Self.[28]

CONCLUSION

Jung described the modern person as being "hemmed round by rationalistic walls" which cut us off from the eternity of nature. Analytical psychology, he writes,

> seeks to break through these walls by digging up again the fantasy-images of the unconscious which our rationalism has rejected. These images lie beyond the walls; they are part of the nature *in us* ... against which we have barricaded ourselves behind the walls of reason.[29]

This article has explored one such image from our Irish ancestors which could help us break through the walls and cultivate an attitude toward our life and work which Jung named "religious," and which our Irish ancestors called *thin*. It is an attitude which expects and honors the holy in the midst of the ordinary; an attitude that the invisible is as *real* as the visible, and often so much more powerful; an attitude that our highest human achievement is not *reason*, but *reverence*; an attitude that allows us to deepen the relationship between conscious and unconscious, seen and unseen. With such an attitude, "in any instant the sacred may wipe you with its finger."[30]

NOTES

1. Clarissa Pinkola Estes, "The Radiant Coat" [Audiotape] (Boulder, Colorado: Sounds True), # A118.

2. Fergus Fleming, Shahrukh Husain, and C. Scott Littleton, *Heroes of the Dawn* (Amsterdam: Time-Life Books, 1996), pp. 28, 55.

3. Edward C. Sellner, *Wisdom of the Celtic Saints* (New York: Ave Maria Press, 1993), p. 25.

4. Steve Rabey, *In the House of Memory* (New York: Dutton, 1998), p. 68. Emphasis added.

5. Tom Cowan, *Fire In The Head* (New York: Harper/Collins, 1993), p. 55.

6. David Clark and Andy Roberts, *Twilight of the Celtic Gods* (London: Cassell PLC, 1996), p.119.

7. Fleming, *et. al.*, *Heroes of the Dawn*, p. 29.

8. William Butler Yeats, ed. *Irish Fairy and Folk Tales* (New York: The Modern Library, 2003), p. 4.

9. Nigel Pennick, *Celtic Sacred Landscapes* (New York: Thames and Hudson, 1996), pp. 132-33.

10. William Butler Yeats, *The Celtic Twilight: Myth, Fantasy, and Folklore* (Dorset: Prism Press, 1990), p. 30.

11. Cowan, *Fire in the Head*, pp. 52, 100.

12. Timothy Joyce, *Celtic Christianity* (Maryknoll, NY: Orbis Books, 1998), p. 29.

13. Margo Adler, *Drawing Down the Moon* (Boston: Beacon Press, 1979), p. ix.

14. C. G. Jung, *Memories, Dreams, Reflections* (New York: Vintage Books, 1965), p. 355.

15. C. G. Jung, *Collected Works,* trans. R. F. C. Hull (New York: Bollingen Foundation, 1958), vol. 11, § 275. Emphasis added. (All future references to Jung's *Collected Works,* abbreviated to *CW*, will be by volume and paragraph number.)

16. Jung, *CW* 18 § 580-81.

17. Rudolph Otto, *The Idea of the Holy* (London: Oxford University Press, 1923).

18. Jung, *CW* 11 § 6, 9.

19. C. G. Jung, *Letters, Volume One: 1906-1950* (Princeton: Princeton University Press, 1973), p. 377.

20. Jung, *CW* 11 § 509.

21. Jung, *Letters, Volume Two: 1951-1961* (Princeton: Princeton University Press, 1953), p. 265.

22. Jung, *CW* 8, § 841.

23. *Ibid.* Emphasis added.

24. Jung, *Letters*: I, p. 172.

25. For further development of the psychological dynamics of *threshold* phenomena, see Donald Kalsched, *The Inner World of Trauma*; James Hollis, *The Middle Passage: From Misery to Meaning in Midlife*; Murray Stein, *At Midlife*; and D. W. Winnicott, *Playing and Reality.*

26. Note: See John O'Donohue, *Anam Cara: Spiritual Wisdom From the Celtic Saints* and *Eternal Echoes,* and Philip Newell, *The Book of Creation.*

27. Jung, *Letters, Volume Two*, pp. 483-484.

28. Donald Kalsched, *The Inner World of Trauma* (London: Routledge, 1996), p. 144.

29. Jung, *CW* 8 § 739.

30. Annie Dillard, *Teaching a Stone to Talk* (New York: Harper and Row, 1982), pp. 67-73. Emphasis added.

STORY AND THE INTERFACE WITH THE SACRED IN IRISH MYTH

> For groups, as well as for individuals, life itself means to separate
> and to be reunited, to change form and condition, to die and to
> be reborn. It is to act and to cease, to wait and rest, and then to
> begin acting again, but in a different way. And there are always
> new thresholds to cross: the thresholds of summer and winter, of
> a season or a year, of a month or a night; the thresholds of birth,
> adolescence, maturity and old age; the threshold of birth and
> death and that of the afterlife—for those who believe in it.
>
> —Arnold van Gennep, *The Rites of Passage*, pp. 189-190

STORY

In order to become a recognized master of his art, the ancient Irish
poet or storyteller had to memorize a long list of tales. In the Book
of Leinster we read:

James Fitzgerald comes from a small village in southern Ireland. After some years
teaching in Primary School in London, he trained as a Jungian analyst in Zurich. He has
a private practice in London.

> Of the qualifications of a Poet in Stories and in Deeds, here follows, to be related to kings and chiefs, viz.: Seven times Fifty Stories, i.e. Five Times Fifty Prime Stories, and Twice Fifty Secondary Stories.[1]

The list of tales is instructive:

Adventures	Loves	Courtship
Elopements	Conceptions & Births	Youthful Exploits
Assemblies	Annals	Prohibitions
Divisions	Feasts	Expeditions
Irruptions	Invasions	Cattle-raids
Battles	Sieges	Slaughters
Destructions	Frenzies	Violent Deaths
Visions	Voyages	Place-lore
Caves		

It seems the stories had their own proper time for telling. Stages of life, initiations, dramatic social or political events, all required the proper story to be told. Seasonal changes, which also represented the crossing of a boundary, had their own appropriate stories. Each set of stories embodies an encounter with another dimension, and an interface with the sacred dimension of being.

The interesting thing is that the list does not sequence the stories by cycles concerning one person or event, as in, for instance, the *Iliad* or the *Odyssey*. Instead, the stories are classed according to type, as modern folklorists classify fairy or folk tales. In fact, the stories record archetypal events, that is, events in which two worlds are constellated and a "boundary-event" takes place. A conception or birth records the crossing of a boundary, from the other world into this one. Battles depict the constellation of opposites that meet and conflict at the boundary place of the battlefield. When an invasion happens, two worlds, two systems interpenetrate. The ordinary, secular world is invaded by an outsider, a stranger, one who embodies the sacred dimension. From the point of view of the invader, however, it is the place invaded that partakes of the sacred.

Whether these interfaces occur in the dimension of space or of time, it is undeniably clear that they were the object of continual, profound fascination for the early Irish. Celtic consciousness has for several millennia been a weakly felt current on the periphery of the prevailing

European psyche. The Graeco-Roman outlook has been predominant, obscuring for the most part the Celtic, which has maintained a continuous but shadowy existence. Those aspects we recognize as basic to the Graeco-Roman worldview have to do with the rational and practical approach to reality. In Jungian terms, we call these the thinking and sensate functions of consciousness. We might suspect, therefore, that the Celtic psyche and worldview pertain more to the intuitive and feeling functions. The Classical attitude places the rational human being at the center, and views the world accordingly. Bruce Arnold, in his article *The Celtic Enigma*, states the issue as follows:

> Classical art works outward from an ideal concept of man. …
> Celtic art works outward from a realistic concept of endless time
> and limitless space towards the frail and peripheral figure of man,
> broken, foolish, feeble and grotesque, achieving … a majesty that
> is still intensely human and limited and of the earth. … In classical
> art man stands at the centre of a circle: he is a god, or a hero,
> perfect in form, omnipotent, supreme. … By comparison, in
> Celtic art man emerges belatedly from a background of abstract
> patterns and symbols, to be a victim.[2]

For almost three thousand years, consciousness has developed according to the model promoted by the Classical attitude, in which the ego has taken the leading, central role, controlling the field of consciousness. So definitive has this model of the ego become that all deviations from it are taken nowadays as pathological, as any cursory glance through the DSM (Diagnostic and Statistical Manual of Mental Disorders) can confirm. The healthy ego is deemed to be single, focused, proficient in control of the will, able to defend its integrity through judicious use of the aggressive instinct, and capable of imparting continuity to life through the sexual instinct. Division, multiplicity, and ambiguity in the ego are usually regarded as symptoms of disease and disorder.

There is an inevitable order in the way the ego comes into existence and maintains its identity during the course of life. However, there are transition times and places when the ego's boundaries prove to be too rigid and restrictive. The life cycle brings naturally occurring moments when we have to cross over into a broader identity: puberty, midlife, and old age are some such times. There are also crises in life—illness, mourning, war, disaster—when we are forced into such transition spaces, when the psyche has to adapt and change and, in the process, move into a new identity. Such times belong to that state called liminality, which is a transition or initiatory stage between identities. Voluntarily or involuntarily, we are forced to immerse ourselves in such borderline states of being, through which we are re-created.

The transition between states of being, however, is not a smooth one. When two different systems or attitudes come into contact, the tension created calls into question the values of the predominant attitude, and the possibility of chaos ensues. Every neurosis is such a possibility. This confrontation between order and chaos is the subject of all creation myths. It is also the basis of the rituals that accompany all major transitions in life, those that are called Rites of Passage.

The cycles of stories listed earlier have a deeply psychological significance. Whenever a traumatic or numinous incident takes place, or a life-cycle episode has to be negotiated, an archetypal field is constellated, bringing with it the intensity of emotion from the unconscious. At times this may possess consciousness and transport the individual into an altered state. At times the effect may be destructive. However, it also seems necessary for purposes of initiation and transformation for these intense archetypal states to be activated. All rites of passage are meant to bring about a state of affect which transforms the individual. It is this emotion that enables the person to cross over the boundary into his new being and identity.

When a boundary in time or space is constellated, reality becomes divided into two dimensions: this world and the other world, the secular and the sacred. The boundary itself pertains to the condition of the liminal, which means threshold. We find constant reference to boundary phenomena in Irish literature and belief. Consciousness is drawn to spaces and times that are liminal, as they have a fascinating effect, belonging as they do to the unconscious realm. They stand for chaos, from which the ordered universe, or cosmos, is created. Every interface has a fascination for consciousness. The pool's surface, the mirror, the film screen, the television, or computer screen all open up a dimension of reality other than this secular world in which we live. In the same way myth, story, and fairy tale create an interface for the imagination to peer into the Otherworld.

CREATION

There is no trace of a creation story in what has come down to us from ancient Irish myth. The closest we have is in a text called the *Leabhar Gabhála Eireann*, usually translated as the Book of Invasions of Ireland, which is an account of a succession of peoples who invaded Ireland from the beginning of time. The word "*gabháil*" has a wide range of meanings, including: the act of taking, performing, conceiving, yoking, mooring, tethering, harnessing, dressing, going, crossing, controlling. It signifies an act of comprehending or apprehending. It stands for the act of making something conscious. One might rename the work as the Book of Making Ireland Conscious.

The last in the series of people to invade the island were the Sons of Mil, the ancestors of the Irish of the present day. It is Amairgen, the poet and judge of this group, who by his words performs a kind of act of creation. Prior to their coming to land, while their ship is still in suspense on the ocean, Amairgen conjures up, in words "that are in the nature of creation incantations,"[3] the island that would be the future home of his people:

> I seek the land of Ireland,
> Forceful is the fruitful sea,
> Fruitful the serried mountains,
> Serried the showery woods,
> Showery the cascade of rivers,
> Casacaded the tributaries of lakes,
> Tributaried the well of hills,
> Welling the people of gatherings,
> Gathering of Tara's king,
> Tara, hill of tribes,
> Tribes of Mil's people,
> Mil's ships and galleys,
> Galleys of mighty Eire,
> Eire, mighty and green.
> A crafty incantation,
> Craftiness of Bres's wives,
> Bres, of Buaigne's wives,
> Great lady Eire:
> Eremon harried her,
> Ir and Eber sought for her—
> I seek the land of Ireland.[4]

This is a magic formula, circular in form, and containing, as it were, interwoven lines that wind round like the spirals on some piece of ancient Irish jewelry. As with many creation stories, it tells of creation taking place out of the primal waters of chaos. The island that is called up out of the waters is an image for the whole of the created cosmos. On the periphery, beyond the ninth wave that defines the boundary of identity for the island, Amairgen by his words of power creates, out of the potentiality of the primal chaos of the ocean, an ordered and fertile kingdom, to be ruled from the central throne of the high king at Tara. Consciousness, identity, is here shown to be generated at the edge and transmitted inward to the center. It presents a different model of identity than the usual, in which, seed-like, it grows from a central point and pushes ever outward.

Ireland was without identity, in fact was still part of the primal chaos, until it was taken, captured in the words of the poet. In this story we can see that the source of identity is not within the island, but that it comes from the people who arrive from over the sea, from the other realm. The "invasions," the "takings," bring identity from the Otherworld to this world. In the words of the Rees brothers:

> From a mythological point of view, nothing really exists until is has been 'formed,' 'defined,' and named, and in as much as *Lebor Gabala Eirenn* is concerned with the origin of physical features, boundaries, and names, it retains some of the essentials of a cosmogonic myth.[5]

In addition to his act of creation, the poet Amairgen provides in his own person a paradigm for the identity that any future king might replicate. As he sets his right foot on the land of Ireland he recites the following:

> I am Wind on Sea,
> I am Ocean-wave,
> I am Roar of Sea,
> I am Bull of Seven
> Fights,
> I am Vulture on Cliff,
> I am Dewdrop,
> I am Fairest of Flowers,
> I am Boar for Boldness,
> I am Salmon in Pool,

> I am Lake on Plain,
> I am a Word of Skill,
> I am the Point of a Weapon
> that poureth forth combat,
> I am God who fashioneth Fire for a Head ...[6]

On the ocean where all things are potential, Amairgen represents multiple possibility, since at this point he symbolizes the totality of creation. This story is a foundation myth, in which the center and the periphery are bound together in an essential manner. The periphery in fact acts as the source of creation for the central place of power, where the king resides. These two polarities, that of unity and multiplicity and that of center and periphery, recur again and again in the ancient Irish tradition, and represent essential components of its world view. The significance seems to be that identity depends both on a center where singularity exists, and a peripheral area which presents multiple possibilities of being. In the psyche, conscious identity is a singular thing, by which we are enabled to define ourselves as "I," but nevertheless it arises out of the multiple possibilities within the unconscious.

You could say that consciousness is generated at every interface between the psyche and reality, whether of the inner or outer world. This interface, the plane of division, is a magical area representative of sacred space, which is the creative source of all secular space. "Boundaries between territories ... are lines along which the supernatural intrudes through the surface of existence."[7] It is contact with this sacred space which is the substance of all rites of passage. This space represents the original point of creation, from which the cosmogonic power inserted itself into this secular world.

Initiation, as Arnold van Gennep says in his book *The Rites of Passage*, consists of three stages: Separation, Transition, and Incorporation. Their aim is to transform the individual from one condition or status to another. The effectiveness of initiation depends on the state of liminality, into which the initiand enters by means of initiation rites, and through immersion in which he or she is transformed into a new being. This state, sometimes called "betwixt-and-between" is a boundary place between being and non-being. All cultures seem to have recognized the necessity of entering this state for the purpose of making the many transitions required by life. There was also a correlation between this state and the first moment of creation, in which the world was brought into being by the gods. As such, the creative powers were instilled in this state, and this gave it the power of recreation and renewal. It was a state sought out on purpose by shamans and visionaries, to which the Celtic druids seem to have belonged. Many of the stories that the ancient storyteller had to recite, particularly those in the categories of "Adventures" and "Voyages," seem to originate in initiatory ordeals of entry into and emergence from this transformative state of liminality.

The Voyage of Bran

One method of entry into this other dimension is highlighted in the following story, "The Voyage of Bran," one of the most famous Otherworld stories of early Irish literature. It is one of that class of stories called Voyage tales, which told of journeys of heroes, or even saints, to an other world across the sea. The beginning of this story, however, is on land:

> One day, in the neighbourhood of his stronghold, Bran went about alone, when he heard music behind him. As often as he looked back, 'twas still behind him the music was. At last he fell asleep at the music, such was its sweetness.[8]

Going about alone suggests that Bran is already in an introverted state, outside the walls of his stronghold, not contained in the safety of the collective, his tribe, and so, open to whatever may happen. The unearthly source of his impending initiation is doubly emphasized at this point—he hears music and it is behind him. With a visible stimulus, one can after all, easily close one's eyes. The ears, however, are an open boundary through which we can most easily be influenced. And music, after all, is invisible, mysterious, as is its effect on us. Bran is possessed, rendered wholly unconscious by the power of this otherworldly music. Sometimes music is a danger to mortal ears, particularly for those at sea, as the story of Odysseus and the Sirens illustrates. Music corresponds to the non-rational and to the emotional base of the psyche. It can bring about an altered state of consciousness. Every interface, even that with cyberspace through the screen of the computer, constellates the possibility of the "possession" of consciousness. Music's great power emanates from its invisibility, and its interface directly with the mind.

> When he awoke from his sleep, he saw close by him a branch
> of silver with white blossoms, nor was it easy to distinguish its
> bloom from the branch. then Bran took the branch into his
> royal house.

Something new has come into his world from Bran's dream state,
something whose essence is of the feminine, as the silver branch with
its white blossoms proclaims. Its otherworldly origin is clearly suggested
in that it is all one, there is no distinction between branch and blossom,
as with blossoms of the secular world. Division pertains to this world
of Ireland and consciousness. When he takes this undivided branch
into his royal house, Bran is already inviting in something not wholly
of ordinary life. Even in my childhood, bringing white tree blossoms
into the house was forbidden, whether it was hawthorn, elder, or apple.
Something of the fairy world was always ascribed to them.

> When the hosts were in the royal house, they saw a woman in
> strange raiment therein. 'Twas then she sang the fifty quatrains
> to Bran, while the host heard her, and all beheld the woman.

Now the other dimension discloses itself visually, openly, publicly. It
is the Anima figure, representing the unconscious, not just for Bran,
but for the collective of men in his house. What was prefigured by the
ravishing music, and then by the miraculous blossom, is now embodied
in the female figure, which has the unearthly power to penetrate the
boundaries of the closed building. The Anima is one of those archetypal
figures of the collective unconscious, who appears autonomously,
disturbing consciousness, and bringing with her the aura of mystery
and magic, bestowing a destiny on the man she favors. She is a
messenger from the Otherworld. She appears at critical junctures of a
man's life, signalling a time of testing, trial, and adventure.

When the Anima appears in this unexpected way to a man, it is clear
that his consciousness is in need of something new, a new goal or vision.
It is not stated in the story what particular need there was for Bran or his
people, but we may get some clue from the verses the woman in "strange
raiment" sang to the assembly. Here are just a few of those verses:

> A branch of the apple-tree of Emne
> I bring, like those one knows;
> Twigs of white silver are on it,
> Crystal brows with blossoms.

> There is a distant isle,
> Around which sea-horses glisten:
> A fair course against the white-swelling surge,-
> Four pillars uphold it.
>
> A delight to the eyes, a glorious range,
> Is the plain on which the host hold games:
> Coracle contends against chariot
> In the southern Plain of White Silver ...
>
> Unknown is wailing or treachery
> In the familiar cultivated land,
> There is nothing rough or harsh,
> But sweet music striking the ear.
>
> Without grief, without sorrow, without death,
> Without any sickness, without debility,
> That is the sign of Emne-
> Uncommon is an equal marvel ...
>
> There are thrice fifty distant isles
> In the ocean to the west of us;
> Larger than Erin twice
> Is each of them, or thrice ...

The woman describes further the wonder of this magical land in other verses of her song. It is a land of health and everlasting joy, full of women, games, music, and wine. Two characteristics stand out, which indicate its difference from this world of Bran and of ours. "Coracle contends with chariot" there; that is, land and sea are one, in a conjunction of opposites. The other noteworthy fact is that the sorrows and troubles of this world do not exist there. It is a place "without grief, without sorrow." And because it is without death, everyone is immortal, "they look for neither decay nor death." It is no wonder then that the strange woman has appeared in Bran's domain: humans are always yearning for health and joy, and a resolution of the conflict of opposites. In another story it says of this land: *There, there is neither "mine" nor "thine."* It is not so much that the opposites are reconciled there, but that there has never been a division into opposites from the primal unity. We are in a divided state in this mortal world, and from that fact flows the grief, sorrow, illness, and death that are our lot.

> Thereupon the woman went from them, while they knew not whither she went. And she took her branch with her. The branch sprang from Bran's hand into the hand of the woman, nor was there strength in Bran's hand to hold the branch.

Bran makes no delay in setting out to find this wonderful land: with the Anima's call, he cannot refuse, it is his destiny now. The very next morning he puts out to sea with "thrice nine" companions. On the third day out, he sees a man in a chariot coming towards him over the sea, as if on dry land. This is the paradoxical vision in which he begins to be initiated into the knowledge of the other world. The man declares himself to be Manannan son of Lir, the god of the sea. He sings thirty verses to Bran, some of which emphasized the supernatural nature of the liminal condition in which Bran is on his sea-voyage. Here are a few of those verses:

> Bran deems it a marvellous beauty
> In his coracle across the clear sea:
> While to me in my chariot from afar
> It is a flowery plain on which he rows about.
>
> That which is a clear sea
> For the prowed skiff in which Bran is,
> That is a happy plain with a profusion of flowers
> To me from the chariot of two wheels ...
>
> Speckled salmon leap from the womb
> Of the white sea, on which thou lookest:
> They are calves, they are coloured lambs
> With friendliness, without mutual slaughter ...

By presenting an alternative vision of reality, Manannan challenges the conscious rational attitude by which Bran has lived his life, and opens up one that belongs to the non-rational condition of being. In the words of the brothers Rees,

> Coincidences of opposites and of other irreconcilables give a shock
> to the understanding and transport the spirit to the gateway of
> the Other World.[9]

Manannan describes further the people who live in this land of paradox, which is as yet closed to Bran's perception:

A beautiful game, most delightful,
They play sitting at the luxurious wine,
Men and gentle women under a bush,
Without sin, without crime ...

We are from the beginning of creation
Without old age, without consummation of earth,
Hence we expect not that there should be frailty;
Sin has not come to us.

The condition of these immortals is free of time and the earthly
dimension, and exists in a state beyond the opposites. Sin is an inevitable
outcome of the separation of the opposites in human consciousness;
in the unconscious the opposites are united in a timeless, immortal
state, in the condition of the archetypes. It is a place of innocence and
unity before the Fall.

The final revelation of Manannan is the promise of an incarnation
from this timeless place of unity in the world of mortals. The god himself
will father a son, whose nature will reveal the multiform potential of
the Otherworld from which he comes:

He will delight the company of every fairy-mound,
He will be the darling of every goodly land,
He will make known secrets- a course of wisdom-
In the world, without being feared.

He will be the shape of every beast,
Both on the azure sea and on land,
He will be a dragon before hosts at the onset,
He will be a wolf in every great forest.

He will be a stag with horns of silver
In the land where chariots are driven,
He will be a speckled salmon in a full pool,
He will be a seal, he will be a fair-white swan.

This revelation conveys the essence of the immortal realm and its
relationship with this world of manifestation. It is an evocation of the
primordial creation story of Amairgen, in which one person contains
the multiple possibilities of being, not limited or "defined" by a single
identity. He will unite in his person all aspects of being, the animal
and human, this world and the other world. By making known all

secrets, he will reveal what is hidden, bring into consciousness what has been secreted into the unconscious. From a Jungian point of view, this son of Manannan will embody the archetype of the Self. Individuation for Jung meant wholeness not perfection, and here we see the wholeness of all creation incarnated in one being.

After this transcendent revelation, Bran goes on with his voyage to find the Land of Women. On his way there, his boat passes by the Island of Joy, where they see a host of people staring and laughing. The loss of one of his men, whom he sends on to the island, and who merges with the laughing crowd, has a significance for their ultimate destination, as it reduces their numbers to the magical number of three nines. This number seems to be the signature number of the Land of Women, since on their arrival, there are "thrice nine beds" available there. To be caught in a state of permanent hilarity—in the land of laughter—is a possession and a limitation of being, as it is a single state, not the totality. One sacrifices the ultimate condition of wholeness if one is overcome by such chaotic affective states. Also, there is no relationship to the other in such self-absorbed, narcissistic conditions.

The method by which Bran comes to the Land of Women is worthy of attention. Although the chief of the women welcomes them, Bran "did not venture to go on shore."

> The woman threw a ball of thread to Bran straight over his face. Bran put his hand on the ball, which adhered to his palm. The thread of the ball was in the woman's hand, and she pulled the coracle towards the port. Thereupon they went into a large house, in which was a bed for every couple, even thrice nine beds.

It is as if Bran's consciousness is captured in the inadvertent, automatic gesture, which is itself a sort of unconscious compulsion, the hand that rises without conscious thought to ward off the missile thrown at the face. Too much thinking brings hesitation and doubt, and prevents us from attaining that land of magic and mystery.

In this place to which Bran is inevitably led, each bed is for a couple, which underscores the essence of the island. It is the Land of Women, but it furthers the *coniunctio*. It thus enables the union of the two worlds, the feminine Other World—that of the unconscious— and the world of Bran—that of the ordinary, rational, conscious world.

It is of necessity, too, a world in which the sense of mundane time disappears, as time represents separation and division, and the Other World dimension is an eternal Now, the Present Moment, in which all things are unified.

But into every paradise there comes a disturbance. Here it takes the form of homesickness, a longing for the land of Erin. The world of consciousness still has a claim that has to be resolved. With the disappearance of Bran from the world, a lacuna or space has been left there that has to be filled. As Jung says in his essay, "Adaptation, Individuation, Collectivity," the person who leaves the collective in order to complete their individuation process, incurs guilt, which they must redeem. He goes on:

> He must offer a ransom in place of himself, that is, he must bring
> forth values which are an equivalent substitute for his absence in
> the collective personal sphere.[10]

A sacrifice will have to be made, as the woman from the Island of Woman warns Bran, saying that none of them should set foot on the land when they come to Ireland. She also says they should take with them the man they left on the isle of laughter. This brings the number back to that suitable for the ordinary world again.

When they come to Ireland at last, the men there ask who it is who has come over the sea:

> Said Bran: "I am Bran the son of Febal."
> One of the men said: "We do not know such a one, though
> 'The Voyage of Bran' is one of our ancient stories."
> One of Bran's men sprang from them out of the coracle. As
> soon as he touched the earth of Ireland, forthwith he was a heap
> of ashes, as though he had been in the earth for many hundred
> years. ...
> Thereupon to the people of the gathering Bran told all his
> wanderings from the beginning until that time. And he wrote
> [it] in ogham, and then bade them farewell. And from that hour
> his wanderings are not known.

Here is a meeting across the boundary of life and death, of past and future. The island of Ireland represents the world of temporality and mortality, and Bran and his companions are on the other side of that boundary, in the immortal realm. The one companion, however, out of longing for that mortal world of appearance, steps ashore, crosses the boundary and becomes the sacrifice that enables Bran's company to regain their mystical number and sail away again.

The ransom to be paid, however, is not only this man's death. Bran leaves behind him his own story for the world. But at this point realities overlap, in a way that appears very modern. The men of Ireland do not know Bran, but they do know his story, from of old. Time has removed him from them, but what has survived through the boundary of time and its limitation is the event through which he has attained immortality, now contained in Story, "The Voyage of Bran." Bran has gone through the process of Rebirth. The symbolic has transformed his identity from mere mortal into one of the Immortals, as he has gone beyond the human boundary of time and space, to achieve the symbolic life. As Jung says:

> You see, man is in need of a symbolic life—badly in need. ...
> But we have no symbolic life. Where do we live symbolically?
> Nowhere, except where we participate in the ritual of life.[11]

Bran has participated fully in what life offered him. He took up the challenge or call that the unconscious made to him through the otherworldly music. He did not refuse, even when he had to go beyond the ordinary bounds of his life and enter an otherworldly dimension. As Jung says, it is only when our identity is resolutely bound, as Bran's was to his voyage, that we are opened up to the archetypal dimension. Bran's identity has become transformed into the symbolic dimension of story which the ordinary world can look to as an example forever after. Bran has attained an identity whose source was the Other World, and which participated in the identity of the Immortal Ones. Both offer the possibility of a new being, if one makes the proper sacrifice at the boundary, the interface with the Sacred.

NOTES

1. From The Book of Leinster, quoted in Alwyn Rees and Brinley Rees, *Celtic Heritage* (London: Thames and Hudson, 1961), p. 208.

2. Bruce Arnold, "The Celtic Enigma," *Dublin Magazine*, n.d.

3. Rees and Rees, *Celtic Heritage*, p. 99.

4. Version quoted in Caitlin and John Matthews, *The Encyclopaedia of Celtic Wisdom* (Shaftesbury, Dorset: Element, 1994), p. 15.

5. Rees and Rees, *Celtic Heritage,* p. 104.

6. *Ibid.,* p. 98.

7. *Ibid.,* p. 94.

8. All quotes from "The Voyage of Bran" are from *Ancient Irish Tales,* eds. Tom Peete Cross and Clark Harris Slover (London: Geo. Harrap & Co, 1935), pp. 588-595.

9. Rees and Rees, *Celtic Heritage,* p. 344.

10. C. G. Jung, *Collected Works,* Vol. 18 (London: Routledge & Kegan Paul, 1977), § 1095.

11. *Ibid.,* § 625.

DEIRDRE OF THE SORROWS

LARA NEWTON

Astriking feature in Irish mythology is the feminine element, the strong female figures who populate the stories: Macha who brings on the curse of the men of Ulster when the king and warriors fail to acknowledge her labor pains, Maive who rules and fights as she loves, with passion and endurance that rival any man, the goddess Danu who rules over the tribes that are a divine race said to have inhabited Ireland before the coming of the Celts. In his introduction to *The Tain,* Thomas Kinsella says that it is women, "on whose strong and diverse personalities the action continually turns... it is certainly they, under all the violence, who remain most real in the memory."[1]

Any naming of heroines in Ireland's lore soon brings us to the tragic romantic women who hovered in uncertainty, caught between the possibility of boundless love and the surety of vengeful destruction. None represents this struggle so nobly and beautifully as Deirdre, often referred to as "Deirdre of the Sorrows." Indeed her story, also known as the story of the "Exile of the Sons of Uisliu," is designated as one of the "three sorrows of story-telling" or the "three tragedies of the Gael." It is a story that grips the heart and begs to be understood.

Lara Newton, M.A., is a Jungian analyst in Denver, Colorado and the author of *Brothers and Sisters: Discovering the Psychology of Companionship* (Spring Journal Books, 2007). She has a Master's Degree in English Literature, attended the Yeats Summer School in Sligo, Ireland, wrote her Master's thesis on James Joyce, and has studied Irish mythology for over 35 years.

"Deirdre's Story"

King Conchobar of Ulster was at a feast held in the home of his bard Fedlimid. As Fedlimid's wife walked through the banqueting hall, the child still in her womb cried out, a piercing cry that rang through the hall. Cathbad the Druid interpreted this mysterious occurrence. He prophesied that the baby would grow to be the most beautiful woman ever seen in Ireland. Because of her, there would be destruction and warfare among the men of Ulster, a splitting of the powerful Knights of the Red Branch. The warriors at the feast all said, "Kill the child!" But King Conchobar said that he would take this baby, have her reared far from other people in a secluded place, and when she had grown to be a woman he would make her his wife. No one dared argue with the King. The baby was born later that same night.

Deirdre grew in the company of only her foster parents and an old woman named Leborcham who loved her with all her heart. The girl had never seen a man, except the King who came to visit rarely. One fateful day, her foster-father was skinning a calf on the snow, and Deirdre saw a raven come to drink the blood. She exclaimed to Leborcham, "The man I could love must have those three colors: hair like the raven, cheeks like blood and his body as white as snow." Leborcham told her that Noisiu, Uisliu's son, was such a man, and Deirdre swore she would be ill until she met him.

When the meeting took place, both Noisiu and Deirdre fell in love. Knowing that she was the intended bride of Conchobar, Noisiu tried to reject Deirdre, but she bound him by requesting that he "take her with him." Noisiu and his two brothers, Anle and Ardan, left with Deirdre that very day, accompanied by a small band of followers.

From that day forward, the sons of Uisliu traveled with and protected Deirdre. The love of Noisiu and Deirdre grew even in their exile, and under the extreme hardships that were put upon them. Conchobar pursued them, and they were never safe in one place for long. They wandered in Ireland for some time, and then crossed the sea to the land of Alba.

In Alba, Deirdre and the sons of Uisliu had a period of relative calm, which was eventually ended by the jealous king of Alba's attempts to win Deirdre from Noisiu. Once again, Deirdre, her lover, his brothers, and their followers were forced to escape to an island in the sea.

When news of these troubles of the sons of Uisliu reached his court, King Conchobar still burned with bitterness toward Noisiu, Anle and Ardan, and desire for Deirdre. As his warriors entreated him to forgive the brothers and welcome them back, the king came up with a cunning plan.

He determined that he would appear to forgive the brothers, in order to lure them and Deirdre back to Ulster, where he could have the brothers killed and take Deirdre for his own. He asked the much-loved and trusted Fergus to be the one to take news to the sons of Uisliu: Their long exile had ended, and they were welcomed home again. Suspecting no deception, Fergus set sail for the island where Deirdre and the three brothers were.

When Fergus came to shore on the island, the brothers were overjoyed to hear the call of an Ulster man. Deirdre, however, had dreamed a horrifying dream the night before, which foretold the deaths of Noisiu, Anle, and Ardan, and she believed that Conchobar was deceiving them. The brothers dismissed her fears, assuring her that she had nothing to worry about. Deirdre sang a sad lament, but went to Ireland with Noisiu and his brothers, because she would not be separated from her true love. She went as a woman doomed.

Conchobar's plan included separating Fergus from Deirdre and the sons of Uisliu, which was accomplished shortly after they reached Ireland's shore. With their main protector gone, they fell into the king's trap, even though Deirdre continued to warn Noisiu and his brothers that Conchobar could not be trusted. She begged them to wait for Fergus, not to put themselves in Conchobar's power, but they still wanted to believe that they were safe. When finally the three brothers acknowledged that her forebodings had been right, it was too late to turn back and they were indeed in a trap.

The fighting which followed was brutal and long. At the end, the three brothers were slain, but not before they had taken many another warrior with them. Deirdre fell at their feet and wept, full of grief. When Fergus heard of the betrayal, he and his men went into exile in the county of Connacht where they joined forces with Queen Maive.

Conchobar took Deirdre to his castle, where she lived for a year. In that time, she neither smiled nor took joy in any activity. So Conchobar saw that the death of the sons of Uisliu had brought him no pleasure, and the desire he had felt for Deirdre wilted under her disdain. At the end of the year, he asked Deirdre whom she hated the most of anyone. She answered that it was he and Eogan mac Durthacht, the man who dealt the death blows to Noisiu, Anle, and Ardan. So Conchobar, all pleasure but malice gone from him, took Deirdre to spend the next year in the home of Eogan mac Durthacht. As they were in his chariot on their way to this meeting, Deirdre flung herself out of the chariot and dashed her head against the large black boulders beside the path.

Deirdre was dead, and as she had wished, she was buried in the same grave as Noisiu and his brothers. From the grave there grew two trees of yew, and their branches and leaves entwined to form an arch.[2]

* * * * *

How are we to understand this story? From the first paragraph, we see the undeniable elements of a "divine child" motif:[3] a baby who cries out from the womb, is sequestered for her upbringing, and is prophesied to bring about an upheaval in the existing culture. She brings new and profound energy to the world in which she arrives. However, the story is also a tragic romance. Such romances always carry a deep significance for the people who hear them. Love that is fated to occur, no matter what obstacles stand in its way, and that is equally fated to end tragically, speaks to us of a psychological necessity. We must look closely at the nature of the lovers, what brings them together and what tears them apart, in order to understand that necessity. Both themes, the divine child and the tragic romance, are harbingers of change. We see them weaving in and out of each other throughout this story. Deirdre is the one who "knows" from the beginning to the end of her tale, and she is also the woman who will die for love.

Long before the two lovers find each other, Deirdre has called to us from the loneliness of the womb. She is somehow drawn to announce herself when her mortal nemesis is near—Conchobar, the king who cannot resist the idea of possessing the most beautiful woman in Ireland, even though he will surely be an old man by the time she is grown. For a ruler to assert his power and demand that which others know is not right, that which will disturb the balance of the kingdom, occurs often enough in life, and certainly often in myth. Time after time, this kind of assertion marks the downfall of kingdoms, as well as the downfall of individual lives. The leader no longer wishes to lead, to grow and develop. Rather, he is ruled by his greed. Intrapsychically, "he" may be my own greedy ego that doesn't want to allow change to arise from any source other than itself; or, in a cultural sense, "he" may be the community I belong to that clings to an image of itself as innovative and prosperous, while watching its borders jealously. Yes, we know this king.

But do we know the baby Deirdre? Although she cries out in awareness of her woe before she is born, she is still powerless to stop it. Again, this is often a feature of the divine child's life. Perhaps her "awareness" is all instinct, with little conscious connection. However, from the moment that she makes herself known, *we* must be aware that this child has abilities, as well as beauty, that are beyond the normal human range. And our awareness increases the pathos of Deirdre's story. For this keen ability, which connects her to the "otherworld" of movement and meaning, is never really appreciated by the others in her story. Some love her and some covet her, but not even Noisiu completely understands her depth. Her ability is medial; she is both a child of the earth and a child of spirit, and her deep feminine connection to those seemingly contrasting realms motivates her actions throughout the story. Deirdre comes into the world with a second sight which guides her to fulfill her destiny, and it appears that her tragic end is just as much a part of her destiny as the love relationship that she has with Noisiu. Neither the prophetic young girl-child nor the beautiful lovers are safe in this world. She is in danger of being taken as the token beauty of an old unloving king, and they are in danger of being torn apart, killed, and tormented by that same figure.

The cry from the womb is an image of suffering that is yet to unfold, but nevertheless is inevitable. Indeed, the Druid Cathbad's focus on predicting the struggles that warriors and kings will endure on her account totally skirts the fact that here, in the midst of a feast, is a woman about to give birth to a child, and the child is crying out with resounding anguish. Deirdre's distress, just as Deirdre's happiness, is never attended to in her story. But it is she who brings about a change in Ulster, a change that begins with her cry from her mother's womb.

If Deirdre and the sons of Uisliu are the transforming agents in the story, Conchobar is the very image of that which needs so desperately to be transformed. Even his loyal warriors recognize his flaws. Yet he persists and destroys the best and most beautiful potential in his kingdom. Conchobar is the rigid tendency in the culture of ancient Ireland *and* the modern western world—and in us as individuals—to control, for the ego's limited purposes, the very potential that could save and change us. Right before him, ready to live and thrive, are beauty and depth, and finally love. But Conchobar allows his baser desire for possession and self-indulgence to control his actions.

As a woman, Deirdre's specialness is twofold. In addition to her deep connection to the otherworld, surely her beauty is astounding. As Yeats puts it, "she'd too much beauty for good luck."[4] Yet her relation to her own beauty is not proud. She only wants to love and be loved. Beauty and love usually go together in myths and fairy tales. Beauty inspires us to the highest emotion, love, which brings about a union of the opposites. Yet it also activates lower urges that must be dealt with, such as greed and covetousness. In Deirdre's story, if she and Noisiu are to find love, they must face these other, baser emotions.

The baser as well as the higher emotions can be seen in relation to Deirdre's resistance to union with Conchobar *and* in relation to the alchemical process[5] that underlies the whole story and seems to draw Deirdre into relation with Noisiu, her intended mate. Union with Conchobar would be, at best, a lesser *coniunctio*[6]—a diminishment rather than an enhancement of Deirdre's potential. The alchemical process or agent of change operates on more than one level in this story. First, Deirdre is the divine child who must be known, accepted, and allowed to live and develop her potential; she is destined to bring about a complete transformation in the kingdom. She is the beginning (catalyst) and end (result) of the transformation, showing us the paradoxical truth of alchemical process. Through her, a sorting out of the true from the untrue, the noble from the base, can occur. Then also, Deirdre grows into the *soror mystica*,[7] who must find her true mate. If she does not, the potential that she brings into the world will die with her.

When the lone Deirdre, far from human society, responds prophetically to the alchemical colors—black (the black crow), white (snow), and red (blood)—with such intensity, we know that she has found her mate. Just as surely, we know that the transformation she seeks is a life and death matter. Her boundless love, if achieved, *will* bring about the end of an era. If we simply follow the story, the old era appears to be one ruled by violence and greed, as well as an era in which the word of the king is followed at all cost. The rigidity of the status quo is all-important. But even in that old era, there are many key figures who assist the movement toward change: Leborcham who values Deirdre, Noisiu her true mate who honors her request to take her away, his two brothers who accompany and protect her, as well as Fergus and many other warriors. The old era has already lost its absolute authority and power. In the new era, the cry of a baby girl and the passion of a beautiful young woman must be attended to as well. And, as with most tragedies, by the end of the story, we all long for a new era.

The love story of Deirdre and Noisiu is both powerful and sweet. It develops so quickly that we are likely to lose the sense of fate that leads up to their encounter. I have stressed Deirdre's response to the alchemical colors (black, white, and red) which serves as her awakening to the possibility of true union. From that moment, she is moved by a driving force that will not be subdued until Noisiu agrees to run away with her. Noisiu is the best that Ulster has to offer in handsome, accomplished young men. He sings and fights with equal finesse, and he devotes his considerable talents to his life with Deirdre. In him is contained all the colors of transformation, and together he and Deirdre change the world. That is, they love. This couple is an image of what good can come when we allow our best potential to develop from within, rather than having it snatched up and possessed by the ego as soon as it is perceived. No child is born from this union, except for the child of our own longing to create a world in which a Deirdre and a Noisiu may live and thrive.

An important aspect of Deirdre's specialness, her ability to see beyond the mundane world, is demonstrated throughout this story, beginning with her first utterance from the womb. Later, she has the prophetic response to the black, white, and red images she sees in nature. Deirdre sees the potential for union and new life. Finally, prior to the arrival of Fergus, she dreams of the danger that awaits her and the three brothers. She warns them, and her warnings go unheeded until the end is near. Deirdre is not only a beautiful woman who attracts all men who see her; she is also a medial woman who sees beyond the surface of this world. When she and the sons of Uisliu are faced with the decision of whether to return to Ireland, Deirdre's choice becomes one between following her inner voice of wisdom and following her love. As we knew she would, she follows her love, thus sealing her place in mythic history as a tragic heroine. She cannot abandon that which gives her life meaning, even if she knows that she is following Noisiu to death.

From the beginning the story of Deirdre pulls us into its drama. Recorded in the eighth century, and believed to have emerged from a heroic period between 200 BC and 250-350 AD,[8] this story and its tragic heroine continue to fascinate and inspire Irish literary greats as well as those of us who stumble upon it unawares. W. B. Yeats was drawn to Deirdre's ethereal, otherworldly qualities,[9] and John M. Synge saw in her an earthy woman of wild nature[10]—both knew this woman spoke to the heart of humanity in a timeless voice. As with Shakespeare's *Romeo and Juliet* or the Welsh myth of Tristan and Isolde, we can't hear her love story without wanting to intervene, to help her and her lover find a way to safety. Equally as powerful is the cry of the baby from the womb, a cry that pierces our consciousness and forces us to listen.

Finally, Deirdre's last year sears our minds. The torment she endures is so painful that some versions of the story have simply changed the ending—she dies of grief when Noisiu dies, or she kills herself rather than live without him. I believe this waters down the tragedy and lets us off the hook. We need to see just how vile the Conchobar in us and in our world can be. As Jung once said in another context, we need to "drink down to the very dregs"[11] this killing force, so that we know it once and for all. At the end of her story, when we see Deirdre's death and the yew trees that grow from her and Noisiu's grave, we are left with the psychological, emotional, and spiritual mandate: To create a world in which love and wisdom can dwell together and not be destroyed.

NOTES

1. Thomas Kinsella, *The Tain* (Oxford: Oxford University Press, 1969 and reissued 2002), p. xv.

2. There are many versions of the story and embellishments that have been added over the years. In many accounts, Deirdre's laments are written out in verse form. My account here comes predominantly from the Kinsella translation, *The Tain* (1969), which is taken from the oldest known written version of the story. Other accounts of the myth that were consulted for this telling are found in: Daithi O hOgain, *The Lore of Ireland: An Encyclopaedia of Myth, Legend and Romance* (Cork, Ireland: Collins Press, 2006); Eoin Neeson, *Deirdre and Other Great Stories from Celtic Mythology* (Edinburgh: Mainstream Publishing Company, 1997); *Irish Sagas and Folk-Tales*, retold by Eileen O'Faolain (London: Oxford University Press, 1954).

3. The alchemical term is *"filius philosophorum* = archetype of the divine child," as mentioned in C. G. Jung, *Psychology and Alchemy* (*Collected Works* 12) (Princeton: Princeton University Press, 1968), § 215. Also discussed in detail in "The Psychology of the Child Archetype," *The Archetypes and the Collective Unconscious* (*CW* 9i) (Princeton: Princeton University Press, 1969), § 259-305. I am also reminded here of Patricia Berry's essay, "Reductionism/Finalism and

the Child," in *Fire in the Stone: The Alchemy of Desire* (Wilmette, Illinois: Chiron Publications, 1997), pp. 79-93. Berry speaks of the child of the current time being the "abused child" and the child of an earlier Jungian time (the time she "grew up" in, so to speak) having been the "divine child." Deirdre, a child arising in the Irish psyche as far back as 200 BC, seems to combine these two aspects.

4. W. B. Yeats, "Deirdre," *The Collected Plays of W. B. Yeats* (London: Macmillan, 1952), p. 172.

5. In Europe, the medieval practice—part science and part philosophy—which hinged on combining substances ("base matter" or *prima materia*) in a procedure that would ideally result in the release or creation of a pure substance (gold). As we know, Jung saw the process of moving from *nigredo* through *albedo*, and finally to *rubedo*, as an image of the individuation process.

6. When the opposites (or one of them) that unite have been imperfectly separated, the result is a contaminated mixture, and further work (*separatio* or purification) is needed before a greater *coniunctio* can occur. In this story, Conchobar's desire for power is a stronger motivator than his love for Deirdre, if in fact he loves her at all. See Edward Edinger, *Anatomy of the Psyche: Alchemical Symbolism in Psychotherapy* (La Salle, Illinois: Open Court Publishing, 1985), pp. 212-215.

7. The female assistant or counterpart to the male alchemist.

8. Neeson, p. 15.

9. Yeats, pp. 169-203.

10. John M. Synge, "Deirdre of the Sorrows," *The Complete Plays of John M. Synge* (New York: Vintage Books, 1935), pp. 211-268.

11. C. G. Jung, "The Negative Mother-Complex," *The Archetypes and the Collective Unconscious* (*CW* 9i) (Princeton: Princeton University Press, 1969), § 184.

MODERN IRELAND: WORDS AND MUSIC

HEART MYSTERIES:
TRADITIONAL LOVE SONGS OF IRELAND

JAMES W. FLANNERY

We stand outside the walls of Eden and hear the trees talking within, and their talk is sweet in our ears.[1]

—W. B. Yeats

—i—

The culture of Ireland, renowned throughout the world for its extraordinary accomplishments in literature, music, film, and, in more recent years, business, has been described as a psychic triumph in the face of material defeat. Normally the loss of a nation's language as the result of a deliberate policy of colonial subjugation leads inevitably to the loss of its native culture and, with that, the destruction of its national pride and identity. That did not occur in Ireland despite

James W. Flannery, Ph.D., is a Yeats scholar, a professor at Emory University, and the Director of the W. B. Yeats Foundation. Dr. Flannery is also a noted interpreter of the famed *Irish Melodies* of Thomas Moore. His critically acclaimed recording *Dear Harp of My Country: The Irish Melodies of Thomas Moore*, may be sampled on the website of the W. B. Yeats Foundation at www.college.emory.edu/wbyeats.

This essay, and its accompanying song lyrics and notes, are taken from a book in progress by Dr. Flannery devoted to the effort throughout the late nineteenth and early twentieth centuries to carry over into English the genius of the Gaelic love song tradition of Ireland. The songs discussed in the text may also be sampled on the Yeats Foundation website.

a systematic effort lasting almost five centuries to uproot and destroy every vestige of the Gaelic heritage of the country.

The reasons why that common colonial strategy didn't work in Ireland are complex. To a considerable extent, they are due to the power and resiliency of the native culture as well as the remarkable courage of the people in determining to hold onto their cultural heritage as a source of sustenance and strength, especially in times of suffering and despair. But equally, the survival of Irish culture into modern times is due to the vision, artistry, and heroic perseverance of a group of men and women who devoted their lives to mining the genius of Gaelic Ireland and carrying it over into the English language where its bounty could be—and is today—shared with the entire world.

The effort to express the genius of the Gaelic soul of Ireland in English really starts with Thomas Moore (1779-1852), the first internationally known Irish artist. Moore's lasting reputation rests with ten immensely popular volumes of folk-song arrangements published as *The Irish Melodies* between 1808 and 1834. Down through the centuries the sense of a distinctive Irish culture was preserved by the bardic order of poets that held an honored place in the assemblies of their chieftains. The bards (or *filidh* in Old Irish) were originally members of the Druid caste and, besides being the repository of the traditional knowledge and wisdom of the Irish tribal system, were also said to possess supernatural powers of divination and prophecy. Bards were expected to have an intimate knowledge of the geography, myths, songs, and stories of Ireland as a whole, but especially the special category of lore known as *faoin dúlraoidh*, or songs in praise of place. Much of this material deals with tales attached to holy mountains, wells, rivers, and other sacred spots. Naturally, the heroes and other exceptional people associated with these places were also included in the *dinnshenchas*, or lore of prominent places, that was also passed down over the centuries. The success of the bardic tradition in fostering a passionate love of place and country helps to explain the fierce resistance of the Irish to colonial rule and exploitation. What it also explains is the fervent attachment to their homeland of Irish exiles stretched across the globe.

The bardic order depended for their existence on the continued survival of the Gaelic nobility, who were their patrons. But beginning in the sixteenth century and continuing throughout the seventeenth century, Gaelic Ireland suffered a series of calamitous defeats, culminating with the Battle of the Boyne (1690) and the ensuing Williamite Conquest of Ireland. The Gaelic Catholic nobility and their armies were forced to go into exile—the tragic "Flight of the Wild Geese"—leaving the bards without any means of support. Now they wandered the countryside, homeless and reduced from places of privilege to near beggary, their collective voice, in the words of poet John Montague, "a long drawn-out death song of an order, monotonous in its intensity, like a dog howling after its master."[2]

The next two centuries were times of devastating loss and humiliation for Gaelic Ireland. Ninety per cent of the land was held by rulers who were alien to the native people in ethnic background, language, and religion as well as profound political, social, and cultural sympathy. Under the notorious Penal Laws enacted in 1695, Irish Catholics could not sit in Parliament nor vote in parliamentary elections. They were forbidden to possess arms or even own a horse worth more than five pounds. Catholics could not keep a school nor send their children to be educated abroad. Ownership of land was subject to another complex branch of the penal code under which an eldest son, by renouncing his Catholic faith and proclaiming publicly his conversion to the Anglican Church of Ireland, could deprive his Catholic father of the management and disposal of his property. Catholic bishops were banished from the country and liable to be hanged, drawn, and quartered if they returned. While a certain number of priests were tolerated, unregistered ones were liable to the same penalties as the hierarchy.

It was out of the horrors of a situation in which the native Irish had become pariahs in their own land that Thomas Moore, a Catholic educated at Trinity College, Dublin (by the end of the eighteenth century some of the Penal Laws had been lifted), began a process of cultural transformation that was to have profound political as well as purely aesthetic consequences. As an accomplished poet, lyricist, and musician, Moore was deeply moved by the traditional music of Ireland then just beginning to be collected. A realist as well as an idealist, however, Moore realized that the past was definitely past, the old order shattered. If Ireland as a nation was to survive at all, the Gaelic culture had to be reclaimed and reborn in another form. Moore took upon himself the daunting task of grafting new words in English onto the ancient modal airs of Ireland. In doing so, he introduced into English verse certain exotic new verse forms borrowed from the original Gaelic.

Thus he brought into English the Celtic note in literature—a magical note that continues to be sounded down to the present day, thereby providing Irish poetry with one of its most entrancing qualities.

Moore can also be credited with introducing into English a number of techniques from the Gaelic song tradition—specifically techniques intended to evoke archetypal responses at the deepest level of the psyche. With their long breath lines and ravishing liquid flow of vowel sounds and consonants blending into one another, this is the language of reverie. In poetry of this nature the qualities of subconscious association take the lead. The poetry becomes hypnotically repetitive, oracular, incantatory, and, in the original sense of the word, charming. W. B. Yeats (1865-1939), with his own desire to transport readers of his poetry and audiences for his plays into the phantasmagorical world of the unconscious, was well aware of Moore's poetic achievement as a latter-day bard. Indeed, the Irish poet Austin Clarke, himself a master of Gaelic prosody, argued that "the slow-delaying rhythms" and the "vowel music" of Yeats's early poetry were inspired directly by Moore as well as the nineteenth-century translators who succeeded him.[3]

Politically, the work of Moore also had a powerful impact. For centuries, in the timeless strategy of colonizers the world over, it was standard propaganda to argue that the Irish were ignorant savages who knew nothing of civilization until they were blessed with English manners and mores. Moore and his nineteenth-century followers countered this charge with the grace and subtlety of their artistry as well as the fierce indignation with which they drew attention to the brutal wrongs done to Ireland by their colonial masters. Moore was not an active revolutionary, but his songs fueled the flames of patriotism in Ireland and evoked a sympathy for the Irish cause throughout the Continent. Moore also drew upon the historic defeats of Ireland as a goad to present action, a tactic that his fellow countrymen were soon to seize upon. At a time when Irishmen were wallowing in despair, he sought to restore a sense of national pride and purpose by celebrating the heroism of real and legendary figures who had sacrificed their lives in preference to servility. Moore's *Irish Melodies* were translated into every tongue of Europe, including Hungarian, Polish, and Russian, where their passionate yearning for freedom stirred hearts with similar feelings.

Moore spent the majority of his life in England where he became the idol of the literary establishment and a welcome guest in the drawing rooms of the nobility, performing his *Irish Melodies* as after-dinner entertainment. Ironically, back in Ireland he would have been arrested for some of the radical sentiments he expressed through the medium of song. Like his bardic precursors in Gaelic, Moore was a public witness-bearer to the greatness and grief of Irish culture. In doing so, he paved the way for the Irish Literary Revival at the turn of the twentieth century—arguably the major literary and dramatic movement of the twentieth century.

—ii—

W. B. Yeats, the founder and leader of the Irish Literary Revival, donned the mantle of Moore in basing much of his own life's work on the treasure trove of imaginative riches contained in the ancient mythology of Ireland and the folklore of the Gaelic-speaking peasantry. Yeats's first major essay, published when he was only twenty-one, was devoted to a two-part elegy on the poet and translator Samuel Ferguson (1810-1886). Ferguson, a Scots-Irishman who loathed Catholicism as well as the nationalist aspirations of the vast majority of the Irish people, nonetheless fell in love with the native culture. Indeed, he devoted his life to enabling the Irish, including members of the Ascendancy class like himself, to "live back in the land they live in" by coming to know the native heritage of the native people.[4] In paying tribute to the ideals and work of Ferguson, Yeats began to formulate a theory of art that shaped not only his own effort as an artist but that of the entire Revival:

> Great poetry does not teach us anything—it changes us. Man is like a musical instrument of many strings, of which only a few are sounded by the narrow interests of his daily life. Heroic poetry is a phantom finger swept over all the strings, arousing from man's whole nature a song of answering harmony. It is the poetry of action, for such alone can rouse the whole nature of man. It touches all the strings—those of wonder and pity, of fear and joy. It ignores morals, for its business is not in any way to make rules for life, but to make character. It is not, as a great English writer [Matthew Arnold] has said, 'a criticism of life,' but rather a fire in the spirit, burning away what is mean and deepening what is shallow.[5]

With his pursuit of life-transforming mystical and occult experience, Yeats was a poetic counterpart to Carl Jung. What Jung called individuation, or the actualization of all one's human faculties, was called by Yeats Unity of Being. But he went beyond Jung in arguing that this state of being cannot be realized without an equivalent realization of all the latent spiritual energies that exist within one's own culture. An impossible ideal, of course, but Yeats was committed to an imaginative process of thought that aimed to give actuality to forms that lie beyond the categories of space, time, and personality. As he once wrote, "It may be that the arts are founded on the life beyond the world, and that they must cry in the ears of our penury until the world has been consumed and become a vision."[6]

Yeats found an initial answer to his own spiritual hunger in the half-pagan, half-Christian beliefs of the Gaelic-speaking peasantry whom he encountered as a young man in the West of Ireland. He was astonished to discover that, in the cosmology of the peasantry, "this world and the world we go to after death are not far apart."[7] Yeats was profoundly moved to find a correspondence for this belief system in a collection of love songs translated and published in 1893 by the Gaelic scholar Douglas Hyde:

> [This] is one of those rare books in which life and art are so completely blended that praise or blame became well-nigh impossible. It is so completely a fragment of the life of Ireland that if we praise it we but praise Him who made man and woman, love and fear, and if we blame it waste our breath upon the Eternal Adversary who has marred all with incompleteness and imperfection.[8]

Many critics have commented on the verbal magic of Irish poetry and song, finding therein a reflection of an entire world conceived of as sacred. The contemporary Irish poet Nualla ní Dhomnaill, in a *New York Times* article explaining why she writes in Gaelic, asserts that only a culture bereft of a life-transforming contact with the otherworld would have to struggle so hard to maintain it:

> The way so-called depth psychologists go on about the sub-conscious now-a-days, you'd swear they had invented it or at least stumbled on a ghostly and ghastly continent where mankind had never previously set foot. Even the dogs in the street in West Kerry know that the 'otherworld' exists and that to be in and out of it constantly is the most natural thing in the world.[9]

A constant fructifying tension between reality and fantasy, life and the dream, Darkness and Light is one of the abiding themes of Irish literature, but nowhere more so than in the traditional love songs of Ireland. Over and over again one encounters descriptions of the beloved as a kind of angel descended to earth from paradise, radiating eternal happiness through a perfect beauty that can only be compared with precious jewels, the fragile luminescence of roses or lilies in bloom, the evanescent rapture of a skylark's song or a white swan drifting over a still lake at evening. Similar imagery is also used to describe the haunting appearance of fairies—particularly the *"leanansidhe,"* or fairy mistress, who often lays claim to the male imagination—especially in moonlight gardens amidst the scent of flowering fruit trees or glimmering among the shadows of a forest at the bewitching hour of twilight or early dawn. Such sensual imagery always carries sexual connotations. And overwhelmed by desire the lover is utterly smitten—afflicted with a wasting sickness that saps him of all his will and energy. Such profound feelings does the beloved inspire that without her presence the love of God is unattainable and only through love is God experienced. The loss of the beloved is the same as the loss of God.[10]

Only a culture steeped in a reverence for nature as a mystical emanation of the Divine could conjure love in imagery and attitudes such as these. Indeed, in the tradition of the eighteenth century *"aisling"* (or vision poem) Ireland herself is personified as a fairy woman fleeing the advances of an unwanted suitor, searching for her one true mate whom she will know by his willingness to die for her sake. No wonder that for two centuries *"aislinghi"* such as these inspired revolutionary activities in Ireland. It is also no wonder that when such forms of romantic all-consuming love—whether directed towards a particular person, place, or an entire island nation—is blocked from fulfillment, severe psychic disturbances can result. In Ireland these disturbances often erupted in the episodes of brutal violence that have marked the turbulent history of the country, leaving in their wake bitter hatreds that continue to fester for generations. One of the missions that guided Yeats's work as a poet and cultural activist was to create a love of Ireland so deep that it ultimately overcame her tragic divisions. In that as in so many aspects of his life, vision and political reality failed to coalesce.

—iii—

It has been said that words make you think a thought and music makes you feel a feeling, but a song makes you feel a thought. The four Irish song lyrics that follow demonstrate the truth of that observation, each in quite different ways. "Down by the Salley Gardens," an early lyric by Yeats, expresses the old Gaelic idea of "*neart*," meaning the creative energy that is evoked when all the forces of nature are summoned in a mission designed to bring healing to the soul. According to bardic tradition, master harpers and singers were employed as intermediaries between this and the other world. With the help of the fairies, their natural allies, they were able to cure many illnesses and ease the pain of childbirth as well as the wounds of warriors injured in battle. Such gifted performers were considered sacred because of their access to the supernatural. This is why, in the Christian iconography of Ireland, harpers and singers take pride of place along with the saints and holy virgins, all of whom sing the praises of God.

"Kilcash" embodies a central aim of the Irish literary Revival, namely to make sacred in the imagination the holy places of Ireland—in this case a sixteenth-century castle and its beloved grounds brought to ruin through the devastation of the Penal Laws. The Druid idea that God is present in the natural world is evoked in increasingly embittered line after line of the lyric, like the axe blows that cut down the once abundant forests of Ireland. The song expresses the "*slí an uaigneas*," or fierce heartbreak, of an entire culture that has been separated from its ancestral roots and way of life.

The Christian mystic Ivan Illich has defined human flesh as embodied love. Just as in Christ, God became flesh, so human beings are called to embrace our neighbors through an act of loving friendship.[11] "The Parting of Friends" expresses the same idea in a threnody of grief that, in its very anguish, also gives testimony to the love that inspired it. The deeper meaning of the song is that it is through love among friends—in this case a group of eighteenth-century patriots who will shortly lose their lives in the cause of Irish freedom—we also engage ourselves with the "*Anima Mundi*," or soul of the world. For it is by embracing the personhood of one another through love that we release divine energy into the world.

"The Gates of Dreamland," by the Irish mystic George ("A. E.") Russell, is a vision of the complete transformation of the modern world made possible through the spiritual power and passion of the Irish Literary Revival. The song could be viewed as emblematic of all that Yeats and his colleagues in the Revival sought to accomplish. The fact that, from the standpoint of Yeats, the movement he founded only partly succeeded in realizing his lofty ambitions should not blind us to the greatness of its achievement. For, in giving voice to what the French Islamic scholar Henry Corbin calls the "*mundis imaginalis,*" Yeats and his fellow artists opened up the possibility of breaking down the divisions between the inner and outer, the psychic and the physical so as to create a new order of being in which, as the Corbin scholar Tom Cheetham avers, "thoughts are embodied and bodies are spiritualized."[12]

Yeats, at the end of his life was asked whether he could sum up his philosophy, and replied, "Man can embody truth, but he cannot know it."[13] From his struggle to create images of an ideal life out of the actions of mundane reality—and vice versa—Yeats came to believe that the artist as well as ordinary human beings can come to know a far deeper understanding of life than that known to either the pure man of thought or man of action. Celebrating the life-affirming energy that can only be born out of a perpetual tension between opposites is the key to the genius of Ireland. That is the "heart mystery" at the core of Yeats's art and of many Irish artists.[14] It is also the mystery at the heart of a tradition of magical Irish love songs whose glory lies as much in their transcendent aspirations as in the compassion wrought out of their soul-disturbing sorrows.

—iv—

DOWN BY THE SALLEY GARDENS
Lyric by William Butler Yeats (1865-1939)

> Down by the Salley gardens
> My love and I did meet,
> She passed the Salley gardens
> With little snow-white feet.
> She bid me take love easy,
> As the leaves grow on the tree;

But I being young and foolish
With her did not agree.

In a field by the river
My love and I did stand,
And on my leaning shoulder
She placed her snow-white hand;
She bid me take life easy,
As the grass grows on the weirs,
But I was young and foolish
And now am full of tears.

In performing Yeats' "Salley Gardens," I sometimes refer to it as a Buddhist song of renunciation. Published in *Crossways* (1889), Yeats's first volume of verse, the lyric was influenced by the quietist philosophy of the Indian holy man Mohini Chatterjee, who provided Yeats with his first experience of the Eastern doctrines and meditative practices that became central to his lifelong spiritual pursuits. Inspired by the teachings and example of Chatterjee, Yeats, with a group of high school friends who included George ("A.E.") Russell, founded in June 1885 the Dublin Hermetic Society where, as he later recalled, Chatterjee sought to persuade his young disciples that "all action and all words that lead to action were a little vulgar, a little trivial. Ah, how many years it has taken me to wake out of that dream."[15]

"The Salley Gardens" is actually based on an eighteenth-century Irish ballad, "The Rambling Boys of Pleasure," that Yeats heard as a youth in Sligo. Following time-honored Irish tradition, Yeats freely adapted the words to his own purposes. The word *saille* in Gaelic means "willow," and there was in Sligo town an actual willow grove where lovers were wont to meet. The other details of the setting—a field by a riverbank, the water flow stilled by the presence of a little dam, or *weir*—lend a languorous enchantment to Yeats's interpretation that is utterly lacking in the original ballad. I was once challenged at a faculty party in Atlanta by a pugnacious, somewhat inebriated visiting poet from Northern Ireland who, knowing my love of Yeats, sang the following verse from the ballad, prefacing it with the claim that Yeats was nothing less than a "literary thief:"

It's down in Sally's Garden,
O there hang Rosie's three;

> O there I met a fair maid,
> Who told me her mind so free;
> She bids me take love easy
> As leaves they do fall from the tree,
> But I being young and crazy
> Could not with her agree.

Replying to his charge, I said that Yeats had described his version as "an old song re-sung," meaning that one rendition of an air need not cancel out another. Then, honoring another venerable Irish tradition, that of *flyting* (or verbal jousting), I proceeded to sing Yeats's exquisite meditation on the need to balance the frenzy of love's longing with the peace that comes only from submitting oneself to the pattern of nature's inexorable ebb and flow.

Yeats may have ultimately come to regret that he failed to heed the advice contained in his own lyric. In January 1889 what he called "the troubling of my life" began with his meeting of the woman who became his own *leanansidhe*, the beautiful Irish revolutionary leader Maud Gonne.[16] Statuesque in form, with a mane of golden hair and alabaster skin, Maud seemed to Yeats like a Celtic goddess brought to life. Instantly smitten, he wooed her in verse, but also by striving to make himself into a man of political action. All to no avail. Many years afterwards, Maud told Yeats that the world should be grateful she had not married him; otherwise all his magnificent love poetry would not have been written.[17]

Yeats, more than any other Irish writer of modern times, was true, both artistically and experientially, to the bardic legacy of Ireland. "Down by the Salley Gardens" may be Buddhist in its implicitly passive doctrine, but the young man who wrote that poem actually lived by a quite different philosophy than that advocated by Mohini Chatterjee and other sages of Eastern thought. Yeats dedicated himself to acquiring a form of wisdom that is only wrung out of the inevitable heartache of living life with passion. For Yeats, as with his bardic antecedents, the greater the limitation the greater the longing for transcendence. In that creative tension between reality and the dream—the latter symbolized by the fairy woman with "snow-white feet" who appears to the stricken lover in his old Sligo "song re-sung"—lies the key to Yeats's quintessentially Irish genius.

—V—

KILCASH

Translation by Frank O'Connor (1903-1966)

Ah! What shall we do for timber?
The last of the woods is down,
Kilcash and the house of its glory,
And the bells of the house are gone.
The Spot where that lady waited
who shamed all women for grace,
When earls came sailing to greet her,
And Mass was said in the place.

My grief and my affliction,
Your gates are taken away,
Your avenue needs attention;
Goats in the garden stray;
The courtyard's filled with water
And the great earls, where are they?
The earls, the lady, the people
Beaten into the clay.

No sound of duck or geese there,
Hawk's cry or eagle's call,
No humming of the bees there
That brought honey and wax for all,
Not even the song of the birds there
When the sun has gone down in the west,
Nor a cuckoo on top of the boughs there,
Singing the world to rest.

There's mist there tumbling from branches
Unstirred by night and by day,
And a darkness falling from heaven,
And our fortunes have ebbed away;
There's no holly nor hazel nor ash there;
The pasture is rock and stone,
The crown of the forest is withered
And the last of its game is gone.

I beseech of Mary and Jesus
That the great come home again.

> With long dances danced in the garden,
> Fiddle music and mirth among men,
> That Kilcash, the home of our fathers,
> Be lifted on high again,
> And from that to the deluge of waters
> In bounty and peace remain.

"Much of what the Irish had—the castles, mills, warehouses, forts, churches, farms—was ruined by wars and by abandonment, so that…we are passing through a land where, in the name of some violent dream or other, real things have been destroyed."[18] When I came across this statement by the English writer V. S. Pritchett more than forty years ago, I had no idea just how forcefully its truth would be imprinted upon me. Even now, I can barely get through the horrible litany of devastation depicted in the song without being overwhelmed.

The destruction of the woods surrounding Kilcash Castle was no isolated act, but the continuation of a two-hundred-year-old strategy aimed at the total conquest of Ireland. At the beginning of the seventeenth century, the island was thickly forested, with oak and elm trees reinforced by groves of ash, whitebeam, cherry, poplar, apple, holly, juniper, arbutus, and yews. The woods had provided shelter in times of war until the ruthless efficiency of the Tudor armies destroyed this last refuge of the people. The words of Edmund Spenser still shock in their stark depiction of raw human suffering:

> Out of every corner of the woods and glens they came creeping
> forth upon their hands, for their legs would not bear them; they
> looked like anatomies of death; they spoke like ghosts crying out
> of their graves ….[19]

Elizabeth I ordered the destruction of all the woodlands of Ireland not only to deprive the Irish of shelter, but as a source of timber. It is no exaggeration to say that the British navy was built with Irish oak. The reason for this is that the English forests had already been depleted by the time of the Elizabethan conquest. Thus timber in Ireland was for the colonists a source of wealth and power. In Munster alone, over one million acres of woodland were forfeited, along with their native wildlife. By the early eighteenth century, Ireland was a treeless wilderness, except for private estates like Kilcash.

For a people who from ancient times had venerated their woodlands this ruination of the land was sacrilege. The pagan traditions of Celtic Ireland are rich in the lore of holy trees, especially the oak, yew, ash, apple, and rowan. Druidism, the nature religion of ancient Ireland, was originally a cult based on the god of the oak tree, which, besides containing ancestral spirits, had the power of making the rain fall, the sun shine, and flocks, herds, and even humans to increase.[20]

Despite the fact that Druidism was often portrayed as hostile to Christianity, many pagan nature beliefs and traditions were absorbed by the early Irish Church. Just as cutting down an oak tree was an offense in pagan Ireland, so St. Columcille (? 521-597) deplored the cutting down of an oak grove at Derry where every leaf was "full of heaven's angels." St. Brigid (d. c. 524), whose very name derives from a Celtic fertility goddess, established her celebrated convent with its perpetually burning fire on an ancient druidic site of worship, Kildare (*Cill Dara*, "the shrine of the oak tree"). But it is in the magnificent prayer-poems composed within the monastic communities of sixth to ninth-century Ireland that one finds the most direct and lovely evocation of God's bounty as inseparable from the wonders of nature:

> A wall of woodland overlooks me
> A blackbird sings me a song (no lie!).
> Above my book, with its lines laid out,
> the birds in their music sing to me.
>
> The cuckoo sings clear in lovely voice
> in his grey cloak from a bushy fort.
> I swear it, but God is good!
> *It is lovely writing out in the wood.*
>
> (*Trans. Thomas Kinsella*)[21]

As the great Celtic scholar Kuno Meyer wrote,

> These poems occupy a unique position in the literature of the world. To seek out and watch and love Nature in its tiniest phenomena as in its grandest, was given to no people so early and so fully as to the Celt ....[22]

The stately, defiant ruins of Kilcash Castle, County Tipperary still stand as a testimony to the glories it once housed. The lady in the song "who shamed all women for grace" was Lady Iveagh (née Margaret Burke), and her name was indeed synonymous with kindness, courage, and generosity at a time, the early eighteenth century, when to be a Catholic in Ireland was to be an outcast. In defiance of the Penal Laws, priests were ordained at Kilcash, and it was a place of refuge for her brother-in-law, Christopher Butler, the Catholic Archbishop of Cashel. For the people of the district, the sixteenth-century castle stood as a solitary symbol of the former greatness of an entire culture, that of Gaelic Catholic Ireland, and of a fervent hope that that greatness would someday, somehow be restored. That hope was totally gone by the end of the eighteenth century.

Frank O'Connor's brilliant translation of "Kilcash" captures, especially in its insistently graphic litany of grief, a reverence for place similar to that evoked in the prayer-poems of early Medieval Ireland. But now what is also being mourned is the loss of an aristocratic way of life. The "great earls" who built the castle and sailed home to greet their lady had fought on the Jacobite side of the Battle of the Boyne in July 1690 and the Battle of Aughrim in 1691. Their calamitous defeat at the hands of the Williamite forces marked the end of the Ireland that they and their people had loved. For a time, a few Catholics like the Butlers maintained their holdings and positions as a kind of "shadow gentry" to the Protestant Ascendancy, the new masters of Ireland. Thus, a semblance of the old ways of life continued with the lavish entertainments for which the Irish were famous, including, no doubt, "long dances danced in the garden." But, by the end of the century the Penal prohibition against Catholics inheriting substantial properties had forced the Butler family to conform to the Established Church. With the 1801 Act of Union that forcibly bound Ireland and England together, Walter Butler, eighteenth Earl of Ormonde and owner of Kilcash, became a lord of the new United Kingdom and left for England. The famous trees of Kilcash were sold in order to support his lavish lifestyle as an absentee landlord living in London.

For the poets as well as ordinary people, cutting down the woods of great houses like Kilcash was a violation of propriety as well as a symbol of subjugation. As Declan Kiberd points out, Edmund Burke in later years, whenever he needed a metaphor for the Irish state or its economy, described it as a slow-growing tree lopped off before it had reached maturity. The poets equated the loss of the trees with their own demise as long-established representatives of traditional Gaelic life and culture. With fury as well as wounded pride, Aogán O'Rathaille (? 1670-1729), whose own life had been reduced from privilege to poverty by the upheavals of the time, lacerated the "upstart" planters for huckstering the woods "at sixpence a tree."[24]

William Butler Yeats, who at one point made a vain attempt to connect his own lineage with that of the Butlers of Munster and modeled his role as a poetic witness-bearer after the bards of ancient Ireland, also understood the huge cultural loss symbolized by the wreckage of the great houses of Ireland. His play, *Purgatory*, written in 1938, a year before his death, is a brooding meditation on the angry ghosts who, in the twentieth century, still seemed to roam the Irish countryside, exacting a frenzied vengeance against innocent and guilty alike. Yeats raged against all those who had cast ruination on Ireland:

> ... to kill a house
> Where great men grew up, married, died
> I here declare a capital offense.[24]

Yeats is not just referring to the "Big Houses" of the Protestant Ascendancy, though he was by then a defender of the values of the Anglo-Irish and the gifts that they, too, had given Ireland. Instead, the symbolic "house" to which he refers is the entire island of Ireland.

Just three years after writing *Purgatory* and two years after his own death, the great house to which Yeats had become most deeply attached was also destroyed. Coole Park, built in 1770 and the home of Augusta Lady Gregory, had since 1894 been a personal refuge for the poet and a hallowed place to which a host of the leading figures of the Irish Literary Renaissance came for solace and inspiration. A huge copper beech still stands in Lady Gregory's garden and on it are carved the initials of her illustrious guests: John Butler Yeats, the poet's father, and Jack Yeats, the poet's brother—both distinguished painters—as well as J. M. Synge, George Bernard Shaw, the painter Augustus John, Douglas Hyde, George ("A. E.") Russell, Sean O'Casey, and, of course, Yeats himself.

Lady Gregory died in 1932. Yeats, foreseeing her imminent death, wrote a poem the year before in honor of all that the two held dear:

> Sound of a stick upon the floor, a sound
> From somebody that toils from chair to chair,

Beloved books that famous hands have bound,
Old marble heads, old pictures everywhere.
Great rooms where traveled men and women found
Content or joy ...

We were the last romantics—chose from theme
Traditional sanctity and loveliness;
Whatever's written in what poet's name
The book of the people; whatever most can bless
The mind of man or elevate a rhyme;
But all that is changed, that high horse riderless.
Though mounted in that saddle Homer rode
Where the swan drifts upon a darkening flood.[25]

Today a visitor can still enjoy the hushed splendor of the walled garden, the shadowy woods so lovingly planted by Lady Gregory and the lake where, as Yeats recorded, "nine-and-fifty swans" once glided on its "brimming waters."[26] The entrance avenue to Coole continues to lift the heart with its soaring archway of ilex trees beckoning the visitor onward towards imaginative glory. But of the house, nothing. As with Kilcash, it remains for us to bow our heads in silent homage to a world of "bounty and peace" whose like will never come again.

—vi—

THE PARTING OF FRIENDS
Translation by Alice Milligan (1866-1953)

Ere long thro' the town my way I had wended,
By hundreds 'twas shown I was truly befriended;
We are now gathered here, yet my spirit is grieving,
The hour draweth near when my friends I'll be leaving.

The winecup goes round and song is invited,
The harpstrings resound to listeners delighted;
Let the gay music swell, till the time comes to sever,
My heart knoweth well we are parting forever.

My father, leaving Ireland in 1926 as a "Diehard" IRA man on the run from the Free State Army, had the audacity to pay a farewell visit to a close friend who was serving time in Mountjoy Prison for his political activities. When I asked what had given him the courage to take this extraordinary risk, he replied that it was "not a matter of

courage but the responsibility of friendship." For the Irish, friendship
is close to being a sacred trust.

There are deep roots for this tradition. Within the monastic
communities of the early Irish Church it was common for men and
women to develop a spiritual relationship with a fellow member of the
community known as an *anam chara*, or soul-friend. In strictly religious
terms this could be one's personal confessor—the individual charged
with imposing an appropriate penance for the sins one had committed.
But the idea of the *anam chara* extended well beyond the conventional
notion of a confessor to include the lifelong responsibilities of a
respected mentor, companion, and guide in whom one could confide
all the hidden intimacies of life. Given the ascetic discipline of monastic
life, such a relationship was vitally important for mental health. This
is recognized in the teachings of Celtic Christianity; as St. Brigid said,
"anyone without a soul-friend is like a body without a head; is like the
water of a polluted lake, neither good for drinking nor for washing."

John O'Donohue, in a recent book inspired by the idea of the *anam
chara*, has argued that the Celtic world view is based on an
understanding of life itself as sacred, with the love between friends a
precious means of realizing how divinity penetrates all of our human
existence. In this mystical tradition, friendship and love enable human
beings to bridge the gap between their own isolated identity and that
of others. As O'Donohue beautifully expresses it: "Love is the threshold
where divine and human presence ebb and flow into each other."[27]

This, of course, is the reason why the experience of love is so often
overwhelming. When we truly fall in love, according to C. G. Jung,
what occurs is that the experience calls forth the destiny of our life;
the very singularity of our passion for someone else opens up to us our
own depths, our own soul's genius. What can also occur is that we
develop in the throes of love a heightened awareness of death. As James
Hillman puts it, the very limitlessness of romantic passion summons
its opposite through emotions that remind us of the fragility and brevity
of life.[28] That may be why people take such extraordinary risks for the
sake of love. And, in the case of people like my father, for the sake of a
friendship exercised with all the responsibilities attached to love.

Many of the Irish love songs exhibit the polar tensions involved in
a supernal passion that transcends all earthly bonds along with a
desolation and despair born of the all-too-human realization that the

goal of one's desire can never in this life ultimately be reached. This dialectical tension is stunningly expressed in a single quote from Yeats's play, *The Shadowy Waters*: "Yet never have two lovers kissed but they/ Believed there was some other near at hand/And almost wept because they could not find it."[29] That overwhelming desire which, in normal circumstances is directed towards a human being, has in Ireland sometimes been transferred into a passionate love for a national idea. Such was the case with my father and many of his Republican colleagues and friends. Hence their devastation at the failure of the Irish Revolution to achieve all of its political goals. In that they were heirs to a long and tragic national legacy of blighted hopes.

On June 12th 1795, a farewell dinner was held in Belfast for Theobold Wolfe Tone (1763-1795), the father of Irish Republicanism, who was about to leave Ireland as an exile bound for the United States. Just a few days before his departure, Tone and a small group of his closest friends ascended to the highest point of Cave Hill at McArt's Fort, a site which provides a spectacular view over Belfast and its Lough. There, according to Tone's memoir, they made "a most solemn obligation...never to desist in our efforts until we had subverted the authority of England over our country, and asserted our independence."[30] The group included Henry Joy McCracken, Samuel Neilson, Thomas Russell, and William Simms. All but Tone were Ulster Protestants; he, too, was a Protestant, but was born in Dublin. All were prominent leaders of the United Irishmen, that gallant and idealistic group of Protestants and Catholics who, during the 1790s, came together in an effort to establish a democratic, non-sectarian Irish Republic where the rights and values of all Irish people would be respected. That effort came to a bloody end with the failed Rebellion of 1798 in which over 30,000 Irishmen lost their lives.

In Belfast, Tone and his family were cheered by the many friends who had rallied round them. Plans were laid for Tone to go to France to gather support for an effort to overthrow English rule in Ireland. Two unsuccessful French invasions were subsequently made; the second in 1797 resulted in Tone's capture and subsequent death by suicide in a condemned cell. McCracken, Neilson, Russell, and Simms were also to die as a result of the 1798 Rebellion. All were in attendance at the farewell banquet for Tone.

Also present at the banquet was Edward Bunting (1773-1843), a young musician whose *General Collection of the Ancient Music of Ireland*, published in 1796, marked the beginning of the effort to revive traditional Irish music. Bunting had attended the 1792 Belfast Harp Festival where he transcribed the airs of ten harpers who had been assembled in order to preserve some fragments of their art before it altogether disappeared. Eight of the twelve airs in the 1808 first edition of Thomas Moore's *Irish Melodies* were taken from the Bunting *Collection* and Moore was to provide lyrics for twenty-six other Bunting transcriptions.

It was customary at the end of such gatherings for a closing song to be played. Sometimes this would be a gay and graceful dance tune or a drinking song so as to send people home on a cheerful note. On the occasion of a death or the possibility of prolonged separation of friends, the air would be much sadder. At the close of the banquet for Tone, Bunting chose an appropriate air, "The Parting of Friends," a lament said to have been written by the Northern poet Cathal McCabe on the death of his friend, the great poet and composer Turlough O'Carolan. The piece is not contained in any of Bunting's three collections but preserved in one of his notebooks under two phonetically inscribed titles, "*Na Cumun*" and "*Scaroon no Gompenaugh*," meaning "The Bond" and "The Scattering of Friends."

It is recorded that the wife of Tone, perhaps sensing the horrors in store for so many in the company, including her husband, burst into tears at the pathos of the music and left the room.

—vii—

THE GATES OF DREAMLAND
Lyric by George ("A. E.") Russell (1867-1935)

It's a lonely road thro' bogland to the lake at Carrowmore,
And a sleeper there lies dreaming where the water laps the shore.
Tho' the moth wings of the twilight in their purples are unfurled,
Yet his sleep is filled with music by the masters of the world.

There's a hand as white as silver that is fondling with his hair;
There are glimm'ring feet of sunshine that are dancing by him there:

And half open lips of faery that were dyed to richest red,
In their revels where the Hazel Tree its holy clusters shed.*

"Come away," the red lips whisper, "all the world is weary now,
'Tis the twilight of the ages and it's time to quit the plough.
Oh, the very sunlight's weary ere it lightens up the dew,
And its gold is changed and faded before it falls to you."

"Tho' your colleen's heart be tender, a tenderer heart is near,
What's the starlignt of her glances when the stars are shining clear?
Who would kiss the fading shadow when the flow'r face glows above?
'Tis the beauty of all beauty that is calling for your love."

Oh, the great gates of the mountain have opened once again,
And the sound of song and dancing falls upon the ears of men;
And the Land of Youth lies gleaming, flushed with rainbow light and
    mirth;
And the old enchantment lingers in the honey heart of earth.

Central to the tradition of ancient Ireland was the belief that music
and poetry possess an occult power to profoundly alter human behavior.
This belief may derive from the mythic idea that the arts have their
origin in the Otherworld, and that through them the fairies sometimes
confer their magical gifts upon mortals. Thus a systematic development
of the imaginative faculties was an integral part of the rigorous training
followed by those who would assume the privileged position of
professional bard.

But what one also finds in Irish folklore is that the actual experience
of the Otherworld can be fraught with terror. Indeed, the abduction
of someone to the fairy world is often accompanied by an hypnotic,
hallucinatory form of music that has the effect of dragging the hapless
victim into a never-ending nightmare. John Synge, an artist not
normally inclined to surrender himself to occult speculation, describes
such an experience in his brilliant memoir, *The Aran Islands*:

---

*Hazel trees are a source of sacred wisdom in Irish folklore. They surround the
Spring of Segais, the source of supernatural wisdom in the Celtic Otherworld. Segais is
itself the mythological source of the two most sacred rivers of Ireland, the Shannon and
the Boyne. When the hazels drop their nuts into the well they are eaten by the salmon,
who then carries their wisdom with him as he makes his way upstream every springtime,
back to the world of humans.

Last night, after walking in a dream among buildings with strangely intense light on them, I heard a faint rhythm of music beginning far away on some stringed instrument.

It came closer to me, gradually increasing in quickness and volume with an irresistibly definite progression. When it was quite near the sound began to move in my nerves and blood, and to urge me to dance with them.

I knew that if I yielded I would be carried away to some moment of terrible agony, so I struggled to remain quiet, holding my knees together with my hands.

The music increased continually, sounding like the strings of harps, tuned to a forgotten scale, and having a resonance as searching as the strings of the 'cello.

Then the luring excitement became more powerful than my will, and my limbs moved in spite of me.

In a moment I was swept away in a whirlwind of notes. My breath and my thoughts and every impulse of my body became a form of the dance, till I could not distinguish between the instruments and the rhythm and my own person or consciousness.

For a while it seemed an excitement that was filled with joy, then it grew into an ecstasy where all existence was lost in a vortex of movement. I could not think there had ever been a life beyond the whirling of the dance.

Then with a shock the ecstasy turned to an agony and rage. I struggled to free myself, but seemed only to increase the passion of the steps I moved to. When I shrieked I could only echo the notes of the rhythm.

At last with a moment of uncontrollable frenzy I broke back to consciousness and awoke.

I dragged myself trembling to the window of the cottage and looked out. The moon was glittering across the bay, and there was no sound anywhere on the island.[31]

One of the basic tenets of mystical belief systems throughout the world is that, by actively pursuing altered states of consciousness, one can develop a deeper awareness of the magical in ordinary life. This remains a key function of Irish poetry and music—and it continues to have a profound impact on many aspects of Irish culture, including a veneration for particular holy sites. In the Irish tradition, visionary experiences such as the one described above give strength to the opinion that there is a psychic memory attached to these places. Such locales—

the sacred sites of both pagan and early Christian Ireland—are called "thin places."

The lyric to this song by George ("A. E.") Russell describes an attempted fairy abduction in the form of an enchanted dream. Its setting is Carrowmore, a peninsula jutting out into the Bay of Sligo which is filled with Neolithic burial chambers overlooked by the greatest cairn in all of Ireland, the mountaintop gravesite of Maeve, the fairy Queen of Connacht. At the very time when the lyric was written, Russell and his friend W. B. Yeats were deeply involved in occult research designed to prepare the way for a spiritual movement of such power and insight that it would transform the consciousness of the modern world. "A. E." wrote to Yeats describing the incredible changes that were about to occur:

> The gods have returned to Erin and have centered themselves in the sacred mountains and blow the fires through the country. They have been seen by several in vision, they will awaken the magical instinct everywhere, and the universal heart of the people will turn to the old druidic beliefs. I note through the country the increased faith in fairy things. The bells are heard from the [fairy] mounds and sounding in the hollows of the mountains. A purple sheen in the inner air, perceptible at times in the light of day, spreads itself over the mountains. ... Out of Ireland will arise a light to transform many ages and peoples.[32]

The same transformative energy evident in this prophetic statement and in "The Gates of Dreamland" also fired the imagination of Yeats as he worked to establish a literary and dramatic movement in Ireland that would take upon itself the fervor of a priesthood in combining two passions ready at hand: "Love of the Unseen Life and love of country."

As a young man, Yeats believed that art is "tribeless, nationless, a blossom gathered in No Man's Land." But writing about Ireland and the arts in 1901, inspired by his own dreams of what Ireland might become at the dawn of the new century, Yeats claimed that it was possible to create a modern Irish version of classical Greece in which artists, drawing upon the history, legendary lore, and religious traditions of their country, would "fix upon their memory the appearance of mountains and rivers and make all visible again in their art, so that Irishmen, even though they had gone thousands of miles away, would still be in their own [imaginative] country."[33]

For Yeats the means to cultural transformation must be immediate, rooted, and practical. As Yeats put it, scholarship and art must function together so as to "make love of country more fruitful in the mind, more a part of daily life." Thus, in the ancient Irish spirit of "*dinnshenchas*," or lore of places, music, poetry, and other works of art would ultimately endow the Irish landscape with a sacramentality lost elsewhere in the modern world. In this way the stories, poems, and songs associated with particular locales would "make every lake or mountain a man can see from his own door an excitement in his imagination." No mere collection of slogans for a catchy tourist campaign, Yeats sought to ground the arts in the ever-changing patterns of actual life. Only thus would Irish art reflect "the passing modes of mankind" and in that, "the face of God." Only thus would "the spirit of man" be wedded to "the soil of the world." And only thus would the Irish race become, over time, "a chosen race, one of the pillars of the world."[34]

Extravagantly utopian if one were to test these ideas against the social, political, and economic urgencies of a nation that had barely begun the process of defining its own identity much less climbing out of the hideous morass of colonial oppression. But without the idealism and courageous enterprise of a Yeats, who knows if the twentieth-century Irish culture that was to produce world-class artists like James Joyce, Samuel Beckett, Brian Friel, Seamus Heaney, Niall Jordan, Jim Sheridan, Louis Le Brocquy, Robert Ballagh, U2, and Bill Whelan would have taken the shape it did. And who knows what kind of an Irish culture might have emerged had Yeats not sought to ground it in a living sense of its past greatness as well as its future possibility—a fusion of the kingdoms of everyday reality and imminent transformation within a mystical oneness.

As fellow art students in their late teens and twenties, Yeats used to accompany George "A. E." Russell into the countryside where his friend painted the fairy creatures who appeared directly to his sight, their nubile white bodies glowing sensuously amidst the shadowy reaches of the woods. Yeats and Russell quarreled, however, because Yeats wanted to question the fairies, thus driving them away. It was symptomatic of other quarrels that would almost destroy their friendship. The most serious of these occurred in 1903 when Russell opposed Yeats's effort to transform the amateur group of actors who comprised the then grandiosely titled "Irish National Theatre Society" into a professional company that within a year would become the world-famous Abbey Theatre. Yeats responded to Russell's objections in an extraordinary letter that defined the differences between the two of them:

> I desire the love of a very few people, my equals or my superiors. The love of the rest would be a bond and an intrusion. ... The antagonism, which is sometimes between you and me, comes from the fact that though you are strong and capable yourself you gather the weak and not very capable about you, and I feel they are a danger to all good work. It is I think because you desire love. Besides, you have the religious judgment to which all souls are equal. In all work except that of salvation that spirit is a hindrance.[35]

The antagonism to which Yeats refers reflected many deeper divisions within Irish society that would damage not only the friendship of Yeats and Russell but also a great deal more that they both held dear. Yeats, always more practical than Russell, realized that the dark side of any cataclysmic change in human affairs is the "Savage God" of violence—the rampaging, raging violence that has marked revolutionary political movements throughout the entire course of the twentieth century, including, of course, Ireland. Still, for all the self-indulgence of so much of Russell's writings, his fairy paintings with their haunting sense of the imaginal remain a glorious legacy. And so does Yeats' magisterial body of work as well as an entire literary movement unparalleled in modern times for its human and spiritual resonance and richness. That movement owes much of its continued enchantment to the deliberate effort of these two inspired artists to recover the magic of the ancient traditions of Gaelic Ireland. As Seamus Heaney has written of a fiddler on the Blasket Islands who claimed to play what came "out of the night:"

> So whether he calls it spirit music
> Or not, I don't care. He took it
> Out of wind off mid-Atlantic.

> Still he maintains, from nowhere
> It comes off the bow gravely,
> Rephrases itself into the air.[36]

NOTES

1. Review of Douglas Hyde's "Love Songs of Coungehtt" (Bookman: October 1893), published in *Uncollected Prose of W. B. Yeats, Vol. I*, ed. John P. Frayne (New York: Columbia University Press, 1970).

2. *The Book of Irish Verse*, ed. John Montague (New York: Bristol Park Books, 1998), p. 26.

3. *Poetry in Modern Ireland* (Cork: Mercier Press, 1951), pp. 15–16, 19.

4. "The Dublin Penny Journal," *Dublin University Review* (January 1840), p. 116.

5. "The Poetry of Sir Samuel Ferguson" ("Irish Fireside," October 9, 1886), republished in Frayne, p. 84.

6. "The Celtic Element in Literature," *Essays and Introductions* (New York: Macmillan, 1961), p. 184.

7. *The Celtic Twilight, Mythologies* (London: Macmillan, 1962), p. 98.

8. Frayne, p. 292.

9. "Why I Choose to Write in Irish," *New York Times Book Review* (January 8, 1995), p. 28.

10. See Seán O'Tuama, "Love in Song," *Repossessions: Selected Essays on the Irish Literary Heritage* (Cork: Cork University Press, 1995), pp. 134–160.

11. Tom Cheetham, *After Prophecy: Inspiration and the Unity of the Prophetic Tradition* (New Orleans, LA: Spring Journal Books, 2007), p. 79.

12. Cheetham, p. 9.

13. "Letter to Lady Elizabeth Pelham (January 4, 1939)," *The Letters of W. B. Yeats*, ed. Allan Wade (London: Rupert Hart–Davies, 1954), p. 322.

14. See "The Circus Animals Desertion," *Collected Poems* (London: Macmillan and Company, 1965), p. 392 for the source of the title of this essay as well as one of Yeats's most powerful poetic statements of his dialectical philosophy. Also see *The Irish Mind: Exploring Intellectual Traditions*, ed. Richard Kearney (Dublin: Wolfhound Press, 1985) for a series of essays arguing that, contrary to the linear, logocentric, and dualistic philosophy that has dominated Western thought, the Irish way of thinking expresses a dialectical logic that embraces opposition, contradiction, and ambiguity—what James Joyce called having "two thinks at a time."

15. *Collected Works in Verse and Prose, Vol. VIII* (Stratford-on-Avon: Shakespeare Head Press, 1908), p. 279.

16. W. B. Yeats, *Memoirs*, ed. Denis Donoghue (London: Macmillan, 1972), p. 40.

17. Introduction to *The Gonne–Yeats Letters 1899–1938*, ed. A. Norman Jeffares (New York: Norton and Company, 1992), p. 19.

18. V. S. Pritchett, "The Irish Character," *Holiday Magazine*, Vol. 33, No. 4 (April, 1963), p. 58.

19. Edward Spenser, *A View of the Present State of Ireland* [1596], ed. W. L. Renwick (Oxford: Clarendon Press, 1970).

20. Eoin Neeson, "Woodland in History and Culture," in *Nature in Ireland: A Scientific and Cultural History*, ed. John Wilson Foster (Dublin: Lilliput Press, 1997), pp. 133-156.

21. *The New Oxford Book of Irish Verse*, ed. Thomas Kinsella (New York: Oxford University Press, 1979), p. 30.

22. Kuno Meyer, *Ancient Irish Poetry* (London: Constable and Company), p. xii.

23. Declan Kiberd, *Irish Classics* (Cambridge, MA: Harvard University Press, 1996), pp. 56, 80.

24. W. B. Yeats, *Collected Plays* (London: Macmillan and Company, 1960), p. 683.

25. W. B. Yeats, "Coole Park and Ballylee," *Collected Poems* (London: Macmillan and Company, 1965), p. 276.

26. "The Wild Swans at Coole," *Collected Poems*, p. 147.

27. John O'Donohue, *Anam Cara: A Book of Celtic Wisdom* (New York: Harper-Collins, 1997), pp. 52-3.

28. James Hillman, *The Soul's Code: In Search of Character and Calling* (New York: Random House, 1996), p. 146.

29. *Collected Plays*, p. 151.

30. Marianne Elliott, *Wolfe Tone: Prophet of Irish Independence* (New Haven: Yale University Press, 1989), p. 258.

31. John Synge, *The Aran Islands* (Marlboro: The Marlboro Press, 1907), pp. 64-5.

32. "Letter from A. E. to W. B. Yeats (February 2, 1896)," *Letters from A. E.*, ed. Alan Denison (London: Abelard- Schuman, 1961), p. 17.

33. "Ireland and the Arts," *Essays and Introductions*, pp. 204–206.

34. *Ibid.*, pp. 208–210.

35. Letter from Yeats to "A. E.," (January 8, 1906), *Letters*, p. 466.

36. "The Given Note," "Door Into the Dark," *Opened Ground: Selected Poems 1966–1996* (New York: Farrar, Straus and Giraux, 1998) p. 36.

THE WISDOM OF W. B. YEATS
"THUNDER OF A BATTLE FOUGHT IN SOME OTHER STAR"

MARK PATRICK HEDERMAN

Kathleen Raine (1908-2003), the British poet, critic, and scholar of William Blake and W. B. Yeats, summed up herself and the century through which she had lived as follows:[1]

> A child of my time, who at Cambridge read Natural Sciences, and rejected my Christian heritage in order to adopt with uncritical zeal the current scientific orthodoxy of that university, I have lived long enough to come full circle. It is all that I learned in my Cambridge days that I have little by little come to reject, by a reversal of premises which has brought me to my own Orient. A slow learner, I have been blessed with a long life which has brought me to a knowledge not taught in our schools.

For W. B. Yeats and for Kathleen Raine, the sages who can teach us a knowledge of another kind are the great poets and visionaries down through the centuries whose wisdom has been harvested in the so-called sacred books from all spiritual traditions. For these two twentieth-

Mark Patrick Hederman has been a Benedictine monk of Glenstal Abbey in Limerick, Ireland, for over 40 years. He was prior of the monastery and headmaster of the school at different times, before embarking upon his present quest: to unearth the presence of the Holy Spirit in our world. He has written an account of this search during the opening years of the 21st century called *Walkabout: Life as Holy Spirit* (Dublin: Columba, 2005).

century protagonists of an alternative world, William Blake (1757-1827) was such a prophet:

> Who beat upon the wall
> Till Truth obeyed his call.[2]

The difficulty is that many people regard Blake as insane and Yeats as not much better. Kathleen Raine is dismissed by this widespread constituency as a lesser poet in her dotage, or a semi-religious quack.

Listen to John Carey, Merton Professor at Oxford University and chair of the Man Booker judges for 2004, who is reviewing the first volume of Roy Foster's biography of W. B. Yeats: "Was he [Yeats], you find yourself blasphemously wondering, really that intelligent?"[3] and he lists the usual proofs of intellectual backwardness:

> He was substandard at school . . . He never learnt to spell: even as a grown man, simple monosyllables foxed him . . . His gullibility was fathomless. Mysticism and magic, to which he was introduced by the half-batty George Russell, occupied much of his waking and sleeping life. He believed he conversed with old Celtic gods and a copious ragbag of other supernaturals.[4]

Such critics may or may not believe that we have taken a major detour from the path of Truth, but they certainly do not regard William Butler Yeats as a trustworthy guide to a better path, and such critics hold the high ground in influential academic circles.

The first half of the twentieth century was a battle for the "soul" of Ireland. The Roman Catholic Church, as the century progressed, became the highest and the loudest bidder. But W. B. Yeats set out to represent an alternative spiritual tradition. His kind of "prophet" is one whom William Blake would have seen as "the awakener," one who, like Kathleen Raine, "speaks *from* the spirit innate in all, *to* the spirit innate in all."[5]

Yeats wrote to Lady Gregory on the 28th of January 1904 describing his first lecture tour in America. He is in Chicago speaking to an almost exclusively Catholic audience in Notre Dame:

> I began of a sudden to think, while I was lecturing, that these Catholic students were so out of the world that my ideas must seem the thunder of a battle fought in some other star ... I think these big priests would be fine teachers, but I cannot think they

would be more than that. They belong to an easygoing world
that has passed away.[6]

Much of Yeats's life was a battle against the "easygoing world" which
Roman Catholicism seemed to him to represent and which he saw as
the paralyzing fate of the new Ireland of the twentieth century. He
believed that one of his tasks was to provide his country and, indeed,
the world of the twentieth century with the elements of a more vibrant
religious life.

> I have mummy truths to tell
> Whereat the living mock.[7]

These two lines summarize in epigrammatic form the huge ambition
and deflating reception of his efforts.

Yeats wrote in his introduction to Lady Gregory's *Gods and Fighting
Men* (1904) "Children at play, at being great and wonderful people"
are the true reality of what we are and what we should become.
"Mankind as a whole had a like dream once; everybody and nobody
built up the dream bit by bit and the story-tellers are there to make us
remember." But the children of the twentieth century had put away
these ambitions "for one reason or another before they grow into
ordinary men and women." But the poets and the artists and the
storytellers are there to keep the dream alive, to keep the path open to
that brave new world.

In his letters W. B. Yeats dated our defection, our detour from the
true heritage opened for us by imagination and religion, to the 17th
century. In 1926 he wrote to Sturge Moore that "what Whitehead calls
'the three provincial centuries' are over. Wisdom and Poetry return."
The twentieth century was the privileged time of reawakening.

The wisdom which Yeats believed to be our most precious heritage
can only be expressed through poetry. The word of God can never be
relayed through prose. If this means that the message is sometimes
obscure that is not because the poet is being deliberately obscurantist,
it is because we are moving in a borderland area for which ordinary
language is not designed. Yeats believed also that the whole person in
the totality of every constituent part was needed to discover and embody
such truth. There is a religion which reneges on its responsibility to
discover such Truth and which becomes a search for immunity against

the shocks of life. Such a fearful attempt to hide from the demands of human passion and human life is, for Yeats, a denial of the two essential mysteries of Christianity: Creation and Incarnation. Such a religion was the one being proposed, in Yeats's view, for the new Ireland of the twentieth century.

Yeats worked on the text of *A Vision* for twenty years. It was published in two versions, the first in 1925 the second in 1937, two years before his death. His own "thinking," if such is the correct term for his work, is neither scientific nor metaphysical, it is mythical. *A Vision* is a "gradually accreted credal construct" which finally emerges as a "massively syncretic mythic system," James Lovic Allen suggested in 1975.[8]

One of the first and most intuitive studies of *A Vision* by Virginia Moore in 1956 recognizes that Yeats's "belief" must influence his poetry. However, her analysis never gets beyond the norms of "good taste" which prescribe for English and American critics that Theosophy is foolishness and all religious mythology eventually Christian.

W. H. Auden was less polite and more dismissive: "In 1930 we are confronted with the pitiful, the deplorable spectacle of a grown man occupied with the mumbo-jumbo of magic and the nonsense of India."[9] And elsewhere: "All these absurd books," and with his irritatingly superior snigger: "but mediums, spells, the Mysterious Orient—how embarrassing."[10] Hugh Kenner granted it, in 1956, the architectural status of a "gothic fortress" which a brief generation of critics had assaulted and "scrutinizing its interior by periscope reported that it was full of bats."[11] Northrop Frye called it "an infernal nuisance" that we "can't pretend doesn't exist."

Critics in the 1960's became more cautious and respectful. Helen Vendler[12] tried to rehabilitate it as a source of poetic imagery, an experience necessary to produce the power of the later poetry and the plays of the mature artist. Harold Bloom, acknowledging the sympathetic brilliance of her salvage operation, wishes he could agree, but cannot: "Jung is a bad romantic poet, Yeats a great one who suffered, in *A Vision*, a failure in vision."[13] Ellmann prolongs the architectural metaphor in 1967: "*A Vision* is a cathedral whose 'symbolic portentousness' seems to liquidate humanity and into which its author is suctioned, 'cocooned' or 'ingested.'"[14] Steven Helming in 1977 suggests that the whole thing is a hoax which confounds all Yeats's enemies and critics and shows him to be a comic genius almost as cunning and perverse as Joyce.[15] Matthew De Forrest in 1991 presents the intriguing possibility that the book is in code form and that, like the esoteric subjects with which it deals, unfolds itself in a secret language for those who can read the signs. The surface narrative is a decoy to deflect cynics and scoffers.[16] Perhaps the most useful work was done by A. Norman Jeffares, whose biography of W. B. Yeats[17] and 1990 edition of *A Vision* and related writings[18] put the texts and the facts at the disposal of anyone interested, in a practical, dispassionate way. At the beginning of the twenty-first century a wealth of biographical and critical work helps us to take a more measured and sympathetic stance.

The variety of bemused interpretation and irritated skepticism which have surrounded *A Vision* ever since its creation are caused, or at least exacerbated, by the coy and deliberate fiction with which Yeats surrounded the origins of this work. The 1925 edition was presented as the essential teaching of an Arabian tribe, the Judwali, who had once possessed a learned book called *The Way of the Soul between the Sun and the Moon* attributed to a certain Kusta ben Luka, a Christian Philosopher at the Court of Harun Al-Raschid. This Sacred Book had been lost and its essential doctrine was explained to younger members of the tribe through the medium of diagrams drawn by old religious men upon the sand. These diagrams were identical with a book called *Speculum Angelorum et Hominorum* which had been written by a certain Giraldus and printed in Cracow in 1594. Two old friends of Yeats, with whom he had quarrelled, Michael Robartes and Owen Aherne, meet in the National Gallery in 1917. Robartes is in possession of this wisdom collected in

> sheets of paper which were often soiled and torn . . . rolled up in a bit of old camel skin and tied in bundles with bits of cord and bits of shoe-lace. This bundle . . . described the mathematical law of history, that bundle the adventure of the soul after death and that other the interaction between the living and the dead.

Michael Robartes is in possession of the wisdom which he wants Owen Aherne to publish. The trouble is that "no man has ever had less gift of expression" than Robartes, and Aherne is incapable of receiving the wisdom without imposing upon it his own Christian interpretation. The two quarrel violently and Robartes decides that they should give the documents to Yeats and ask him to write them down. Robartes had originally intended to do this but balked at the prospect, saying to Aherne: "I have great gifts in my hands and I stand between two enemies; Yeats that I quarrelled with and have not forgiven; you that quarrelled with me and have not forgiven me."

In the second edition of 1937, Yeats admits that this introduction was made up by him because the real truth of the origin of *A Vision* involved his wife and she had not been prepared to have her name associated with the text at that time. Now, he is able to tell the real story: Four days after his marriage when he was in a state of gloom, mostly because he was thinking of Maud Gonne and her daughter Iseult, his wife began to act as a medium, through a process of automatic writing, and this was the beginning of those revelations which he later edited into their final form in *A Vision*. He describes the strange occurrence of these revelations in the Introduction to the second edition, under the heading "A Packet for Ezra Pound:"

> What came in disjointed sentences, in almost illegible writing, was so exciting, sometimes so profound, that I persuaded her to give an hour or two day after day to the unknown writer, and after some half-dozen such hours offered to spend what remained of life explaining and piecing together those scattered sentences. "No," was the answer, "we have come to give you metaphors for poetry."

Early readers of these texts can be forgiven for suspecting that the whole thing was humbug, and for accusing Mrs. Yeats of inventing her mediumship as a way of shaking her husband out of a depression four days after their marriage.

It would have been difficult for the average Irish person in the forties and fifties of the last century to understand the relationship between Yeats and his wife Georgie Hyde-Lees. He married her at the age of 52 when she was 26, in the same year during which he had already proposed to Maud Gonne for the umpteenth time and to her daughter, Iseult, for at least the second time. Maud Gonne and he had been "mystically" married according to themselves, and Yeats remained obsessed with her throughout his life. Yeats also had several love affairs before and after he was married. Such facts are hard for those of us who live in "an easygoing world that has passed away" to understand; they certainly sound like "thunder of a battle fought in some other star." According to Yeats's own account:

> I was saying to myself, "I have betrayed three people," then I thought, "I have lived all through this before." Then George spoke of the sensation of having lived through something before (she knew nothing of my thought). Then she said she felt that something was to be written through her. She got a piece of paper, and talking to me all the while so that her thoughts would not affect what she wrote, wrote these words (which she did not understand), "with the bird" (Iseult) "all is well at heart. Your action was right for both but in London you mistook its meaning."

To suggest that either or both these extraordinary people were guilty of fraud in these circumstances is to misunderstand the reality which is being touched upon here. Mrs. Yeats was a much more creative and impressive partner to W. B. in all their many pursuits together than early uninformed gossip and speculation allowed. Her portrait emerges much more positively in the biography of Yeats by A. Norman Jeffares who describes her as

> very well educated, being a good linguist by aptitude and very well read ... They had a lot in common. She was studying astrology . . . Like many of his friends, she shared his interest in tarot cards. She was reading philosophy. She was attending seances with him and she was admitted—probably in 1914, with Yeats as sponsor—to the *Stella Matutina* section of the Golden Dawn.[20]

They were together in the making of *A Vision*, and research by George Mills Harper presents us with over 4,000 pages which were transmitted through Georgie Yeats, sometimes while she was asleep but mostly while she was awake. More subtle instruments and methods are needed to understand this phenomenon. Both Margaret Mills Harper and Elizabeth Butler Cullingford hold that many of the seminal ideas of *A Vision* originated in the mind of George Yeats and that its communal genesis destroys the possibility of individual authorship or control over the text.[21] Ann Saddlemeyer's biography of Mrs. W. B. Yeats establishes all this authoritatively.[22]

Whatever we say about *A Vision* we have to recognize that both Yeats and his wife believed that the text came to them from "unknown instructors" in a dimension other than our workaday consciousness. It represented the event for which Yeats had been waiting and preparing himself during all the weary and frustrating hours of discipleship to various orders and societies. It was a moment of revelation during which Yeats "received" a wisdom which he felt bound to record without interpretation or elaboration. His reception of it was dependent upon his wife, and at the time of their commitment to this audition they experienced a blending of their souls which put them in touch with a much larger psychic reality, stretching both in time and in space beyond the limited circumference of the historical life of each or of both of them. This, then, is the source of *A Vision*. That one of its results was to inspire Yeats to more effective poetic endeavor seems also to be indisputable. The structure of *The Tower*, the book of poetry he published in 1928, is based upon the revelations which also informed *A Vision*. The book of poetry was named both for the poem of that title and for Thoor Ballylee, the ancient tower house which still stands and which Yeats and his wife were converting into a symbolic home for themselves. Yeats wanted this book of poetry, named after Thoor Ballylee, to be an icon in itself, and as itself. The real tower in which he lived, and the book of poems called after it, were the most important legacy he would leave behind him. He had asked Sturge Moore to create the design for the cover: "The Tower should not be too unlike the real object or rather . . . it should suggest the real object. I like to think of that building as a permanent symbol of my work plainly visible to the passer-by."[23] Both the building and the book are congruent to the structure of *A Vision,* published three years earlier in 1925. The poem "All Souls' Night" serves as epilogue to both books.

The question which haunts in the presence of such texts is: are we here in possession of something which has succeeded in pushing back a little further the frontiers of human ignorance? Has Yeats's genius, coupled with the genius of his wife, allowed all of us to make a breakthrough to areas which had been unavailable to the realm of human discourse? Is this writing something in the order of a prophecy heralding a new age of religious consciousness? This is what Yeats fervently believed and this is what it is our duty to explore. In the touchingly arrogant words of our potential master, speaking of "Ireland and the

Arts," and quoting his friend Mr. Ellis: "It is not the business of a poet to make himself understood, but it is the business of people to understand him. That they are at last compelled to do so is the proof of his authority."[24]

Are we to take *A Vision* seriously on its own terms, on Yeats's terms? If so, then it is a revolutionary document; if not, it may be of interest to literary criticism but it is not essential to life. In examining the total phenomenon we must recognize both its dual authorship and the particular poetic genius of the one who gave it definitive and enduring expression. Yeats was essentially a poet and all his great work is given to us in the language of poetry. The text of *A Vision* is, therefore, irretrievably connected to Mrs. W. B. Yeats as source, and to the later poems and plays of W. B. Yeats as collateral.

Of the more recent biographies and studies of Yeats's life and work, Terence Brown's captures certain nuances and subtleties in this regard. "To the institution of an occult marriage," he suggests, "Yeats as poet owed a great debt, as do we his readers, who discover in his later writings a body of work which confronts in its heroic and radically disturbing fashion, the crisis faced by the religious imagination in the modern world."[25]

When we ask why did Yeats not come out into the open and say to his readers: "I am a prophet. I have just received a divine revelation which I am now communicating to you in a work called '*A Vision*,' which has taken much of my life to elaborate in its now definitive form, and which, of all my works, is the one containing the most important wisdom it has been given to me to impart,"[26] we must look for answers in at least three sensitive areas: Yeats's awareness of the hostility of others, and his own timidity and lack of self-confidence. These were little appreciated facts at the time, but have been perceptively presented by one of his early biographers, Richard Ellman. Denis Donoghue sums it up:

> In Ireland, it is fair to say, Yeats is resented; not for his snobbery, his outlandish claim to the possession of Norman blood, or even for his evasion of history by appeal to two classes of people who existed only as shades—Gaelic Irish and Anglo-Irish—but because he claimed to speak in the name of "the indomitable Irishry." De Valera claimed to speak for Ireland, and the claim was tenable: he has had, in that capacity, no successor. In the

> present confusions, readers of Yeats resent his appeal to Irishness, and his assertion that he knows the quality of Irishness when he meets it. That resentment is so inclusive that little or nothing survives in its presence.[27]

According to Elizabeth Butler Cullingford, "Yeats knew that his name had become a byword for paganism, anti-Catholicism, opposition to Gaelic culture, and snobbery" among his Catholic counterparts, and especially in the Catholic culture being supported and diffused by such publicity organs as *The Catholic Bulletin*.[28]

Roy Foster's biography[29] shows the persistence and depth of antagonism between Catholic Ireland, as incarnated in the newly established Free State and expressed in *The Catholic Bulletin*, and the "New Ascendancy" which they saw as "epitomized by people like WBY [W.B. Yeats], Gogarty, Plunkett, and Russell, and entrenched in institutions such as the Royal Irish Academy, Trinity College, and the Senate." The Bulletin described the Nobel Prize which Yeats won in 1923 as "the substantial sum provided by a deceased anti-Christian manufacturer of dynamite." "It is common knowledge," this report continues, "that the line of recipients of the Nobel prize shows that a reputation for Paganism in thought and word is a very considerable advantage in the sordid annual race for money, engineered, as it always is, by clubs, coteries, salons and cliques."[30]

Secondly, Yeats was obsessed by mysticism, in awe of those whom he knew to be geniuses in this sphere, and aware that he was not one of them, but rather a poet. Those who idolize the man and worship his poetry find it difficult to understand this hierarchy of values. However, the circle of Yeats's most intimate friends shared it. In this esoteric work, which Yeats fostered for most of his life with dedication and energy, there were others who were more gifted and capable than he was. Yeats was interested in creating a Celtic Order of Mysteries which would "select its symbols from all the things that had moved people 'through many, mainly Christian, centuries.'"[31] However, Yeats seemed to have been aware at all times of his dependence upon others for his own mystical life. He was something of an orphan in the spiritual realm and did not possess the self-contained visionary faculty which, he believed, others like A.E. (George "A.E." Russell), Blake, and MacGregor Mathers embodied. Yeats's wife said when A.E. died that he was "the nearest to a saint you and I will ever meet." She was addressing her husband, and went on to say, "You are a better poet, but no saint."

Thirdly, Yeats was brought up by his father, John Butler Yeats, whom he "admired ... above all men" as an enlightened agnostic. Darwin and Huxley had put paid to Christianity and all the superstitious mythology of pre-scientific humanity. The discoveries which ushered in the twentieth century in both science and art allowed John Butler Yeats to be optimistically humanist. He wanted his children to avail of the freedom and knowledge to which they now had a right, and was anxious to defend them from the destructive and guilt-ridden complexes which established churches had foisted upon their contemporaries. John Butler Yeats's biographer suggests that had he lived to read *A Vision,* "the shock would surely have killed him."[32]

His son believed that true Christianity should be grafted to the indigenous religion of a country, that each country became a "Holy Land" only when its imagination had been captured and its Old Testament led towards the expansive and comprehensive fulfilment of the new. Europe had no older or greater religious tradition than that embodied in the rites, the sites, the pilgrimages of prechristian, Celtic Ireland.

Byzantium, which symbolized for Yeats that perfect fusion of Christianity with the human imagination, in its early period, was contemporaneous with Patrick (396-469). The "unity of being" within a "unity of culture" which Yeats regarded as the goal of religious reconciliation, was evident in the Book of Kells and other art works of this period of Celtic culture.[33] Later he said in a B.B.C. Broadcast in Belfast [8 September 1931]:

> Now I am trying to write about the state of my soul, for it is right for an old man to make his soul, and some of my thoughts upon that subject I have put into a poem called 'Sailing to Byzantium.' When Irishmen were illuminating the Book of Kells [in the eighth century] and making the jewelled croziers in the National Museum, Byzantium was the centre of European civilisation and the source of its spiritual philosophy, so I symbolise the search for the spiritual life by a journey to that city.

One of the major differences between this earlier Christianity and later manifestations of it, especially in the version being institutionalized in Ireland after independence, but also in various protestant variations, was its capacity to integrate the sexual as a sacred mystery central to all life of whatever kind. The character of Crazy Jane in Yeats's imagination (an old woman whom he invokes in a series of poems including one called "Crazy Jane Talks to the Bishop") represents the Old Testament of the Celtic race crying out against the bishop, representing institutionalized religion, especially its contemporary Irish Catholic variety. Sexual prudery and puritanism were major enemies in Yeats's crusade for a more integrated and wholesome Christianity.

There is sufficient evidence to suggest that the source of Yeats's mystical writings is the blending of the collective unconscious with the corporate personality achieved by his wife and himself through satisfactory sexual communion, involving frequent intercourse which had to include female orgasm. "Collaboration between the sexes was the enabling precondition of Yeats's achievement, and the topic of sexual love dominated his conversation with the spirits."[34]

The sexual was "the sixth sense" which could tune into the unconscious, creating the balance between creativity and sexuality which brought about "unity of being." Anne Saddlemeyer has provided the most convincing account of this common source of "the script" which was communicated to W. B. Yeats and his wife George during so many hours of their married life.[35] Such contact with the sacred is germane to a long tradition of mystical experience which, even in the Judaeo-Christian versions, from the book of Genesis, through the Song of Songs, to the writings of so many poets of mystical "marriage," employs the image of male/female union to describe relationship with the divine.

Elizabeth Butler Cullingford sees the "Supernatural Songs," which were written after Yeats had had an operation to restore his sexual potency, as "the verses of a ribald iconoclast who is out to disturb musty piety, but is nevertheless serious about reconciling divine love with the natural emotion of human passion."[36] She also suggests that Yeats found in Indian Tantric philosophy "the acceptance of sex as a road to divinity" and an affirmation of his own insistence upon "an alliance between body and soul" which "our theology rejects."[37]

Yeats's work in *A Vision* is the desert geometry, the abstract sketch, the "frozen music," which his later work fleshes out. The poem, "The Gift of Harun Al-Rashid," explains the relationship between the poet's marriage and his initiation into the mysteries which constitute *A Vision*.

It tells the story of Yeats's marriage at the age of 52 with a young woman and how the ensuing ecstasy revealed through her was nothing less than the infrastructure of the universe. The extraordinary world into which both he and his partner were introduced, through the everyday event of their sexual communion, is also conveyed by the unreal and antique nature of the story. As Yeats had said of Maud Gonne that his earlier poetry "shadowed in a glass/ What thing her body was," so *A Vision* was a cubist representation of the body of his wife. "The Gift of Harun Al-Rashid" is possibly the nearest we shall get to unscrambling that cubist encodement: "Perhaps," as he said in 1934, "now that the abstract intellect has split the mind into categories, the body into cubes, we may be about to turn back towards the unconscious, the whole, the miraculous."[38]

Anne Saddlemeyer's painstaking biography of George Yeats has shown too that she was, perhaps, the more important partner in the eventual achievement of the scripts. Yeats regarded himself as both the dispositive and the final cause of these revelations. He believed that it depended on him to make whatever use might be made of their common "script." But the script as it finally emerged is probably more beholden to George's contributions than it is to W. B.'s, although neither he nor she, nor for that matter any of the critics, would have believed this; nor would they have any interest in it—the only important thing about it was the affect it had on one of the great poets of the twentieth century.

The marriage of Yeats and George Hyde-Lees was more a sacred tryst than a romantic alliance. She was, in fact, the perfect partner to the apprentice mage, and his union with her was probably the most important energy in his life both as person and as poet. His connection with Maud Gonne and her daughter Iseult was more absorbing and stimulating in terms of literary gossip, romantic obsession, and early poetry, but the deep sexual intimacy of his relationship with George was of a different order and became the source of whatever happiness he achieved, mystical insight he attained, and great poetry and drama he wrote in his later years.

A Vision is the map of another country. It is a country to which access was given to Yeats through sexual communion with his wife. It is a country which is wider and deeper than individual consciousness. In their case it became apparent that she began to speak the words from a more extensive consciousness, shared by at least the two of them, but more importantly extending beyond even this expansion of normal understanding, to one shared by the dead. It holds and provides an imagery, a geometry, a symbolism which can be shared by those who have gone before us. It allows the possibility of communion, commensalism with the dead. It goes further and suggests that there is a whole area of consciousness, not just between birth and death, but between death and birth, which can be logged into by an art which lures us to the borders of trance. In itself *A Vision* does not "do" this. Art is the doer of such deeds.

Yeats's ghosts told him that they were bringing him images for poetry. This has often been interpreted as a diminishment in religious terms of his original project in the work of *A Vision*. Such interpretion reads the statement as dismissal of the whole occult experience in his life and his marriage as simply convoluted and fantastic pantomimes and gymnastics to provide him with paraphernalia for his poems, animals for his circus. However, the statement can be understood differently.

Providing images for poetry can be more than fodder for a harvester. Images are not simply manageable units to be included within a predictable tapestry. Images are like diamonds which need the expertise of poetry to display in their multifaceted polyvalence. And here we have to take seriously the parallel work of Ezra Pound, who influenced not only Yeats but also T. S. Eliot and many other pioneers of twentieth-century poetic practice, especially in his almost neurotic attempt to guide this particular idiom through the movements of "*imagisme*," first of all, and then "vorticism," to prevent it from being contaminated by lesser, more popular, and thereby more compromising versions of itself.

Pound had defined the Image as "that which presents an intellectual and emotional complex in an instant of time" and later expanded this attempt to corral and to brand the original species of wildness which he knew had been eliminated almost to the point of extinction by the twentieth-century manufacturers of thought, and which he believed passionately it was the task of the poet to revive and to rehabilitate. "The Image is more than an idea. It is a vortex or cluster of fused ideas and is endowed with energy. If it does not fulfil these specifications, it is not what I mean by an Image."[39]

So, when we say that the later poems of Yeats were vehicles for the Images which he received from the 20-year process of religious endeavor, recorded more prosaically in *A Vision,* we are saying more than that the contents of these poems are full of strange and bizarre pictures which make them more piquant and esoteric. Yeats is attempting to formulate an inspiration received from elsewhere in a shape and structure of language which demand an originality, an ingenuity as idiosyncratic and pliable as that employed by Byzantine artisans, required and permitted for the first time to hammer out the mystery of a God become Man.

We have been educated out of myth and magic. We are able to symbolize as children, but this faculty is erased by our learning the three Rs, our so-called system of education. Civilized societies of the 20th century democratized the languages of reading and writing. These became fundamental currency in the West. They also became the criteria for "intelligence" as we see from the above assessment of W. B. Yeats by professors at Oxford in recent years. Only those who have fallen between the bars of the grid know the extent to which they are marginalized and deprived by illiteracy. We imagine that reading and writing are natural to us, whereas, in fact, they must be two of the most unnatural activities ever undertaken by creatures on this planet.

People of Western Europe in the 20th century were not only able to read and write more or less instinctively, they translated everything that presented itself to them into this narrow network. We read music, art, cinema, life, and love. Everything we did was a story, an alphabet, a grammar, a plot, a chapter, a closed book, a best seller. We read and we wrote our lives. My diary was my day translated into linear modules of coherent literacy. From four years of age all our children are condemned to a bookish, commercial education. Recent meetings of the United Nations seem determined to inflict this myopia on all children of the world in the name of equality of opportunity and universal education.

Walter Ong has examined this restricted vision in much detail. He shows how a language such as High Latin which was never a "mother tongue" [taught by one's mother] to later generations of Europeans, became their only access to so-called Higher Education. Obviously Latin was once a spoken language, but it became a "school language," completely controlled by writing, once it ceased to be a vernacular tongue for those who used it. It became the *lingua franca* of the

universities based in academia and suffusing an exclusively male
environment.

> For well over a thousand years [Latin] was sex-linked, a language
> written and spoken only by males, learned outside the home in
> a tribal setting which was in effect a male puberty rite setting,
> complete with physical punishment and other kinds of
> deliberately imposed hardships. It had no direct connection with
> anyone's unconscious of the sort that mother tongues, learned
> in infancy, always have . . . Devoid of baby-talk, insulated from
> the earliest life of childhood where language has its deepest
> psychic roots, a first language to none of its users, pronounced
> across Europe in often mutually unintelligible ways but always
> written the same way, Learned Latin was a striking
> exemplification of the power of writing for isolating discourse
> and of the unparalleled productivity of such isolation . . . making
> possible the exquisitely abstract world of medieval scholasticism
> and of the new mathematical modern science which followed
> on the scholastic experience. Without Learned Latin, it appears
> that modern science would have got under way with greater
> difficulty, if it had got under way at all. Modern science grew in
> Latin soil, for philosophers and scientists through the time of Sir
> Isaac Newton commonly both wrote and did their abstract
> thinking in Latin.[40]

Only those, like W. B. Yeats, for instance, escaped the net and retained
their imaginative faculties by default. Only those marginalized from
our education system stumbled upon the alternative and, in many cases,
became what we term great artists or geniuses of one kind or another.
Yeats's intelligence was essentially mythic. Such intelligence weaves its
way through symbols and has a very different perspective on the universe
from that of the scientist, for instance. Our generation has been
innoculated against such balderdash.

A seminal work in providing such awareness of our symbolic
blindness is *The Crane Bag and Other Essays* by Robert Graves.[41] The
title essay is the review by Graves of a book by Dr. Anne Ross called
Pagan Celtic Britain. Graves believes that this highly qualified academic
celtologist is barred from understanding the very material she is writing
about because of her university education and scientific mentality. "As
a girl of seventeen Dr. Ross had done what anthropologists call 'field-
work' by learning Gaelic for six months in a West Highland peasant's

hut. Then after graduating at Edinburgh, she took an educational job in the same Goidelic region, but later returned to Edinburgh for a degree in Celtic studies and a Ph.D. in Celtic archaeology." Thus, according to Graves "she forgot . . . how to think in Gaelic Crofter style, which means poetically." He makes his point by quoting her treatment of an important Celtic Myth about "The Crane Bag" of the sea-god Manannan Mac Lir. This bag had been made for the Sea-God from the skin of a woman magically transformed into a crane.

> This crane-bag held every precious thing that Manannan possessed. The shirt of Manannan himself and his knife, and the shoulder-strap of Goibne, the fierce smith, together with his smith's hook; also the king of Scotland's shears; and the King of Lochlainn's helmet; and the bones of Asil's swine. A strip of the great whale's back was also in that shapely crane-bag. When the sea was full, all the treasures were visible in it; when the fierce sea ebbed, the crane-bag was empty.

Dr. Ross is like the rest of us, trained out of our poetic sensibility. She has lost the art of reading the signs of the times. According to Graves she "can make nothing of such fairy-tale material." He has to interpret for her:

> What the fabulous Crane Bag contained was alphabetical secrets known only to oracular priests and poets. The inspiration came, it is said, from observing a flock of cranes, "which make letters as they fly." And Hermes, messenger to the Gods, afterwards reduced these to written characters. Cranes were in fact totem birds of the poetically educated priests . . . That the Crane Bag filled when the sea was in flood, but emptied when it ebbed, means that these Ogham signs made complete sense for the poetic sons of Manannan, but none for uninitiated outsiders. The Crane Bag was not, in fact, a tangible object, but existed only as a metaphor.

Dr. Ross as an academic archeologist has the job of digging up "things" from the past, dating and comparing these. But as a trained scientist "she can accept no poetic or religious magic." Anything that falls outside the scope of her "academic conditioning" is "branded as mythical—mythical being, like Pagan, a word that denies truth to any ancient non-christian emblem, metaphor or poetic anecdote." We too have been overly trained in scientific prejudices. We no longer see the

world as symbol. We are incapable of reading the signs of the times, of
unearthing the Spirit at work in our world. Our world is like the island
of Shakespeare's *Tempest*: a confusion of bewildering lights and sounds
to Caliban, but "clear signals from a different order of experience" to
Prospero's eyes and ears. We have to decide whether "to turn tail on it
all like howling Caliban or to develop new powers of attention and
perception capable of orchestrating this mad music."[42]

Symbolic intimation in poetic form is Yeats's strategy of expression.
"We would seek out those wavering, meditative, organic rhythms, which
are the embodiment of the imagination," he proposes in the
"Symbolism of Poetry." This idiosyncratic and comprehensive idiom
has been masterfully examined by Denis Donoghue:

> His instrument is rhythm, presumably because human feeling,
> which seeks release in words and is outraged by the poor release
> it finds, sways to rhythm as to music.[43]

Yeats learnt much from Arthur Symons who dedicated his book
The Symbolist Movement in Literature (1899) to him. "To name is to
destroy, to suggest is to create," was Mallarmé's principle, according
to Symons, and the most subtle instrument of suggestion was rhythm,
"which is the executive soul." Sartre has argued in his Preface to
Mallarmé's *Poésies* that Mallarmé's devotion to the imaginary arises from
his resentment against reality, and the poems written in that mood
are symbolic acts of revenge: the poet's words are designed to undo
the work of the first Creation, the poem being a second and higher
version.

"An image becomes a symbol," Donoghue explains,

> on being touched by value or significance not attributable to its
> own set. For example: think of an event in narrative as a moment
> or a position along a line, straight or crooked, and then think of
> it as being crossed by another line of value from another source.
> Each line is a set, a paradigm. But the event which occurs at the
> point of intersection between two sets is an image in both; its
> duplicity constitutes its symbolic force. Interpreted in one set, it
> declares itself unrestrained by that interpretation; it is part of the
> other set as well. When we find an image becoming a symbol,
> we feel in it this double potency; its allegiance expands, as if
> answerable to both idioms, ready to participate in both sets of
> relations. This marks its freedom and its suggestiveness; we have

a sense in attending to it that there is no point at which we can
say for sure that its force has come to an end.[44]

However, Donoghue suggests that "Yeats started out as a Symbolist
and ended as something else." In "The Symbolism of Poetry" Yeats says
that "all sounds, all colours, all forms, either because of their
preordained energies or because of long association, evoke indefinable
and yet precise emotions, or, as I prefer to think, call down among us
certain disembodied powers, whose footsteps over our hearts we call
emotions." And in "The Philosophy of Shelley's Poetry" he speaks of
the Great Memory as "a dwelling-house of symbols, of images that are
living souls." Therefore "the aura we feel in the symbol marks for Yeats
the presence of the supernatural in the natural. The poet is therefore a
mage, adept in secret but traditional knowledge. The poet must
become an alchemist of the word. Symbolism is the poet's form of
magic, except that what the mage does consciously the poet does half
consciously and half by instinct. The ancient secret is common to both
disciplines. Magic was congenial to Yeats's mind for many reasons, but
especially because it exerted the heuristic [serving to discover; *heur* =
"find" in Greek] power of language, the common grammar of mage
and poet.

This goes some way to account for the incantatory note in Yeats's
hieratic style, where his lines are more readily acceptable if we take
them as rituals, prescriptions, or interdictions than as secular utterances
delivered from a high horse. Morton Irving Seiden[45] suggests that Yeats
saw great art in general and his own poems in particular as embodiments
of the supernatural. His symbols have theurgical power; his poems and
plays are sacred rites. "In a number of his essays, but notably in
'Speaking to the Psaltery,' first published in 1902, he urges that his
poems be chanted or intonated as though they were (it seems) Orphic
prayers." By means of these supernatural poems "he tried to recreate
in the modern world the mythologies of ancient India, Eleusian Greece,
and pre-Christian Ireland."

The ring-master in this circus of imagery has a task as complicated
as shunting carriage loads of sparkling and exploding jewelry along
converging railway lines from a signal box at a junction in an antique
railway station. The signal box or cabin from which all such direction
occurred was called, appropriately, "The Tower." Originally all such
signalling was done by mechanical means: cables or rods, connected

at one end to the signals and at the other to the signal box, run alongside the railway. The guts of such a system is a signalling frame, complex cabling arrangements with linkage to levers and controls. A railroad switch is an installation at a point where one rail track divides into two further tracks. It can be set in either of two positions, determining whether a train coming from A will be led to B or to C. If we adapt this image to the "system" which Yeats was trying to install, we find him in a Tower overlooking a junction where many more than three "trains of thought" are merging. "Central to the development of this elliptical and mysterious series," says Foster about the poem "A Last Confession," for instance, "is the subtle patterning whereby the interpenetrating gyres and cones of occult astrology are equated to the physical act of love: a fusion of the spiritual and the erotic which for Yeats connects not only to Swedenborgian cosmology but also to his early (and future) interest in Indian philosophy."[46]

The Image is the vehicle, almost the stunt artist, which allows such ambidexterity to be conveyed without losing its integrity or betraying its illusivity. Can it be translated into logical thought? Helen Vendler certainly thinks so. Her book, *Poets Thinking*,[47] defends poetry, because it is "a feat of ordered language" as, therefore, "something one can only call thought."[48] Her "criticism" of poetry has tried to elucidate the thinking of a poem as "an exemplification of its own inner momentum," and in her chapter on "W. B. Yeats Thinking" she claims to have cracked the code of his system of thought which she calls "Thinking in Images" and which she uses as the subtitle of the same chapter. In justice, she claims "we must call what [poets] do, in the process of conceiving and completing the finished poem, an intricate form of thinking, even if it means expanding our idea of what thinking is." This "thinking" cannot be revealed by "a thematic paraphrase," for instance, but it can be excavated by the conscientious critic. Such a critic must be able to translate the subtle calculus of concatenated imagery into however distended an epistemology. What she describes as "the complex architectonic assembling of images by Yeats" can be shown as his "style of thinking" because even though it may become "instinctual" in "the heat of composition" it still "issues from an extensive repertoire of image-memory and intellectual invention, coupled with an uncanny clairvoyance with respect to emotional experience."[49] So, "if we are to understand a poem, we must reconstruct the anterior thinking [always in process, always active] that generated its surface, its 'visible core.'"[50] Such "thinking," described as "the evolving discoveries of the poem," Vendler admits "can be grasped only by our participating in the process they unfold." However, in my view, she has already prejudiced such participation by limiting it to four comprehensive fields which she names as "psychological, linguistic, historical, philosophical." These exclude the very possibility, which the whole process was established by Yeats himself to explore, namely contact with a world outside all these fields which would come under the heading of "religious, mystical, spiritual, magical." Without at least countenancing such contact, there is little possibility of reconstructing "the anterior thinking" of W. B. Yeats at whatever time or in whatever process he was engaged during most of his poetic life. In such a context as his, "thinking" becomes a weak even though indispensable filter for wisdom from another source, and poetry establishes itself as the multifaceted container which alone can salvage from such depths the treasure which inspiration detects. The later poems of W. B. Yeats embody and transcribe the contours of such revelation.

NOTES

1. Kathleen Raine, *W. B. Yeats and the Learning of the Imagination* (Golgonooza Press, 1999), pp. 5-6.

2. W. B. Yeats, "An Acre of Grass," *Collected Poems* (London: Macmillan, 1955), p. 347.

3. R. F. Foster, *W. B. Yeats: A Life, I: The Apprentice Mage 1865-1914* (Oxford University Press, 1997); II: *The Arch-Poet, 2003.*

4. John Carey, "Poetic License," *The Sunday Times*, 9 March 1997, sec. 8, p. 1.

5. Kathleen Raine, *W. B. Yeats*, p. 121.

6. *The Letters of W. B. Yeats*, ed. Alan Wade (1954), p. 422.

7. From the poem "All Souls Night," which Yeats wrote at Oxford in the Autumn of 1920 and which he included in his book of poems, *The Tower* and used as Epilogue to *A Vision.*

8. James Lovic Allen, "Belief versus Faith in the Credo of Yeats," *Journal of Modern Literature*, 4, 1975, pp. 692-716.

9. W. H. Auden, "Prosecution and defence," quoted in Elizabeth Butler Cullingford, *Gender and History in Yeats's Love Poetry* (Cambridge: Cambridge UP, 1993), p. 249.

10. W. H. Auden, "Yeats as a Example," *The Permanence of Yeats*, ed. James Hall and Martin Steinman (New York: MacMillan, 1961).

11. Hugh Kenner, "Unpurged Images," *The Hudson Review*, 8, 1956.

12. Helen Vendler, *Yeats's Vision and the Later Plays* (Cambridge, MA: Harvard UP, 1963).

13. Harold Bloom, *Yeats* (Oxford: Oxford UP, 1970).

14. Richard Ellmam, *Eminent Domain: Yeats among Wilde, Joyce, Pound, Eliot and Auden* (Oxford: Oxford UP, 1967), p. 80.

15. Steven Helmling, "Yeats's Esoteric Comedy," *The Hudson Review*, 30, 1977, pp. 230-246.

16. Matthew De Forrest, unpublished MA Thesis, University College Dublin, 1991.

17. A. Norman Jeffares, *W. B. Yeats: A New Biography* (London: Arena, 1990).

18. A. Norman Jeffares, *W. B. Yeats: 'A Vision' and Related Writings* (London: Arena, 1990).

19. Letter to Lady Gregory, 29th October 1917, *Letters of W. B. Yeats*, ed. Alan Wade (London: Delectus, 1951).

20. Jeffares, *Yeats: New Biography*, p. 146 and p. 175.

21. Elizabeth Butler Cullingford, *Gender and History in Yeats's Love Poetry* (Cambridge, Cambridge UP, 1993), p. 106.

22. Anne Saddlemeyer, *Becoming George, The Life of Mrs W. B. Yeats* (Oxford University Press, 2002).

23. *Ibid.,* p. 314.

24. W. B. Yeats, *Essays and Introductions* (London: MacMillan, 1961), p. 207.

25. Terence Brown, *The Life of W. B. Yeats* (Dublin: Gill & Macmillan, 1999), p. 266.

26. As indeed he wrote in a private letter to T. Werner Laurie, 20th April, 1924, quoted by Saddlemeyer in *Becoming George,* p. 341: "Such wisdom of life, results of much toil and concentration, as has been granted me, that part of me that is a creative mystic, that made out of the shadow of Swedenborg is in this book."

27. *We Irish, Essays on Irish Literature and Society* (University of California Press, 1986), p. 66.

28. Cullingford, *Gender and History,* p. 144.

29. Foster, *Yeats, A Life*, I: The Apprentice Mage 1865-1914; II: The Arch-Poet, 2003.

30. Foster, II, p. 256.

31. Jeffares, *Yeats, New Biography*, p. 77.

32. William Murphy, quoted in Brenda Maddox, *George's Ghosts: A New Life of W. B. Yeats* (London: Picador, 1999), p. 204.

33. Cf. Kathleen Raine, *Yeats the Initiate* (London, 1986).

34. Cullingford, *Gender and History*, p. 111 f.

35. Saddlemeyer, *Becoming George*, pp. 119-123.

36. *Ibid.,* p. 248.

37. *Ibid.,* p. 253.

38. W. B. Yeats, *Explorations*. Selected by Mrs. W. B. Yeats (London: Macmillan, 1962), p. 404.

39. Quoted in *Imagist Poetry*, ed. Peter Jones (Penguin Books, 1972), p. 40.

40. Walter J. Ong, *Orality and Literacy: The Technologizing of the Word* (London & New York: Routledge, 2000), pp. 113-114.

41. Robert Graves, *The Crane Bag and Other Essays* (London: Cassell 1969), pp. 1-8.

42. Alan McGlashan, *Savage and Beautiful Country* (New York: Hillstone, 1966).

43. *We Irish*, pp. 35–51.

44. *Ibid.*

45. Morton Irving Seiden, *The Poet as a Mythmaker 1865-1939* (Michigan State University Press, 1962), pp. 286-7.

46. Foster, *Yeats: A Life*, II: The Arch-Poet, p. 319.

47. Helen Vendler, *Poets Thinking* (Harvard University Press, 2004).

48. *Ibid.,* p. 3.

49. *Ibid.,* p. 118.

50. *Ibid.,* p. 119.

THE RAG AND BONE SHOP OF THE HEART:
YEATS'S PATH FROM PUER TO WISE OLD MAN

JAMES HOLLIS

"Do the people in the orange jumpsuits individuate, and if so, how"? According to the student lore at the Jung Institute in Zurich, this question was likely to come up in an exam, though I never heard of anyone who had been asked that question. The point behind this rather Zen-like query was to oblige the trainee to define *individuation*, whatever that is, and to be able to differentiate that individuation did not in any way depend on intelligence, station in life, or even consciousness. The people in the orange jumpsuits were the street cleaners—the ubiquitous presences in the salubrious streets of Zurich—where I often saw them scrubbing streets, public buildings, and trams in the midst of downpours.

So, what, then, was, is, *individuation*? Briefly put, it is incarnating the fullest possibility one can become, fulfilling the intent of nature, or the gods, a process far more likely achieved through natural unfolding than conscious intent or a conceptual grasp of Jungian principles. The folks in the orange jumpsuits, in other words, had a much better chance at it than the splendid neurotics we were as trainees.

James Hollis, Ph.D., is a Jungian analyst in Houston, Texas, the author of twelve books, and director of the Saybrook/Jung Center graduate program in Jungian Studies.

The individuation process is an unfolding in service to a numinosity, a *telos*, a possible destiny, a movement of soul toward something indefinable. When on track with this possibility, we are not spared suffering, nor do we win the plaudits of our tribe, but we may feel an inner confirmation, perhaps a sense of a supportive energy. When we do not feel these accords, some are driven to Jungian analysis.

* * * *

This article illustrates aspects of an individuation process as exemplified in the life and work of one man, William Butler Yeats (1865-1939), whose productive life spanned the late romantic, Victorian, and high modernist periods of Western culture. He won the Nobel Prize in 1925, not for his poetry, but for his revival of the Irish theatre and for his contributions to the preservation, even resurrection, of a fading Celtic language and culture. When I was a callow youth in my 20s, I chose Yeats for my doctoral dissertation. I believed at the time it was because his poetry was memorable and resonant for me, though I could not explain why. Intuitively I chose the theme "patterns of opposition and reconciliation in the life and work of Yeats," a very Jungian leitmotif. (One chapter of that dissertation, the sole copy of which I have long since misplaced, was a "Jungian" interpretation of his work, in addition to literary, biographical, theological, and symbolic chapter foci to satisfy the expectations of a diverse committee.) In retrospect, I think I chose Yeats because something in my soul intuited that his journey, which he described as articulately as anyone could, foretold my own. He had traveled that path, and left articulate mentoring tracks for me and others.

In the course of research I learned that there is an incredible overlap between his concepts, his psychology, and symbology, and Jung's, a convergence which I described in an early article published and reprinted recently by *Psychological Perspectives*.[1] Jung had once consulted a translation of the *Upanishads* which Yeats had edited, and Yeats referred very tangentially to Jung, but they had no direct or sustained contact or even mutual influence. What they had in common was a rejection of the reductive materialist features of modernism, an appreciation for the symbolic life, and a special interest in occult studies as a path to Gnostic experience. Thus, as intuitives, they mined the same depths, whether as psychologist or as artist. No wonder their insights so often coincided.

Through the years I have drawn upon Yeats at different times in my personal journey as I arrived at junctures similar to which he had earlier traversed. While many casual acquaintances of Yeats will cite a line or a poem from one stage of his life or another, the serious student of Yeats will recognize that there was no single Yeats. There are many. He periodically reinvented himself and launched a whole new style, new subject matter, new psychology, new aesthetics. On one occasion, criticized for his changes, he replied,

> My friends have it I do wrong
> Whenever I remake my song.
> They should know what issue is at stake:
> it is myself that I remake.

This remaking of his identity is how Yeats's individuation organically unfolded. Articulate as he was, and remains, we can track that developmental process through his writing.

* * * * *

Yeats was born to a minority Protestant family in Ireland the last year of the American Civil War, the year Lincoln died, into a largely Catholic culture, an occupied nation, and a country in great danger of losing its soul. How can one sustain one's connection to one's tribal history, one's connective mythos, when the use of one's language is forbidden, when one groans in poverty, when the laws of the occupiers are exploitative, and when one's martyrs are fading memories in the onslaught of a seductive materialism? (His countryman James Joyce described Ireland as "an old sow that eats her farrow.") For Yeats, the aristocracy who supported the arts and transmitted cultural values, and the peasants who tilled the soil and sustained the rich faery world through story and belief, were being replaced by a nation of shop keepers, of petit bourgeoisie, who "fumble in the greasy till" and "add half pence to the pence." His personal journey of psychological development would necessarily have to play out in the context of a social, religious, political, and aesthetic *Zeitgeist* he considered vulgar, diminishing, and antithetical to his soul and the soul of ancient Eire.

His Father, John Butler Yeats, was the premier portrait painter of his era, a flamboyant non-conformist, a man whom Yeats found impossible to rebel against because his old man had already led the rebellion. This artistic spirit and iconoclastic talent spread through the family for William's brother Jack succeeded his Father as probably the most important painter in Ireland, and his sisters Lilly and Lolly founded the Cuala Press which produced lovely, artistically rendered volumes of verse that remain collectors' items to this day. (Only the Wyeth family, with their generations of succeeding talent, offer an analogy to the Yeats tribe). In this context William betook himself to an art institute for a few semesters but found that his talent was in a different medium. This brief education constituted his only formal learning although he was widely, if eccentrically, reading all his life.

As flamboyant as his Father was, Yeats's Mother, Susan, was quiet, reserved, spiritual, and wholly lacking in aesthetic interest.

> Sensitive and deep-feeling but undemonstrative, she always considered her birthplace, the romantic county of Sligo, the most beautiful place in the world, and she passed on the feeling to her children....she stood for a different kind of life, where an ignorant peasant had more worth than a knowledgeable artist.[2]

Between these poles of extravertive artist and political rhetorician, and an introvertive, myth-ridden, dreamer, W. B. Yeats lived his life. Theirs was a life of genteel poverty in Dublin and London. Just after they arrived in London, his Mother had a stroke which deprived her of her faculties and invalided her the last fourteen years of her life.

Yeats's earliest poetry, from 1885-1903, is characterized by nostalgia for a simpler life, by ambivalence toward the harsh demands of daily reality, a rejection of materialism as a value, and a general tentativeness toward virtually everything conflictual. His is the psychology of the eternal youth, the *puer*, who is bound still to the Mother, not necessarily the personal Mother, but to an overweening desire for security, satiety, and satisfaction: "O sick children of the world....words alone are certain good." ("The Song of the Happy Shepherd") "Come away, O human child / For the world's more full of weeping than you can understand." ("The Stolen Child")[3]

In that same period he affiliates with the Irish Republican Brotherhood, which morphs into the later IRA, joins occult groups such as "The Order of the Golden Dawn," and meets the love of his life, Maud Gonne, a fiery revolutionary. He believes that her commitment to political solution and his to cultural resurgence might together provide a healing energy to their stricken nation. He proposes marriage to Maud several times over the next decades but she repudiates his life style by marrying a soldier of fortune and abuser named John McBride. Yeats never gets over this wound. He pines, he complains, he idolizes the Beloved by exalting her in his verse to the status of Helen of Troy and presciently wonders if her political incitements will lead to still another burning city as it does in the Easter Rising of 1916. At times he approaches the pathetic. In "He Wishes for the Cloths of Heaven," he laments that he can only offer the beloved his plaintive entreaties, for

> ... I, being poor, have only my dreams;
> I have spread my dreams under your feet;
> Tread softly because you tread on my dreams.

Finally, he is pulled out of the dreamy world of romance by being sexually initiated by a married woman, Olivia Shakespear, whose daughter later marries Ezra Pound. The first hint of concrete sexuality and of engagement in the concrete world appears: "The horses of Disaster plunge in the heavy clay: / Beloved, let your eyes half close, and your heart beat / Over my heart, and your hair fall over my breast." ("He Bids His Beloved Be at Peace")

By 1903 Yeats is much changed. Maud has married his rival. He has found other lovers. He has co-founded The Abby Theatre with Lady Gregory and launches the revival of an independent Irish theatre, drawing heavily upon Celtic mythology and peasant lore for its subject matter. The daily demands of running a theatre, engaging in political and cultural clashes which their plays provoke, and suffering Maud's rejection, matures him, and his verse hardens in diction. Like other *puers*, he is called to the differentiation and grounding of his libido, to learn his craft, and to get a job.

When he reaches mid-life he acknowledges the cost of being a high flyer. In his poem "Pardon Old Fathers," he begs,

> Pardon that for a barren passion's sake,
> Although I have come close on forty-nine,
> I have no child, I have nothing but a book,
> Nothing but that to prove your blood and mine.

* * * *

So, how do we change? Do we change at all? Do we stay pretty much the same throughout? The answer surely is yes to all of the above. Sometimes we change because our nature is naturing; we succumb to an insurgency from below, throbbing and pushing us into life. Sometimes we change because we are carried by the rites, the instructions, the institutions of our culture. Sometimes trauma changes us, if it does not stick us, fixate our growth. Yeats changed from all of the above, and something else, a growing consciousness which brought him *intentionality*, the intentionality to find his own authority, to risk rejection, and to stand for something, even if he were standing alone. At mid-life, asking himself what he has brought to the table of life, he writes "A Coat."

> I made my song a coat
> Covered with embroideries
> Out of old mythologies
> From heel to throat;
> But the fools caught it,
> Wore it in the world's eyes
> As though they had wrought it.
> Song, let them take it,
> For there's more enterprise
> In walking naked.

For a person who so carefully cultivated the aesthetic, who reveled in "song" for song's sake, his boldness is a step out into an unprotected place. He has cast off the dreamy Celtic twilight (what Joyce cynically called "the cultic twalet") for a more direct presence in this world.

1916 brings the world crashing back down upon him and upon Ireland. The revolution erupts. Dissidents occupy the General Post Office in Dublin and after a few heroic, confusing days are shelled into submission by English gunboats diverted from the Great War. But the British badly stumble in the court of public opinion by ceremoniously executing the sixteen rebel leaders, among them Yeats's nemesis, John McBride. That, followed by an occupation by the hated constabulary troops, known as the Black and Tans for their motley uniforms, creates a groundswell of resistance for six years, leading in 1922 to the partition of Ireland into the two regions we know today. Out of this catastrophe Yeats writes the magnificent "Easter, 1916," in which he oxymoronically sees in the crimson effusion of blood the reinvigoration of Irish green, whereby "a terrible beauty is born."

Shortly after the death of McBride, Yeats proposes marriage again to Maud Gonne, who once again demurs, whereby he foolishly proposes to her daughter, Iseult, who has the good sense to decline as well. So much for idealized projections.

In 1917 Yeats finally marries a much younger English woman, Georgiana, whom he met in an occult society, and they construct a reasonably happy marriage with two children. On the fourth day of their marriage, Georgiana, seeing that Yeats is still pining for Maud, begins automatic writing which purportedly contacts the spirit world and brings enormous revelations. Yeats is so excited that he offers to give up his literary career to be the secretary of these immanent powers, but fortunately for modern literature they reply that they have rather come to provide him metaphors for his poetry. From that point on, many of Yeats's poems can be read at two levels, a surface level available to the casual reader, and a Gnostic level which alludes to a whole cosmology, a theory of personality types, and an interpretation of history which he published in 1927 as *A Vision*,* and revised and republished in 1934. The well known poem, "The Second Coming," is but one of these twin-tiered structures.

For his many articulations of political vision, Yeats is appointed a Senator in the first Irish parliament. He serves conscientiously for two terms between 1922-1928. But what most characterizes the last two decades of his life is that familiar Jungian theme—the tension of opposites. So many of his poems are dialectic structures in which he argues the opposites within his own nature. As he writes in "Ego Dominus Tuus,"

> By the help of an image
> I call to my own opposite, summon all
> That I have handled least, least looked upon.

Jung spoke of the work of analysis as an *Auseinandersetzung*, the setting of one thing over against another. Throughout the life and work of Yeats one finds this recurrent dialectic. I have concluded that the

---

Editor's Note: A Vision is discussed extensively in the preceding article by Mark Patrick Hederman.

most important conversation we will ever have is with ourselves over the polysemous meaning of our unfolding journey. Out of the quality of this conversation, the quality of all other conversations necessarily follows. In his "Dialogue of Self and Soul" this conversation culminates in a profound affirmation. Surveying his tortuous, tumultuous life, he concludes, "I am content to live it all again." How many of us can reach the end of our journeys and affirm all that has been, *all* that has been?

No young person is granted leave to write those concluding words. When Yeats wrote them he was ailing in body and suffering in spirit, yet full of that towering affirmation which signals an elision from the *puer*, afraid of the world, to the wise old man who has entered it, suffered in body and spirit there, and come through.

> When such as I cast out remorse
> So great a sweetness flows into the breast
> We must laugh and we must sing,
> We are blest by everything,
> Everything we look upon is blest.

In the 1930's Yeats declines in body but not in soul. On his death bed he writes still of Maud Gonne, the great unrequited love of his life, and two poems of the many he included in *Last Poems* (1936-39) stand out for honoring the great dialectic of his journey, and ours: a loving commitment to this world, and an affirming release from it. (As Frost said of himself, Yeats also had a lover's quarrel with the world).

In "Lapis Lazuli" he considers the social disorders of his time, anticipates another world conflagration (which commences in fact the year he dies), and achieves a buddhistic "releasement" from the ten thousand passing things of this world. His adumbration that "aeroplane and Zeppelin will come out" proves prescient in the imminent Blitzkrieg, even as these alarms and discords transmogrify into an old, old story for "there struts Hamlet, there is Lear. / That's Ophelia, that Cordelia" who "do not break up their lines to weep. / They know that Hamlet and Lear are gay." Above and beyond history an archetypal drama plays out, and above the troubled plain, the sages sit and "on all the tragic scene they stare," but, and it is a profound *but,* after years of public opposition, political hurley-burley, vituperation, jealousy, and defeat, he is able to affirm this tension of opposites, and let go.

> Their eyes mid many wrinkles, their eyes,
> Their ancient, glittering eyes are gay.

Again, only oxymoron, only the paradox of "tragic gaiety" is large enough to embrace the very opposites the *puer* sought to avoid through his aesthetic flight. Only "tragic gaiety" embraces wisdom by transcending polarities through the paradox of accepting/release and relinquishing/ affirmation.

In this same period, late Fall of 1938, Yeats rises from his bed, asks about Maud, and writes his political and aesthetic will, "Irish poets, learn your trade, / Sing whatever is well made," and consigns himself to the dust beneath his beloved County Sligo mountain Ben Bulben:

> Under bare Ben Bulben's head
> In Drumcliff churchyard Yeats is laid.
> An ancestor was rector there
> Long years ago, a church stands near,
> By the road an ancient cross.
> No marble, no conventional phrase;
> On limestone quarried near the spot
> By his command these words are cut:
>> *Cast a cold eye*
>> *On life, on death.*
>> *Horseman, pass by!*

So, is this the final word from this passionate man, this breezy detachment from what he once called "the fury and mire of human veins"? Perhaps.

Yeats died in Roquebrunne, France in January of 1939 where he was buried in a communal grave. The outbreak of the second World War that same year meant that the world turned to other things until 1948 when the Irish government sent the corvette *Macha* to the Riviera to bring his remains home in state. When his body was piped off the ship in Galway harbor, filled still today with the swans he loved for their archetypal beauty and hint of longevity, his body was received by the Irish Minister of the Interior, one Sean Gonne McBride, the son he never had with Maud.

(Subsequent research has indicated that Yeats's remains were identified from the communal grave by the fact that he was wearing a metal truss for a hernia condition. At the same time an Englishman was buried in the same grave as Yeats, also with a metal truss, so that today it is a fifty-fifty chance that Yeats's grave in Drumcliff Churchyard is occupied by that Englishman, one Alfred N. Hollis).

Yet, I think that the same Yeats who during the last years of his life, described himself as a wild, wicked, passionate old man, the one who wrote a series of bawdy ballads spoken by a "Crazy Jane" persona, is more to be found among his last poems in "The Circus Animal's Desertion." In this poem, Yeats reviews his life and compares himself to a ringmaster at a circus, one who summoned many personnae in his tour, many stunning animalia, many high wire balancing acts, and now knows that the show is closing. The aesthetic sleight of hand which once offered the *puer* the means of escape, what he terms the "ladder" up and out of the muck and mire, has disappeared. But then he considers from whence those early images of flight, those mid-life images of conflict, and those late life images of acceptance and transcendence emerged. Yes, all those images once

> Grew in pure mind, but out of what began?
> A mound of refuse or the sweepings of the street,
> Old kettles, old bottles, and a broken can,
> Old iron, old bones, old rags, that raving slut
> Who keeps the till. Now that my ladder's gone,
> I must lie down where all ladders start,
> In the foul rag-and-bone shop of the heart.

Does this sound like the youth who sought refuge in the imaginary, or escape through the transports of aesthetic sleight of hand? The raving slut who tends the till on all of us is time, death, and desiccation, and she returns us all to elemental earth. But encased in this rag/flesh and bone/cage, the heart beats on. We are left with our humanity, our yearning for love, for divinity, for release, yet are returned finally to the heart which, thumping its disquietude still opens to life, to death, and to the great mystery of it all.

Yeats moved from the eternal youth to the wise old man. He earned his way. We who follow must beware of seeking wisdom, lest we have to earn it too. We are grateful for the markers he left behind in the dark wood we all enter, but each of us must find our personal way through as he did his.

NOTES

1. Jame Hollis, "Convergent Patterns in Yeats and Jung," *Psychological Perspectives*: Vol. 4, Issue 1, pp. 60-68, 1973, and Vol. 48, Issue 2, pp. 288-297, 2006.

2. Richard Ellmann, *Yeats: The Man and the Masks* (New York: E. P. Dutton and Co., 1948), p. 23.

"Instead of adapting itself, as is necessary, to its new surroundings, the libido…regresses to the sheltering ease of the mother's arms and fails to keep pace with the passing of time….When a person remains bound to the mother, the life he ought to have lived runs away in the form of conscious and unconscious fantasies…." C. G. Jung, *Symbols of Transformation,* 2nd edition (Princeton: Princeton University Press, 1956), § 465.

3. All poetry citations are drawn from William Butler Yeats, *The Collected Poems of W. B. Yeats* (New York: Macmillan, 1963).

The Venom of Destiny:

Reflections on the Jung/Joyce Encounter

JOHN HILL

There were three encounters between C. G. Jung and James Joyce. The first concerned money, the second Jung's essay on Joyce's seminal work *Ulysses,* and the third revolved around several conversations between Jung and Joyce about the mental condition of Joyce's daughter, Lucia, the contents of which are mostly known through notes by Carey Baynes and later comments by Jung. All three encounters ended in disappointment. In this paper I will examine these encounters and some of the major reasons why these two great men failed to meet on deeper levels, despite the fact that both struggled in different ways to embody soul through the world of mythic imagery.

"Encounter" stems from the Latin "contra" and implies a meeting "by chance," "in conflict," "with an adversary" or "with the unexpected." Deep encounters initiate a meeting with otherness, the not I, in ways where one feels exposed, vulnerable, and uncertain about one's own identity. Often such encounters bear within themselves conflicting mythologies, fates, and collective patterns that either reinforce defenses

John Hill, M.A., is a graduate of the C.G. Jung Institute in Zurich and a Training and Supervising Analyst at the International School of Analytical Psychology (ISAP) in Zurich. He grew up near Dublin, and received degrees in philosophy at the University of Dublin and the Catholic University of America. He is the author of articles on The Association Experiment, Celtic myth, James Joyce, home, dreams, and Christian mysticism.

This essay was presented at the International Association of Analytical Psychology (IAAP) Congress in Cape Town, South Africa, in the summer of 2007.

against otherness or encourage surrender to the strange, unfamiliar, or unwanted parts of the self.

Joyce cast Jung as an antagonist in the role of literary critic, scientist, diagnostician, and perhaps even priest, while Jung saw Joyce as a visceral avant-garde artist and as a patient's father. Joyce, the artist, disliked science, failed his medical studies, and remained sceptical of any claim to absolute truth; he trusted and received most of his inspiration through an embodied anima that was brought to consciousness through the midwifery of Nora, his wife and partner. Jung, psychologist and scientist, at one stage repressed the artist in himself, claiming it would end in a destructive surrender to the anima.

It appears that both protagonists of this drama resorted to mutual projection and were only able to appreciate each other's veiled mythologies in vicarious ways. Yet both men pursued an individual calling that brought them into conflict with the collective, both struggled to embody life experience in terms of mythic narrative, and both saw life as an odyssey, the goal of which could no longer be limited to the traditional images of heaven or hell.

While their encounters first awakened in each other soul landscapes that were experienced as poison, the venom could later be appreciated as a call of destiny.

THE FIRST ENCOUNTER: A POISONED RELATIONSHIP

Joyce's first encounter with Jung in 1919 was indirect, but it was enough to cast Jung, in Joyce's imagination, as a powerful antagonist who sought to improve Joyce's conduct through analysis. Joyce had been receiving financial support from Mrs. Edith McCormick, who was the daughter of John D. Rockefeller and in analysis with Jung. McCormick wanted Joyce to analyze with Jung, too, at her expense, which Joyce flatly refused. Shortly afterwards, McCormick cut off his credit, and Joyce, noted for his suspicious, paranoid fantasies, first of all suspected his friend Weiss, who was acquainted with Jung, and then Jung himself as having a hand in her decision. In support of that fear, Joyce knew that Jung had encouraged McCormick earlier to withdraw subsidies from the musician Ermanno Wolff-Ferrari, a move which actually had the beneficial result of pulling him out of alcohol and inertia so that he could compose again.[1]

THE SECOND ENCOUNTER:
JUNG'S AGONIZING STRUGGLE WITH JOYCEAN ALCHEMY

In 1931, Daniel Brody, owner of the Rhein-Verlag, a well-known publishing company in Zürich, asked Jung to write a preface either for the third German edition of Joyce's *Ulysses* or a later study of *Ulysses*. Jung accepted. At the time Joyce had this to say about Jung's essay: "He [Jung] seems to have read *Ulysses* from first to last without one smile. The only thing to do in such a case is to change one's drink." When Joyce later met Brody, we can already hear how Jung's essay had activated shadows of Joyce's Catholicism: "Why is Jung so rude to me? He doesn't even know me. People want to put me out of the church to which I don't belong. I have nothing to do with psychoanalysis." Brody replied, "There can only be one explanation. *Translate your name into German.*" When this is done, "Joyce" becomes "Freud," give or take a last letter or two. The matter was somewhat patched up later on when Jung wrote an improved second edition of his essay, did not publish it as a preface, and wrote an appreciative letter to Joyce.[2]

The associative language of *Ulysses* can be compared to a landscape of ruined edifices, inviting those who behold them to imagine how those buildings could be re-created in different ways. Similar to the Association Experiment, which Jung originally devised, the novel's linguistic vacuum invites readers to free themselves from intellectual restrictions and project their own mythological structures into the novel's unfinished sounds and images. This is precisely what Jung eventually attempts to do. His approach to *Ulysses* is personal, at times even confessional, yet it follows a mysterious innate structure of which he is scarcely conscious. Jung keeps lamenting that he must read this book, and only does so because he is asked to do so by a publisher. He falls asleep, is bored to tears, and could just as well read the book backwards as forwards. He cannot rely on his usual intellectual skills of interpretation. There is no clear object to interpret. All his defenses are activated. The work is one great void, empty of meaning. It is the work of a tapeworm, the creation of visceral thinking, and an example of a saurian, cold-blooded, unrelated mind. It is confined to intuition and perceptual processes and is devoid of feeling and thinking. One is kept waiting for something to happen, but nothing happens. In fact, according to Jung, it is a work of destruction and appears to be the creation of a schizoid mentality:

> We also find an atrophy of feeling that does not shrink from any depth of absurdity or cynicism. Even the layman would have no difficulty in tracing the analogies between Ulysses and the schizophrenic mentality.[3]

Jung's critical essay becomes an odyssey, a radical encounter with the otherness of Joyce, and, according to Susan Rowland, an enactment of his own individuation.[4] Only towards the end of it does he seem to liberate himself from the prejudices he has harbored towards Joyce and realize that his essay embodies a process of creating a new edifice, a strange combination of Joycean Dublin and Jungian Alchemy.

After venting his frustration, Jung, the experienced clinician, rightly notes that stereotypical expression, a clear indication of schizophrenic behavior, is, in fact, completely absent from *Ulysses*. Unlike schizophrenics, nothing is repetitive, rather

> The presentation is consistent and flowing, everything is in motion and nothing is fixed. The whole book is borne along on a subterranean current of life that shows singleness of aim and rigorous selectivity, both being an unmistakable proof of the existence of a unified personal will and directed intention.[5]

The discovery of a subterranean current of life also indicates that Jung's encounter with the dark, saurian underworld of *Ulysses* is beginning to constellate the hidden elixirs of the alchemists, a process which he later described as being both physical and spiritual.

> The physical goal of alchemy was gold, the panacea, the elixir of life; the spiritual one was the rebirth of the (spiritual) light from the darkness of Physis.[6]

Jung claims *Ulysses* is built on the wreckage of Joyce's boyhood. It ruthlessly destroys all remaining sentimental attachments to the gods of the Middle Ages and, in particular, the authoritarianism of the Catholic Church. And, indeed, towards the end of *A Portrait of the Artist as a Young Man,* Joyce writes:

> I will not serve that in which I no longer believe, whether it call itself my home, my fatherland, or my church: and I will try to express myself in some mode of life or art as freely as I can and as

wholly as I can, using for my defence the only arms I allow myself to use—silence, exile, and cunning.[7]

According to Jung, Joyce in *Ulysses* chose a style of writing that initiates a practice of radical detachment in order to achieve a work of destruction. Jung finds that it is impossible to become attached to any figure or event in the book, except perhaps Molly of the last chapter. There is no appeal to our sympathy or judgement with the figures that appear or disappear on the stage of life with no apparent meaning. In this anti-world of no-man the readers' forced detachment liberates them from worldly entanglements and spiritual delusions. Jung does not even believe the work is symbolic. Symbols connect us with the hidden depth of the unconscious. *Ulysses* is a work of conscious intention. The work does not dwell on this archetypal background but "veers away in the opposite direction and strives to obtain the utmost objectivity of consciousness."[8] In fact, Jung goes on to say that it should not be symbolic for that would deny its underlying purpose. If it were so, the symbol with its numinous power of attraction would drag us back into "world and spirit,"[9] bound to the world by love or hate, bound to spirit through conviction or prejudice.

For Joyce, the source of the symbol originates in biographical visceral impressions. A conventional language could not express the bodily experiences and memories of a lifetime that represented an affirmation of ordinary life. Memories of Dublin and the life of the people of Dublin became the virginal material of his work. In order to impregnate these impressions with new life, he had to destroy conventional language and create new linguistic forms that could not be defined with one clear meaning. His language was a language of sounds and images with multiple meanings that were designed to stimulate the imagination and release the powers of Eros. Jung, the scientist, let his intuition guide him and spent much of his lifetime linking the symbolic imagery of the unconscious within a relatively tight theoretical framework of meaning. Joyce, the poet, seemed to have worked the opposite way. He let his experiences of everyday life and everyday people guide him, molding them with new form and meaning, fashioning them into artistic creations and infusing them with a mythical imagery that contains echoes of a common human heritage. Joyce's Dublin and all the figures in that Dublin became an archetypal cosmos, pregnant with multiple meanings.

Joycean symbolism does not simply represent an unknown other, the customary Jungian understanding of symbolism; rather, it is more specific and embodies the denied and unknown flesh of humanity. In the Linati schema, each section of *Ulysses* expresses a specific part of the body. (The Linati schema, written by Joyce and sent to Carlo Linati in 1920, showed the parallels between *Ulysses* and Homer's *Odyssey* as well as other amplifications.) For Mark Patrick Hederman, Joyce's language reveals a new incarnation, in which the word is made flesh.

> This is not the language of the mind, it is a visceral language that rushes out of the intestines from a nervous substrate like the sympathetic system, which is quite different from the cerebrospinal system which produces the rational language of ordinary discourse…[it] is the discovery of language as that gesture of being which establishes a new dimension of humanity, from which these two supposedly antagonistic principles of the spirit and the flesh can achieve a hypostatic union.[10]

Given that the cerebrospinal system does not only produce rational language but also a fair share of visceral thought, we may conclude that Joycean language is open, undefined, concrete, inspiring, even seducing the attentive reader to connect with his or her living flesh in ways that bring delight to soul and spirit. Joycean symbolism becomes an embodied experience, not as an enactment of brute physical pleasure, but rather as a purgative process that furthers an embodiment of soul and an ensoulment of body.

One cannot be sure when Joyce first discovered the symbolism of alchemy. It probably was through Jung. In one paragraph of *Finnegans Wake*[11] one finds traces of a Joycean struggle with alchemy, implying also a struggle with his own flesh. The passage refers to the creation of *Ulysses*. It begins with Joyce comparing *Ulysses* to Virgil's Aeneas. Similar to Jung's agonizing struggle with *Ulysses*, Joyce struggled with his own body and soul, and was involved in a process that was

> brought to blood heat, gallic acid on iron ore, through the bowels of his misery, flashly, faithly, nastily, appropriately, this Essuan Menschavik and the first to last alshemist wrote over every inch of the only foolscap available, his own body, till by its corrosive sublimation one continuous present tense integument slowly unfolded…

A visceral language of bodily experience unfolds, expressing utterances of a tormented body that has been cheated of its birthright (Esau), but within which lies the birth of humanity, free from the fanaticism of inhuman ideologies (the moderate Menschaviks as opposed to the fanatical Bolsheviks). Joyce's work is not a psychological interpretation of alchemical symbolism as with Jung. True to his vocation as artist, he creates a new alchemical language, voiced from the stuff of the body, expressed from reflections on primal instinct, by a "squidself which he had squidscreened from the crystalline world…" In this vision of alchemy, Joyce's work embodies psyche's transformation as a process of polymorphous copulations with the world's manifold substances, a sung celebration of the archetypal fecundity of human existence, described as *"marryvoising moodmoulded cyclewheeling history."*

As Jung's encounter with Joyce's *Ulysses* draws to a close, it appears he is overcoming his resistance to it and beginning to perceive the meaning of the work through an alchemical lens. This process is not without struggle. At times one has the impression that he has dismissed Joyce's ego consciousness and attributes his creative writing to a higher self. This interpretation would have, of course, been anathema to Joyce who rejected the notion of a transcendental, disembodied self. At other times Jung, quoting the heretical alchemical maxim "as above, so below," likens Joyce's self to the alchemical Hermes that contains ego and non-ego, mind and matter. One can conjecture that Jung is beginning to perceive the radical otherness of Joyce's world. This statement implies the relative nature of what is conscious and unconscious, and approximates to a view which is now current in contemporary neurobiology and recent research on implicit memory.[12] The conscious mind is woven from many unconscious elements that were formed in long forgotten or repressed attachments of early childhood to real existing caretakers. These highly emotional elements are stored in implicit memory and continually influence thinking, feeling, and patterns of behavior in visceral ways. In Joyce's creative writing there is no strict separation between ego and self. Consciousness cuts across the usual dichotomy of subjective and objective, animate and inanimate, conscious and unconscious. Even contemporary dream research will testify to the existence of two states of consciousness: waking and dreaming.[13] Likewise, in a later work, Jung re-defines the unconscious complexes as "luminosities," consisting of another kind of consciousness, not identical with the waking self.[14]

Imagination, in Joyce, possesses a consciousness that bridges opposites and makes the world come alive in new and refreshing ways. This is nowhere better brought to our attention than in Molly's final monologue.

> I know them well... who was the first person in the universe before there was anybody that made it all... who ah that they dont know... neither do I so there you are... they might as well try to stop the sun from rising tomorrow... the sun shines for you he said the day we were lying among the rhododendrons on Howth...[15]

Joyce, through the voice of Molly, is reminiscing about God and philosophy in a non-intellectual way. He is probably referring to Hume's philosophy. Hume dismissed causality and is well known for his rejection of any attempt to prove that the sun would rise tomorrow. Molly does not care about this kind of philosophy. Consciousness in her mind is not identified with disembodied thinking but arises within a post-modern sensuous context. Her attachment to the world and to the sun is sensual and erotic. The sun rises tomorrow because her lover said it rises for her. Here implied is an affirmation of the human mind that includes Eros and the intentional dimensions of embodied existence.

Molly is an artistic re-creation of Joyce's relationship with his wife, Nora. Joyce was called to destroy old myths and recreate them anew. In order to do this his muse dictated that he was to live a homeless life. As a Mercurial Ulysses he had to identify and de-identify with one home after another. His life and art were dedicated to pay homage to the soul as the source of life, the creator of form, and, like the waters of the rivers and oceans, forever moving, forever changing. In view of the theories of the German philologist, Phillip Wegener, who described the process whereby language becomes a system of faded metaphors,[16] Joyce felt compelled to destroy a conventional language that had lost touch with its life source, and to re-create language anew. His wandering soul found no home in the airy, fairy realms of imagination. It had to subject itself over and over again to fleshy incarnation. In Joyce's theory of art, the virginal soul, in and through life's experiences, suffers defloration. Having being deflowered by reality, artistic imagination can father new creations. True art is copulative, a union of imagination and experience, a union of liquid soul and solid earth, a process in which the artist has "to live, to err, to fall, to triumph, to recreate life out of life." (*A Portrait of the Artist as a Young Man*) This imaginative language was not made flesh by Joyce alone, but through his wife. Nora's body, Nora's mind, Nora's writing, and Nora's language remained a pillar of strength and support, strong enough to contain the soul's projections, mature enough to keep it anchored in reality, vital and teasing enough to inspire new horizons. She became his mistress, his whore, his wife, his goddess. She enabled him to join the sublime with the ridiculous, imagination with reality, heaven with earth, myth with reality. "You were to my young manhood what the idea of the Blessed Virgin was to my boyhood—a vessel of salvation."[17] She indeed became his chief source of inspiration. It was a relationship destined to last a lifetime.

Jung too seems to have been deeply touched by the voice of Nora, linguistically embodied in the final monologue of Molly. For Jung this voice came from below the earth, from Ireland, from an embrace of Eros and the goddess of life who has transformed the barren world into a garden or paradise. Jung ends his short essay on *Ulysses* with a burst of glowing respect and praise, relieved that the hero, the demiurge Joyce himself, has "turned back towards the place where was his home:"

> O Ulysses, you are truly a devotional book for the object-besotted, object-ridden white man! You are a spiritual exercise, an ascetic discipline, an agonizing ritual, an arcane procedure, eighteen [chapters] alchemical alembics piled on top on one another, where amid acids, poisonous fumes, and fire and ice, the homunculus of a new, universal consciousness is distilled! Penelope need no longer weave her never-ending garment; she now takes her ease in the gardens of the earth, for her husband is home again, all his wanderings are over. A world has passed away, and is made new.[18]

Jung's *Ulysses* is not to be understood as an outline of Jungian grand theory but contains elements of a personal myth that is undergoing a process of change. Similar to his paper on Job, his essay on *Ulysses* is a creative articulation of his own struggle, his own individuation process, even a precursor of his later work in alchemy. He agonizes over this book, hating it, but intrigued by it. He has to work through his resistance. It represents a very different world than his own, hard for him to accept, difficult for him to believe. He cannot apply his usual method of interpreting symbols of the unconscious. Like the many nations who banned it from publication, he is tempted to damn it and deny it serious consideration.

One can decipher three distinct moods in Jung's appreciation of *Ulysses*, corresponding to three distinct passages of an alchemical process, which he later interpreted as a model for individuation. Anyone who has read Jung's alchemical treatises will inevitably come across the words *"Nigredo," "Albedo,"* and *"Rubedo."* They describe a process in which the soul, having faced its own darkness, despair, and depression, can achieve a spiritual standpoint transcending collective attachments to the past that have inhibited its development. Through a process of detachment, the dark matter *(Nigredo)* is distilled and rarefied so that a new spiritual attitude is gained *(Albedo, Unio Mentalis)*. Once this attitude is secured, a meaningful return to reality, to body and to life itself can take place *(Rubedo, Unio Corporalis)*. Jung believed that these alchemical texts intimated an archetypal blueprint concerning the death and renewal of psychological life.

The parallels between Jung's struggle with *Ulysses* and the alchemical process are obvious. Jung starts by confessing he dislikes reading the book; he encounters a massive resistance having to confront the desouled void that the book seems to offer. He admits that Joyce has aroused his ill will. He even analyzes himself and asks what is behind his irritation. Pursuing a path of introspection, he concludes that it is Joyce's visceral, cold-blooded, and unrelated mind that turns all to stone. Jung, whose being is encompassed in a dark state of sleep, appears to be immersed in an alchemical *Nigredo*. Despite boredom and vexation, he does not give up, recognizes that as a psychiatrist he is prejudiced, and struggles to gain an inkling of "a mental health which is inconceivable to the average understanding; it may even be a disguise for superlative powers of mind."[19] Immersed in a process of creative destruction, it appears that he is now appreciating Joyce's work through the lenses of the alchemical *unio mentalis*, which is described as a process of overcoming the body, a voluntary death, the soul's alignment with spirit and an objectification of affects.[20] Jung begins to understand Joyce's radical detachment from the collective influences of the past as a necessary stage of development in order to shake off the old gods and initiate a restratification of consciousness. One can feel the relief in Jung as he senses Joyce's detached mind return home to its source of origin. This part of Jung's odyssey foreshadows his own work on the final stage of the alchemical process, described as the *rubedo*, when through *solificatio* the sun shines on the process[21] and a reunion of spirit with body is accomplished.[22] The synonyms of the ultimate goal of alchemy are many: the union of the whole man with the *unus mundus*, the ground of empirical being, a window into eternity, a vision of the divine in matter.[23] Alchemy attempted to change base matter into gold, liberate spirit from imprisonment in matter in order to bring about a new incarnation, and transform the hells of this world into gardens of paradise. Understood from a Jungian and Joycean viewpoint, alchemy provides a foundation for a post-modern attitude that respects and celebrates the sacredness, beauty, and fecundity of the human body, the non-human, and the material world in general.

THE THIRD ENCOUNTER:
NO CONSOLATION FOR TORMENTS OF HELL

Lucia, Joyce's only daughter, began to show clear signs of mental illness in her early twenties. Her mind was increasingly in disarray, her thoughts jumbled, her emotions violent. Joyce was concerned and wondered if the unsettled life, the continual change of residence (Trieste, Zurich, Locarno, Paris), the learning of languages in different schools (Italian, German, French, English), and the variety of careers (piano, singing, dancing) were too much for her young mind.[24] By 1929, she became obsessed with a squint she suffered from and insisted she have an operation, which was not a success. Giorgio, the brother whom she adored and her stable companion throughout the upheavals of Bohemian family life, had left home to live with Helen Kastor. Lucia, in her early twenties, was alone, still living with her parents. She then began a series of sexual escapades with famous writers and artists, including Liam O'Flaherty and Ernst Calder. Lucia also fell in love with the young writer Samuel Beckett, who on noticing her passion for him told her bluntly that he came to Joyce's flat primarily to see her father.[25]

As Lucia's illness became worse, she broke down in public on several occasions. Once when she and her parents were about to get on a train for London, she fell into a fit of howling, which lasted 45 minutes in the Gare du Nord, Paris. Joyce later called this incident her "King Lear scenes."[26] The parents panicked and dreaded the newspaper reports, which affectionately reported: *"Ils aiment Paris trop."* As the drama continued, Lucia acted with great hostility towards her mother and became excessively preoccupied with her father. She cut the phone lines on several occasions, would paint her face black, hurl furniture at her parents, and later set fire to her room. Joyce was determined that she would not be locked up in an institution and so began another odyssey from doctor to doctor, from clinic to clinic, from country to country. All to no avail. Lucia, 25 years old, was showing clear signs of schizophrenia, diagnosed by one doctor as catatonic and by another as hebephrenic. As Lucia's illness worsened, the more desperate her father became. He refused to believe she was incurable and refused to have her locked up. Over the next years, he spent three quarters of his income trying to find relief for her. He felt he alone was responsible for her cure. On the one hand he was fascinated with her ramblings and saw his own genius in her: "Whatever spark of gift I possess has been transmitted to Lucia."[27] On the other hand he worried about the influence he had on her, especially the effect of the nomadic life he had enforced upon the family. In September 1934 Joyce put her in the Brunner clinic in Kusnacht and asked Jung to treat her, hoping for a psychiatric miracle.

Jung only saw her for a few sessions and was met with fierce resistance. He then placed her under the care of Carey Baynes, an experienced, independent woman in midlife and known as Jung's "Rock of Gibraltar." She was supposed to bring about a positive transference that would heal Lucia's problematic relationship with the mother. At first the treatment seemed to work. Lucia spoke freely, seemed happier, and put on weight. Baynes took her on drives and tried to get her interested in work, but could not consolidate the relationship or win Lucia's trust and confidence, despite her initial improvement and some moments of wit and laughter. Baynes noted the parents' resistance to any probing in the family history, Lucia's deep attachment to the father, and the intense animosity between daughter and mother.[28] By the end of the year, Lucia had lost all interest in Jung, commenting later: "To think that such a big fat materialistic Swiss man should try to get hold of my soul!"[29] During that autumn, Jung and Joyce had several conversations about Lucia's condition, the contents of which are unknown as Jung destroyed all his former patients' files.[30] Some parts of this exchange are known indirectly by reference to Baynes' notes. Other parts can be pieced together by later comments of Jung and Joyce.

Jung did not believe that Lucia could be cured and advised against an analysis. He pointed out the schizoid elements in Lucia's poems and, according to Jung's later testimony, Joyce replied that they were anticipations of a new literature. Jung agreed that Lucia's use of language was remarkable but that the connection between words was random.[31] These sparse sources support the conjecture that Jung attempted to help Lucia gain distance from her father. Based upon a letter of Lucia and later remarks of Joyce, Jung's approach met with fierce resistance from the family. Yet that was not all that happened in the encounter. At some level the two men must have understood each other vicariously. Joyce was pleased that Jung did not insist that Lucia be shut up in a psychiatric hospital. He inscribed Jung's copy of *Ulysses* with a note of gratitude: "To Dr. C. G. Jung, with grateful appreciation of his aid and counsel."[32]

One is now tempted to ask if further unconscious patterns influenced the unfavorable outcome of this third Jung/Joyce encounter. Most certainly Joyce was troubled; unresolved complexes were activated. He had surely not forgotten what Jung had written earlier about *Ulysses*. That problematic encounter with Jung continued to occupy Joyce. Now, in this third encounter, Joyce the artist was confronting Jung the psychiatrist about his daughter. Jung was in a position of power and authority, a position that was a loaded issue for Joyce, a position that represented the post-Enlightenment dominance of the scientist's mind over the artist's narrative competence. Joyce took objection to Jung's attempt to separate father and daughter, which he described in a letter as an effort "made by more than one person to poison her mind against me."[33] We can also detect some of Joyce's ill humor and vituperation about *Ulysses* and a potential transference of Lucia on Jung in a condensed passage in *Finnegans Wake*, "We grisly old Sykos who have done our unsmiling bit on alices (Ulysses) when they were yung and easily freudened in the penumbra of the procuring room..."[34]

From a psychological point of view it is most interesting to note that Joyce later referred to Jung as "The Reverend Doctor Jung."[35] Joyce as a young man suffered at the hands of priests who proclaimed a religion of power and fear. The Jesuits proposed to him that he might have a vocation and join the order. In *A Portrait of the Artist as a Young*

Man, the main character, Stephen Dedalus, who represents Joyce himself, imagines his new name as: "The Reverend Stephen Dedalus, S. J."[36] The appellation of Jung appears to indicate that the old Jesuit complex was re-activated in Joyce.

This same complex probably prevented Joyce from being objective about the true state of affairs concerning his daughter. Given the inevitability of Joyce having to confine his daughter to a mental institution, Jung was seen in the robes of a priest, and that reminded Joyce of those sinister figures from the past who threatened his soul with eternal damnation.

After having listened to a Jesuit's long lecture on the torments of hell, the hero, in a state of utmost guilt, cries out:

> And the glimmering souls passed away, sustained and failing, merged in a moving breath. One soul was lost; a tiny soul: his. It flickered once and went out, forgotten, lost. The end: black, cold, void waste.[37]

In *A Portrait of the Artist as a Young Man*, Stephen compares the souls of humanity to the stars in heaven. Light became a symbol of the soul. Joyce named his daughter "Lucia." He was terrified that "Lucia" would be locked up in an asylum for the rest of her life. He refused to send her to a place of imprisonment and torture. It is reasonable to conjecture that he projected onto Jung, the scientist and priest, terrifying figures of the past that had threatened to destroy his freedom and destiny to become an artist. He could not accept any final diagnosis of Lucia, for that would have meant condemning the soul to hell. Their light would go out—a final triumph of the religion of fear, a religion that destroys human freedom and the capacity to love.

CONCLUSION

This brief survey of the encounters between Jung and Joyce cannot do justice to the complexity of the life and work of these great men. Encounters provoke the reality of otherness. Jung's encounter with Joyce activated in him memories of the rejected artist anima. That other life that Jung could have lived had to be sacrificed on the altars of science and psychology in order that his insights be acceptable in a social, professional, and theoretical framework. Joyce's encounter with Jung constellated in him memories of a fear-provoking, Jesuit Catholicism and his failed medical studies. That other life, encountered in the psychiatrist Jung, which Joyce might have lived, had to be ignored in order that the soul be saved from the fires of hell. Both men divined in each other aspects of their unlived lives in vicarious ways. Encounters are not relationships. Encounters are fragmentary and constellate the unexpected and the incomplete. The contextual framework of the Jung/ Joyce encounters did not allow them to achieve a mutual understanding of each other. Their radically different upbringings, their contrasting approaches to myth, and their mutually exclusive destinies to be scientist and artist did initiate them into an experience of otherness.

The encounters activated the hidden potentials of the soul as other, not just in the outer presence of their personalities. In reading *Ulysses*, Jung experienced a moment of final homecoming, a return to a poetic anima, a vision of a pregnant earth, and a distillation of a new consciousness that could be understood as a precursor to his later research in alchemy. In the encounter with Jung, Joyce relived memories of an authoritarian world that threatened the existence of his soul. Jung did not threaten or use force to keep Lucia in a sanatorium. He entrusted the daughter to the care of her father. The encounter with Lucia's tragic madness and the unclear, at times bewildering, diagnosis of the twenty or more specialists had its toll and effected a deep transformation in the mind and heart of the father. Joyce was no longer the narcissist who sacrificed the health of his family for the sake of art. He had become a man of compassion who spent the rest of his life concerned for the well being of his beloved daughter, Lucia, the bearer of light, the "wonder wild." Following his calling, Joyce learnt to pursue the ways of the heart not only in the excitement of youth and beauty but also in the sorrows of illness and death.

Jung and Joyce held up a mirror to one another. They could hardly recognize what was facing them. Nevertheless the encounters impacted upon them the hidden, often misinterpreted force of otherness. In different ways they spent the rest of their lives working on what had been activated—Jung in alchemy, Joyce as the caretaker of his lost daughter. Encounters accentuate otherness and are not meant to smooth out differences. They revive memories of a lost wholeness and reconnect us with the mystery of our being and the world around us. They are never complete. They may initiate a regression, constellate shadow, and certainly mediate unconscious material. Encounters may break us, but also permit insight into those hidden mythologies of self and other. They continually happen in relationships, particularly analysis. Encounters force us to reframe our attitudes, avoid a language of faded metaphors, and inspire us to create our model of the world anew. Like the search for wholeness, they are forever a work in progress.

NOTES

1. Richard Ellmann, *James Joyce* (London: Oxford University Press, 1982), p. 468.

2. *Ibid.*, p. 628.

3. C.G. Jung, *Collected Works*, tr. R. F. C. Hull (Princeton: Princeton University Press, 1953), vol. 15, para. 173 (all future references to Jung's *Collected Works*, abbreviated to *CW*, will be by volume and paragraph number).

4. Susan Rowland, *Jung as a Writer* (London: Routledge, 2002), p. 22.

5. Jung, *CW* 15 § 173.

6. Jung, *CW* 14 § 104.

7. James Joyce, *A Portrait of the Artist as a Young Man* (Harmsworth: Penguin, 1960), p. 247.

8. Jung, *CW* 15 § 185.

9. Jung, *CW* 15 § 186.

10. Mark Patrick Hederman, *The Haunted Inkwell* (Dublin, Columba Press, 2001), pp. 156-157.

11. James Joyce, *Finnegans Wake* (London: Faber, 1975), p. 185.

12. Margaret Wilkinson, *Coming into Mind: The Mind-Brain Relationship* (London: Routledge, 2006), p. 58.

13. J. Allan Hobson, *Dreaming* (Cambridge: Oxford UP, 2005), p. 58.

14. Jung, *CW* 14 § 358.

15. James Joyce, *Ulysses* (New York: Modern Library Edition, 1992), p. 782.

16. Suzanne K. Langer, *Philosophy in a New Key* (Cambridge, MA: Harvard UP, 1996), p. 139-140.

17. Brenda Maddox, *Nora* (London: Minerva, 1990), p. 48.

18. Jung, *CW* 15 § 201.

19. Jung, *CW* 15 § 173.

20. Jung, *CW* 14 § 672.

21. Jung, *CW* 14 § 441.

22. Jung, *CW* 14 § 677.

23. Jung, *CW* 14 § 534-537.

24. Ellmann, *James Joyce*, p. 612.

25. *Ibid.*, p. 649.

26. Maddox, p. 381.

27. Ellmann, *James Joyce*, p. 650.

28. Carol Loeb Shloss, *Lucia Joyce: To Dance in the Wake* (New York: Farrar, Straus, Giroux, 2003), pp. 281-291.

29. Ellmann, *James Joyce,* p. 679.

30. Schloss, *Lucia Joyce*, p. 293.

31. Ellmann, p. 679.

32. Deirdre Bair, *Jung: A Biography* (New York: Little, Brown & Co., 2003), p. 407.

33. Shloss, *Lucia Joyce,* p. 292.

34. Joyce, *Finnegans Wake*, p. 115.

35. Ellmann, *James Joyce,* p. 680.

36. Joyce, *Portrait*, p. 161.

37. *Ibid.*, p. 141.

OTHER VOICES, OTHER RUINS: BECKETT'S SPECTRAL WOMEN

MARY ASWELL DOLL

> The night reveals to the wanderer the things that are hidden by day.
>
> —Theodor Reik, *Listening with the Third Ear* [1]

Samuel Beckett is irascible. He has bones to pick and then he throws them over his shoulder or lets them stick in your throat. He is funny; but not just funny—he is hilarious, in an insouciant sort of way. Beckett could haunt your dreams, as he has mine. I write about this writer, whom I can't not write about and can't not think about, because for me he is like one of those Irish figures that looms up from the depths—Finn McCool's Salmon of Knowledge perhaps—that offers wisdom in quirky ways.

Depth psychology has a curious Beckettian quality of entering the vaporous region of no return. His is the world of maddening sames: characters who insist that no matter who they are—old man, old woman, young woman—something MORE needs to be said. But how to access that something more is the question. Beckett's work is like a

---

Mary Aswell Doll, Ph.D., teaches World Mythology and Literature of the Absurd at Savannah College of Art and Design. She is the author of several books, including *Beckett and Myth* and *Like Letters in Running Water: A Mythopoetics of Curriculum.*

dream we cannot quite understand: it repeats patterns, the basic one being what Jung called the search for soul. For fifty years Beckett's work has focused on soul-searching, taking us to where the soul is felt at its zero point. Empty rooms and ancient ruins, garbage bins and sand dune heaps become the places that Beckett chooses to force awareness out of its stupor. If it dares. Beckett's characters are not heroes or anti-heroes, but they quest, they quest. And in that questing we readers or viewers find ourselves in a territory where few writers have ventured, because Beckett speaks not to the rational mind but to the mind awaiting another source, since the soul has so long been absent.

Attending a Beckett performance or attending to the flat page of a Beckett text, we are drawn into the lure of absence. Tramps wait, women pace, spoken words echo. Nothing happens on the surface of things. *Waiting for Godot* transformed modern theater in the 50s not just because nothing "happened" (twice!), but because an entirely different kind of action presented itself. Commenting on his art form, Beckett once contrasted himself to James Joyce, with whom he had a loving, if sometimes complicated, friendship for over a quarter of a century. Both writers were Irish exiles living in France in the 20s. Joyce, whose eyesight was failing, hired Beckett to take dictation and do research for what later became *Finnegans Wake*. Because of his close understanding of Joyce's style and erudition, Beckett realized that

> Joyce had gone as far as one could in the direction of knowing more, [being] in control of one's material. ... I realized that my own way was in impoverishment, in lack of knowledge and in taking away, in subtracting rather than adding.[2]

Beckett's subtractions present a conundrum to his audience: We must use our heads differently. We must listen harder. We must unhinge ego control. We must become ignorant in the face of not knowing. Although he won the Nobel Prize in 1969 for a vast body of work that included stage drama, film, television plays, radio plays, fiction, poetry, and criticism, Beckett was a minimalist: a master of No(h).

I invoke Noh, Japanese classical drama of the fourteenth century, because of Beckett's similar theatrics. Characters are not meant to represent humans any more than the vocalizations are meant to represent speech. Rather, the stylized patterns and rhythmic vocalizations found in Noh and Beckettian drama seem otherworldly, the characters more like empty vessels[3] through which access to another dimension of reality can be "sounded."

In Noh, as Yasunari Takahashi has written, the rhythmic patterns of dance help to prepare an empty space for the coming forth of unappeased spirits.[4] With Beckett, I see something similar happening but with a twist. Beckett's women characters are inhabited by voices they cannot understand issuing from a place they cannot visit. These tormented souls express an experience of extreme destabilization. On the threshold of breakdown, their verbal and actual pacings trace a Mobius strip, with subjectivity on one side and objectivity on the other. The characters are literally caught inside their own not-thereness. Distracted, off center, disassociated, they are removed spiritually and psychically from the archetypal core of being.

In *Not I* (1974), *Footfalls* (1976), and *Rockaby* (1981), for instance, each play features a woman and her voice. Voice rather than the woman before our eyes compels attention. Bodies seem ghostly. The "character" called Mouth in *Not I* is just that: an orifice containing teeth and tongue, face obscured by dim light, placed eight feet above stage. This play emphasizes the non-human aspect of Beckett's characters. Meaning must be located beyond, beneath, or within, requiring a deeper attention if the characters are to get born properly. May, in *Footfalls*, appears forlorn and lost and in tatters. In *Rockaby*, Woman in a rocking chair is described as "Prematurely old. Unkempt grey hair. Huge eyes in white expressionless face." She is dressed in best black with sequins that glitter and with "Incongruous frivolous head dress set askew."[5] What is going on here? The space that the characters prepare by pacing, rocking, or listening is for the breakthrough of a self that has not yet been born in a language that speaks as if by itself.

Beckett demonstrates what Jung revealed as a peculiarly modern dilemma: the human search for soul. Our era, removed as it is from the myths that once grounded culture, is experiencing an impoverishment of symbol. Beckett's ghostly females are so impoverished that they seem entirely disappeared from themselves, their sourcing. Still, they "feel the rings"[6] that tie them to the Mobius strip of their predicament. They do not know what still stirs them, or stirs them still. Beckett's punning is one way language captures the force of both/and, the word "still" for instance suggesting both quietude and ongoingness, as in his *Stirrings Still*.[7] The puns turn ego's volume down to let meanings double. Vowel substitution achieves the same effect: Characters are both tortured (rack) and secured (rock) by some Thing from below. This Thing is none other than the psyche begging to get born through the "womb of the ear."[8]

One of Beckett's biographers tells us that Beckett was at the Tavistock Clinic in 1935 under the psychiatric care of Wilfred Bion when he heard Jung deliver a lecture. Jung was describing the strange case of a little girl who had amazing mythological dreams. Her death, Jung surmised, was a result of her never having been born entirely.[9] The young girl's psychic forces were so strong, so unchannelled, that they completely overpowered her other inner system of ego control. A direct reference to this case is made in Beckett's *All That Fall* (1957, 84).

The motif of the unborn self haunts Beckett's female characters. Of course, Beckett's commitment to the great No means that we find no rebirth, only moments of listening to "scraps of an ancient voice in me, not mine."[10] Note resistance to the comfort of metanarrative ideas like "change of personality" or "goal of the psyche" or "mandala formations." Rather, Beckett's great No moves into the territory of depth psychology as understood by such post-Jungians as James Hillman, David Miller, Jerome Bernstein, and Stanton Marlan, emphasis on going into the thicket, not getting out of the woods.

Beckett's visual images of the thicket present two sides of the self that battle each other for attention. In *Not I* there are two figures, a Mouth and an Auditor, the latter of whose purpose is to listen with compassion to Mouth's rantings. In *Footfalls* there are two characters, one seen and one unseen, both of whom tell stories that echo one another strangely. And in *Rockaby* a Woman listens to a recorded Voice, played by the same actress. This doubling/echoing/mirroring of character has been recognizable with such male figures as Didi and Gogo (*Waiting for Godot*), Krapp and his tape recorder (*Krapp's Last Tape*), Ham and Clov (*Endgame*), Listener and Recorder (*Ohio Impromptu*). But the female doublings seem more attuned/tortured by what Jung described as "a secret life [that] holds sway in the unconscious."[11] In one of his comments about his artistic intentions, Beckett said that the doublings are, in his words, simple. "It's all symbiosis."[12]

"Symbiosis" is defined by Webster as "the living together of two dissimilar organisms." This dissimilarity is certainly felt in *Not I,* where Mouth is the "mouth" or source of the suffering soul to which its female self is tied. The play throws us into a situation of grief for some inexplicable loss. We hear of a hellish life lived without release from torture. But just when life seems most lost, at rock bottom, the wellspring gushes forth in a frenzy of images. A life that was once lived mechanically and surfacely, is now lived suddenly, fiercely. Imagination holds sway and won't let Mouth stop its spewings. Words provide ritualized acts put into language-spewings that to Mouth seem obscene, literally "off the scene."[13]

Emerging patterns give new meaning to an old myth of mother searching for the lost child. This is the Demeter myth as reimagined by Beckett that recalls a female pattern of earth mother searching for maiden child who was raped by Hades. The myth explores the very dynamic that expresses a Beckettian symbiosis between body and soul, ground and undersurface, seen and unseen, sudden action and long, long suffering. Although the central event is the rape of Persephone, the central impact of the abduction is on the mother. Demeter, goddess of pigs and corn, has always been oriented to earth and rootedness. But this orientation shifts with the disappearance of her daughter, whose rape is a necessary darkening of innocence. But whose innocence? Beckett's focus is on the old ones, especially the mothers, who must acknowledge their once-ancient, mythic symbiosis with chthonic darkness. Beckett re-reads the Demeter myth, giving new emphasis to the need for darkness and the demand by darkness that it be "picked up."

Mouth, as I read the play, recalls Demeter trying to understand this alien darker self. She suddenly becomes consumed by absence, giving the sense that it is *her* rape away from a too-secure rooting on surfaces. Rape is myth's metaphor for the thrust of an Other world, the *necessary* rape of an unwilling ego to be led down to the dark side. In the myth, Demeter surrenders her earthly orientation by emptying out her body. She searches for nine days, does not eat, does not wash. In one motif of the myth Demeter sits by a well, or wellspring, as if to access better the darkness so as to await what will come from below. This inbetween waiting condition is the very territory of Beckettian drama.

Not I is a hard play to watch. It is meant to be beyond rational comprehension, in accordance with Beckett's design to work on the nerves, not the intellect. The play lasts only fifteen to seventeen minutes during which time we hear of a hellish life lived without emotion, "always winter for some strange reason" (1976, 18). We deduce a bit of plot: The speaker was born illegitimately. Or rather, she has never been born. She just began, as an "it." Now in her late years, she tells us between halts (she is listening to a voice that corrects her every utterance) that her routine existence of not talking was interrupted suddenly one day when, Persephone-like, she wandered into a field "looking aimlessly for cowslips" (1976, 15). That is when an interruption to her pattern of not talking occurred. Suddenly she found herself in the dark with a rupture in her brain that caused words to erupt. But she had "no idea … what she was saying! … till she began trying to … delude herself … it was not hers at all … not her voice at all" (1976, 18).

With the constant blubbering of lips harkening back to the sudden moment, Mouth says she thinks she is beginning to feel feeling, an "awful thought" (1976, 19). Feeling, long repressed by a mechanical existence, bursts forth as a stream of words. With this explosion of feeling, Mouth with teeth becomes a *vagina dentata* and the stream becomes the breaking of the womb waters wherein images of an unfathomable, ancient story are bodied forth.

This intense drama ends with what is a familiar motif in Beckett's plays. Mouth repeats a phrase that has been uttered twice before. The repetition serves a ritual speak-act function shifting attention to what is off the scene. It harkens back to a Persephone moment just before the rape with images that suggest springtime and comfort:

> God is love … tender mercies … new every morning … back in
> the field. … April morning … face in the grass … nothing but
> the larks … pick it up—(1976, 23)

The passage has eight phrases forming a kind of rhythmic chant such that "it" needs to be picked up. "It" could be the refrain, the memory of innocence, the mechanical self, or the unborn self. The phrases recall Persephone, the mythic maiden daughter, with words like April, morning sun, larks, field, and grass. But if, as T. S. Eliot writes, April is the cruelest month, then the comfort is indeed ironic. For what is of comfort is the pacing of language with its soothing beats and lovely spring images. What is cruel is the suffering which the Demeter-mother experiences as her daughter-self's rape. Both are necessary.

Beckett has Mouth imply that her suffering is punishment for having been born illegitimately:

> out into this ... before her time ... godforsaken hole called ...
> called ... no matter ... parents unknown ... unheard of ... he
> having vanished ... thin air ... no sooner buttoned up his
> breeches .... (1976, 14-15)

As long as Mouth can keep "it" under control she can continue with
the mechanics of living. Beckett remarked once that "the old ego dies
hard... it betrays its trust as a screen to spare its victim the spectacle of
reality."[14] What I see happening in this tortuous piece is Beckett's
presentation of the reality of unseen forces which, if repressed, will come
back with a vengeance, like Freud's return of the repressed. And when
"it" returns, it is completely unintelligible to the thinking brain. It
feels obscene (off scene).

Ancient earth goddess figures were like the unconscious itself,
ambiguous and capable of doing harm if not propitiated. The goddess
was the *yin*, the prime matter, containing both dark and light, death
and life. Without the goddess there could be no life. It would seem
that Beckett's earth goddess reference is a much troubled modern
Demeter who is so conflated with Persephone that the essential tension
between the two is no longer creative. Rather, what is reflected in the
scraps of language issuing from Mouth are the remains of a once-
supportive myth, now offal because so long dead.

Ironically, Beckett shows us beauty in these moments of despair.
Footfalls, first performed four years after *Not I*, again focuses meaning
on the word "it," doing so as May paces back and forth in nine carefully
cadenced steps. The strip that May traces as she paces is illuminated,
so that our eyes and ears are drawn downward. We are meant to hear
her steps rather than see her face. And as May paces she is trying to
make sense of a story, revolving "it all" in her body as well as her mind.
May's pacing reflects a need to move about the night until its claim
can be registered in her body (feet and ears), since mind has caused
the problem. What we see in this play suggests more than what is
"there." In our capacity as auditors and viewers we become transposed
into listening receptacles, hardly able to sort out the threads of plot
and so resigned to let them in if we can bear to stay still.

According to the rehearsal notes for the German premiere of
Footfalls, Beckett intended the dramatic experience to be auditory. The
walking up and down was to be the central image, the words built
around the footsteps. As the director, Walter Asmus, relayed, Beckett

helped the actress playing May to understand her character by telling her the story of Jung's Tavistock lecture. May wears a ghost costume, Beckett explained, because, like the girl patient of Jung, she is not living, not having been born properly.[15]

This play is a softer rendition of *Not I* but tells again, with variation, the obsessive search of one character for her other inexplicable self. I am interested in the nine steps, which once again recall Demeter's search for nine days. What we see is a slow twisting of movements tracing a Mobius strip or a Gordian knot, so that the character is caught inside her own predicament. The vision is a strangely beautiful rendition of the *via negativa*, as if the character is an initiate, attempting to call forth the other side. May must fully feel the space she is creating. She must get back in touch with underworld life. When she paces and twists on a narrow strip of stage, May draws herself into the circle. She is May, daughter-mother in one; May, the daughter doing the pacing; May, whose anagram Amy, is the daughter in May's story; May, the real mother of Beckett; May, the springtime that disappears in winter but comes again; May, the lost youth of ourselves that is our wellspring and our despair. Mother and daughter echo each other: one seen, the other heard. They are ghosts to each other. The daughter May embodies the image of Homer's Demeter dressed in a dark cloak cast down from both shoulders, walking over land and sea like a wild bird.[16]

As she paces, May tells a story which moves the drama even farther into imagination's realm. The story she tells is this: An old Mrs. Winter one autumn evening sits down to a supper for which she has little appetite and asks her daughter of her opinion of the Evensong service. Was it not strange? Did she observe anything strange? Her daughter disagrees:

> No, Mother, I myself did not, to put it mildly. Mrs. W: What do you mean, Amy, to put it mildly, what can you possibly mean, Amy, to put it mildly? Amy: I mean, Mother, that to say I observed nothing... strange is indeed to put it mildly. For I observed nothing of any kind, strange or otherwise. I saw nothing, heard nothing, of any kind. I was not there. (1976, 48)

This chilling story of nonunderstanding and dead-end communication contains in the middle the daughter's question: "Just what exactly, Mother, did you perhaps fancy it was?" (1976, 47-48). The word "exactly" juxtaposed with the words "fancy" and then "perhaps" is fecund. It suggests, at the heart of this bare-bones world, at the heart of autumn's night, that fancy, only a perhaps, nevertheless energizes psychic departure.

May's story ends with Amy's poignant question:

> Will you never have done ... revolving it all? (*Pause.*) It? (*Pause.*) It all. (*Pause.*) In your poor mind. (*Pause.*) It all. (*Pause.*) It all. (1976, 48)

These words echo the words of Voice in the beginning, described as May's mother, who speaks off stage. Voice says the same thing as the story-mother. Rings within rings tie the story tighter and tighter around itself. That May's sequel, as she calls her story, does not actually accomplish anything is an ironic comment on the pun "seek well." Seeking well should be seeking by the well and seeking from the wellspring, which is the archetypal fundament of human experience. That nothing comes from the seeking is Beckett's comment on the impossibility of accessing completely the other side, since its absence has been so prolonged.

Footfalls is like *Not I* but only a little like. In both, women seekers tap a mythopoetic basis of their mother-daughter pairing. In both, there is the sense of doubling, echoing, and twoness. In both, there is the play of seasons: autumn in one and spring in the other. In both, there is either a story or threads of a story. In both, the story is the connective tissue that binds the two to themselves and to a vague past. In both, the word "it" is important. While the feeling in *Not I* erupts, action in *Footfalls* revolves. Glen Slater's observations about the film *Volver* could serve as a commentary on Beckett's work in this regard: "It shows... how the spirit never completely escapes the pull of the flesh."[17] To revolve into an ever tighter Gordian knot takes us back to the Platonic riddle, "our body is the tomb in which we are buried."[18]

While creating a space for the under world is central to the impact of *Footfalls,* similar attention to spacing words is seen in *Rockaby.* The play focuses on Woman sitting at a window in her rocking chair, rocking back and forth, dressed as for a party. She is at the end of her days. Life on earth has been, to put it mildly, a disappointment. Subjects have failed her, so it is to objects that she turns for comfort, like the arms of her chair. The stage directions make explicit the chair's structure that must give what humans cannot: "curving arms to suggest embrace"

(1981, 22). Woman is empty. Whereas May's words feed her starving soul, here Woman's eyes are described as "famished" (15, 19), never having been able to be seen by another. Woman rocks to and fro, an action that imitates her life-long searching high and low for "another creature like herself/ a little like" (1981, 10). The ambiguity of the word "little" can mean a few things: one who is almost like her, one who is little—a child perhaps, or the lost child of herself perhaps. Keeping ambiguities open, like puns, deepens the poignancy.

The juxtaposition of festive costume and haunting sadness reminds me of Virginia Woolf's Mrs. Dalloway at the end of a day of preparation for her party (1925/1981). We read of her early morning trip to get flowers, of people in the park, the airplane overhead, the busses. Later, she sews her dress and waits for the evening. When the party is in full swing she cannot be happy as she was before because Septimus Warren Smith had committed suicide that afternoon by hurling himself out a window. His death, although she did not know him, haunts her. Woolf shows us that lives and deaths are connected in mysterious ways by motifs often invisible to the eye, like a spider web of interconnections. She has thought her party would be a brilliant bringing-together of acquaintances from her past, where, as with other parties of her past, she could lose herself in the process of living. But the suicide! Even here, at her own nice party, death is in the midst.

Mrs. Dalloway goes to the window in her evening dress and looks out, as is her habit. Her day had been filled with moments of going to the window or having others go to a window. Woolf's window motif symbolizes the lack of transparency we offer to one another, but more significantly offer ourselves. When at the end of her day, in the midst of her party, Mrs. Dalloway goes to the window, it is as if reality stares her back in the guise of an old lady in the room opposite:

> She parted the curtains; she looked. Oh, but how surprising!—
> in the room opposite the old lady stared straight at her! She was
> going to bed. ... She was going to bed, in the room opposite. It
> was fascinating to watch her, moving about, that old lady,
> crossing the room, coming to the window. Could she see her? It
> was fascinating, with people still laughing and shouting in the
> drawing-room, to watch that old woman, quite quietly, going to
> bed. She pulled the blind now.[19]

Mrs. Dalloway does not consciously know that the old lady's straight stare was Mrs. Dalloway's only real connection to anyone. Yet the connection does not actually exist. Mrs. Dalloway is as invisible to the old woman as she is to herself. Like Mrs. Ramsay of *To the Lighthouse*, Mrs. Dalloway had the experience but missed the meaning, to borrow Eliot's phrase. This is a difference with Beckett's Woman in *Rockaby* who knows she yearns for a straight stare. She yearns for the parting of curtains or the lifting of blinds. She knows she is damned in a way that Mrs. Dalloway does not. Knowing is all.

I have been able to detect in the spacing of Beckett's Woman's words a pivot point that signals a turning. This pivot occurs nine times in the text. Each turning of the text, with variation, contains the phrase "high and low," following the refrain "all eyes/all sides," to suggest a synchronistic movement both of eyes searching high and low and chair rocking high and low. The effect is curious. Although Woman's eyes remain unblinking according to the stage directions, making her like a stilled object, the chair is constantly active, making it like an animated presence. It seems that if Woman is to find the Other she seeks—a face, a semblance—she will have to search beyond subjects to objects; that is to say, objective reality.

The nine pacings of phrases once again suggest to me a grounding of this drama in the Demeter myth. Modern consciousness has become so far removed from the ancient stories that their recall must "sound" a different pattern if they are to be heard. I think this is why refrain, pun, and irony are so significant in Beckett's work. Buried in language are not words that give single meaning but words that offer patterns, repetitions, resonances that give multiple meanings. As Mircea Eliade has commented, the language of the ancients did not have words for the big ideas like "reality" or "being;" their meanings came through symbols and myths.[20] The Demeter myth expresses a female connection of opposites but it also expresses *search* as a basic necessity. With Beckett's female questers, search begins and loss is felt and the effort to continue *even within* the tension never stops. *Rockaby's* Woman is not telling herself any evening lullaby when she rocks herself "into the old rocker/mother rocker/where mother sat/all the years/all in black/best black" (1981,17). She is repeating a pattern that is familiar, perhaps with the hope that its familiarity will birth resolution. The utter fascination of Beckett's work is that when the lights fade out on stage, the darkness remains.

Myths are stories that never end. The tramps in *Waiting for Godot* say they are going to leave, but they never do. They continue to wait. The doublings with Beckett's women never release character into a single identity, simple search, or finalized action. This situation could be read mythically, archetypally, even alchemically, as Ronald Schenk expresses it:

> Through the eyes of alchemy, the presenting problem is a matter of appearing in unfinished form, the ore—unrefined, the metal—imperfect, its soul in pain, ugliness or disquiet. Alchemy considers these external situations to have an internal correlative; *nature is always doubled, both within and without at the same time.* … Something is concretely there, but something else is also happening.[21]

Woman in *Rockaby* tells herself it is time she stopped but the words end on an echo. We seem to be at rock bottom. But in the spaces and pauses of Beckett's beautiful texts, meaning hovers like a ghost in images, actions, objects. Among those lie layers of hidden, other worlds.

NOTES

1. Theodor Reik, *Listening with the Third Ear* (New York: Garden City Books, 1948/1951), p. 147.

2. In James Knowlson, *Damned to Fame: The Life of Samuel Beckett* (New York: Simon & Shuster, 1966), p. 319.

3. This idea is expressed in the *Tao Tê Ching*: "The Way is like an empty vessel/That yet may be drawn from/Without ever needing to be filled./It is bottomless; the very progenitor of all things in the world." See Arthur Waley, trans. and ed., *The Way and Its Power: Lao Tzu's Tao Tê Ching and its Place in Chinese Thought* (New York: Grove Press, 1958), p. 146.

4. Yasunari Takahashi, "The Theatre of Mind: Samuel Beckett and the Noh," *Encounter* 58 (April 1982): 67.

5. All references from these works will be from the following editions: *Not I* in *Ends and Odds: Eight New Dramatic Pieces* (New York: Grove Press, 1976), pp. 13-23; *Footfalls* in *Ends and Odds*, pp. 39-50; and *Rockaby* in *Rockaby and Other Short Pieces* (New York: Grove Press, 1981), pp. 8-23.

6. In *Come and Go*, three women sit on a bench clasping hands in a Mobius strip formation. Although none wears a ring, one of the women says she can "feel the rings." Samuel Beckett, *Come and Go,* in *Cascando and Other Short Dramatic Pieces* (New York: Grove Press, 1969), p. 69.

7. Samuel Beckett, *Stirrings Still* (New York: North Star Line, 1988/1991).

8. This felicitous phrase I owe to Stanton Marlan's wonderful essay, "Pre-Texts of the Imaginal in the Hermetic Play of the Dream: The Ontotheology of Bean," *Spring 77—Philosophy and Psychology* (2007): 101-116.

9. Deirdre Bair, *Samuel Beckett: A Biography* (New York: Harcourt, Brace, Jovanovich, 1978), p. 96.

10. Samuel Beckett, *How It Is*, trans. from the French by Samuel Beckett (New York: Grove, 1964), p. 7.

11. Jung, *CW* 9i § 50.

12. In Knowlson, *Damned to Fame*, p. 376.

13. Tom Moore, *Rituals of the Imagination* (Dallas, TX: The Pegasus Foundation, 1983), p. 7.

14. Samuel Beckett, *Proust* (New York: Grove Press, 1931), p. 10.

15. Walter D. Asmus, "Practical Aspects of Theatre, Radio and Television: Rehearsal Notes for the German Premiere of Beckett's *That Time* and *Footfalls* at the Schiller-Theater Werkstatt, Berlin (directed by Beckett)," trans. Helen Watanabe, *Journal of Beckett Studies* 2 (Summer 1977): 82-95.

16. Homer, "The Homeric Hymn to Demeter," *The Homeric Hymns and Homerica*, trans. Hugh G. Evelyn-White (Cambridge, MA: Harvard University Press, 1964), pp. 42-43.

17. Glen Slater, Review of *Volver*, a film written and directed by Pedro Almodovar, *Spring 77—Philosophy and Psychology* (2007): 283-288.

18. Plato, *Gorgias,* 493A.

19. Virginia Woolf, *Mrs. Dalloway* (New York: Harvest, Harcourt, 1925/1981), pp. 185-186.

20. Mircea Eliade, *Cosmos and History: The Myth of the Eternal Return,* trans. Willard R. Trask (New York: Harper, 1959), p. 3.

21. Ronald Schenk, "The Alchemical Attitude of the Analytic Mind: An Introductory Primer on *Prima Materia* for Initial Beginners at the Start, *Spring 74—Alchemy* (2006): 151-174. Emphasis added.

CONTEMPORARY IRELAND: PRESENT-DAY BARDS, IRISH ART, AND THE CELTIC TIGER

THE SUBLIME IN THE ORDINARY:
AN APPRECIATION OF EAVAN BOLAND
AND HER POETRY

CHRISTINA MULVEY

Editor's Note: Internationally acclaimed Irish poet, Eavan Boland, was born in Dublin on September 24, 1944. Her books of poetry include *New Collected Poems* (2008), *Domestic Violence* (2007), *Against Love Poems* (2001), *The Lost Land* (1998), *An Origin Like Water: Collected Poems 1967-1987* (1996), *In a Time of Violence* (1994), *Outside History: Selected Poems 1980-1990* (1990), *The Journey and Other Poems* (1986), *Night Feed* (1982), and *In Her Own Image* (1980). In addition to her books of poetry, she is also the author of the prose memoir *Object Lessons: The Life of the Woman and the Poet in Our Time* (1995), and co-editor of *The Making of a Poem: A Norton Anthology of Poetic Forms* (2000). She is married with two daughters, and is currently a Professor in the Humanities at Stanford University.

Eavan Boland established her reputation as a writer on the ordinary lives of women and on the difficulties faced by women poets in a male-dominated literary world. The themes of her work include issues

Christina Mulvey is a Jungian analyst in Wicklow, Ireland, who received her Diploma from the G. G. Jung Institute in Zurich. A consulting psychologist and lecturer, she is involved in training and professional development in the fields of education, psychology, and psychotherapy. She has a strong background in literature and the arts, and lectures frequently at the Jung Institute in Zurich and in Canada, the UK, and the US. Her book and CD, "The Woolgatherer—the Poetry of Analysis," was published in 2004.

concerning Irish identity, the dilemma of being a woman and a poet, and the hidden and frequently undervalued experiences of everyday life. She explores these issues within the context of recent Irish history and Irish literary tradition. Her use of language is intelligent, elegant, and frequently highly visual.

This article explores how Boland's work can give voice to what might be discovered within the work done in analysis.

* * * * *

Analysts become good at keeping secrets. Perhaps this was already your inclination, now it becomes a professional necessity. People trust you with their stories, their searchings, and their discoveries. As you sit, listen, and absorb the details and nuances, you become filled with the sorrows and joys of their explorations. Because of the nature of the analyst's work you can never fully express or even acknowledge the impact such sharings have on your way of being. It is in art and literature, especially poetry, I find both solace and inspiration to maintain an openness towards the stories I hear but can never speak.

> The needful thing is not to know the truth but to experience it.
> Not to have an intellectual conception of things but to find our
> way to the inner and perhaps wordless irrational experience—
> that is the great problem.[1]

It is of course paradoxical that we need words to go beyond them. In the analytic setting, we can find ourselves thinking and talking about ordinary things, yet once our feelings are also engaged, there is the possibility of transformation. It is as if something other, even something sacred, has been activated. People can learn how to access such healing spaces—spaces that are traditionally associated with religious or spiritual practices, but not necessarily so.

Jung's own appreciation of myth, image, and symbol greatly influenced him and the psychology he developed. He was also very impressed with poetry, especially Goethe's. The Irish poet Eavan Boland has had a similar and deep influence on me and my work. In my practice, I observe time and time again that what touches and moves us, changes us. While I cannot describe how this comes about, I do recognize it when it happens. It is not unlike what one can experience in hearing a piece of music or reading a poem. In the following poem,

Boland illustrates the complex space which can open up within and without when we are so profoundly engaged.

"The Women"

> This is the hour I love; the in-between
> neither here nor there hour of evening,
> The air is tea-coloured in the garden
> The briar rose is spilled crepe-de-Chine.
>
> This is the time I do my work best
> going up the stairs in two minds
> in two worlds...
>
> The hour of change, of metamorphosis
> of shape-shifting instabilities
> My time of sixth sense and second sight
> when in the words I chose the lines I write
> they rise like visions and appear to me.[2]

When Boland wrote these lines, she was still raising a family. She lived on a small, quiet suburban street in County Dublin. Her two worlds of mother and poet were held in a constant conscious tension which is seldom so beautifully and evocatively understood and revealed.

If we choose to look and to see ourselves, then anyone or anything can be a mirror for us. The American poet, Adrienne Rich, has said "what we see, we see and seeing is changing."[3] In a formal analytic session, the analyst can be a mirror. But a poem, a picture, or a piece of music can also reflect ourselves back to us. In an extraordinary way, Boland's poetry gives the reader, and women in particular, the gift of not only seeing but valuing the ordinary details and often hidden creativity of their lives.

Boland lived these experiences yet could also sit apart to record and honor the often unacknowledged work of cleaning, feeding, giving birth, and healing.

"Woman in Kitchen"

> Breakfast over, islanded by noise,
> she watches the machines go fast and slow.
> She stands among them as they shake the house.
> They move. Their destination specific.

> She has nowhere definite to go,
> She might be a pedestrian in traffic…
>
> The wash done, the kettle boiled, the sheets
> spun and clean. The dryer stops dead.
> The silence is a death. It starts to bury
> the room in white spaces. She turns to spread
> a cloth on the board and iron sheets
> in a room white and quiet as a mortuary.[4]

Perhaps we know these moments or perhaps not. Yet we can share them with Boland or, as in the following excerpt, accompany her as she calls the children in from the garden or pause with her in reverie as she gazes into the distance.

> The last dark shows up the headlights
> of cars coming down the Dublin mountains.
> Our children used to think they were stars.[5]

To know oneself fully, we may need to find our way back to our childhood and understand its subsequent influence. Growing up may force us into certain ways of being which, though they serve us well, may not always express our full potential. Jung saw part of the work of analysis as encouraging and enabling the client "to play with his own nature." In the following excerpt from one of Boland's poems, we are reminded that sometimes we all need an invitation to play and explore. How enticing it is to hear her addressing her child in the gentle poem "In the Garden."

> let us go out now
> before the morning
> gets warm
>
> get your bicycle
> your teddy bear–
> the one that's penny-
> coloured
> like your hair
> and come…
>
> I want to show you
> what
> I don't exactly know.
> We will find out…[6]

There are many ways to embark on or continue the inner journey. What I am certain of is that it needs love and attention. We can acquire the skill of the poet who knows how to look, look again, and look even closer. When we try to remember and understand our own life and being, there are the personal circumstances and details to contemplate, but we also need to take into account the wider social and historic contexts in which we live. I love the ease with which Boland can move from present to past, from herself to all women, in a moment.

"The Unlived Life"

"Listen to me" I said to my neighbour,
"how do you make a hexagon-shaped template?"
So we talked about end papers
cropped circles, block piece work
while the children shouted and
the texture of synthetics as compared…

Suddenly I could see us
calicoed, overawed, dressed in cotton
at a railway crossing watching
the flange-wheeled iron omen
of another life passing, passing
wondering for a moment what it was
we were missing as we turned for home.[7]

The phrase "the unlived life" is used by Jung to describe what might be missing in our sense of ourselves and in our lives. In the analytic process, images and dreams can invoke and help us recall some talent or interests which may lie dormant in our unconscious. This can be the starting point for a whole new adventure. In her semi-autobiographical book, *Object Lessons: The Woman and the Poet in Our Time*, Boland describes how

For many years I could make little sense of a remembered image
of a girl in a jumper and skirt leaving her flat, climbing onto the
open rocking platform of a bus and going into the heart of a city.
For years pieces of the journey and the destination would come
back to me like missing sections of a photograph…[8]

In art and literature as in analysis, recollection can become the basis of creation. An aid to this is the idea of the muse. The muse has been a much valued way of working with and inviting inspiration. Often the artist must woo the muse. And this is best done in solitude. Seldom are we so single-mindedly engaged as artists, but perhaps we have something to learn from them in this regard.

In attempting to recall and retrieve the energy and power which may have been lost or forgotten, we may also need to grieve whatever losses have occurred. Consciousness and its pursuit are not easy, they demand much of us and they also bring new responsibilities. Then must we ask or even pray for help. In the following poem, "Envoi," listen how Boland pleads with her muse.

"Envoi"

It is Easter in the suburb, Clematis
shrubs the eaves and trellis with pastel.
The evenings lengthen and before the rain
the Dublin Mountains become visible.

My muse must be better than those of men
who made theirs in the image of their myth.
The work is half finished and I have nothing
but its crudest measures to complete it with...

What I have done I have done alone
What I have seen is unverified.
I have the truth, I need the faith.
It is time I put my hand in her side.

If she will not bless the ordinary
if she will not sanctify the common
then here I am and here I stay and then am I
the most miserable of women.[9]

What is so striking and unusual about Boland is her early and consistent idea of herself as a poet and her determined pursuit of the development of this part of herself. She recalls,

> I know now that I began writing in a country where the word woman and the word poet were almost magnetically opposed. One word was used to invoke collective nurture, the other to sketch out self-reflective individualism...I became used to the flawed space between them. In a certain sense, I found my poetic voice by shouting across the distance.[10]

Object Lessons gave further articulation to the themes and challenges of her life. She not only gave voice to her inner journey, she also inspired and affirmed many others in their creative pursuits. While such a model may ignite and even propel us forward in our own endeavor to be conscious, we need to find what might sustain us. After the initial euphoria, complacency can set in; we write that first paper, join the painting class—a bit like New Year's resolutions failed by February. In analysis, it is frequently the moment when people want to stop the process and leave analysis. Often, enough ground has been laid but we are still only working on the excavations before beginning to build the actual house. This can be a time of turmoil and self-doubt—we cannot go forward, we cannot go back. "There were times," Boland writes in *Object Lessons*

> when I felt like a poet and times when I did not. I felt like a poet in the kitchen of the flat. There with the coffee mug and my copybook I felt equal to the definition. There, where no one could see me, I found parts of myself which only the strange working and reworking made visible.[11]

The image of a creative space Boland once inhabited is recalled again and again throughout her writing. The idea of the waiting copybook, the invitation and readiness to regularly take up the pen, catches for me Jung's suggestion that we circumambulate dreams, returning again and again to the space where we give undivided attention to ourselves and to our souls.

The example of the poet, honoring all aspects of her life—not only the specially happy or sad events, but equally the mundane and the regular—can teach us the importance of observation, patience, and reflection. In a way, the poems of Boland themselves might serve as canvases or copybooks for us to record and elaborate what we discover within ourselves. Her art can turn the ordinary into the sublime which itself can hold and nurture us.

"Night Feed"

> This is dawn
> Believe me
> This is your season, little daughter,
> The moment daisies open,
> The hot mercurial rainwater

> Makes a mirror for sparrows
> It's time we drowned our sorrows.[12]

Both her prose and poetic reflections on her life gently lull us into a new security which can awaken our urge and ability to look, wonder, and even luxuriate in our simplest experiences and thoughts.

In Boland's poem, "Midnight Flowers,"[13] she describes a descent and evokes a wondering about paradox. Suddenly we are face to face with a child who is closely examining a snapdragon which is the color of her hair. Such moments of intimacy and surprise can break open our hearts. This opening is what is most deeply desired in the creative process and analysis but is frequently avoided or even feared and frequently with good reason. Emotions are often held in the fine detail, the minutiae of our everyday life and memories. Soft and harsh experiences can become so enmeshed that we forget them both, losing in the process some of what we may need to expand and fulfil our potentialities.

Sometimes in moving forward we need to look back. Boland does this beautifully in "Then."

"Then"

> Where are the lives we lived
> When we were young?
> Our kisses, the heat of our skin, our bitter words?
> The first waking to the first child's cry.[14]

That our lives change is inescapable. What we can do is develop our capacity to flow and grow with those changes, initiating those that would serve us well.

Much of an analyst's work is about waiting, about attending. Perhaps this is why, for an analyst, the way Boland describes sitting up with a poem, as if with a patient with a fever, is so powerful.

"Inheritance"

> …I stayed awake, alert and afraid, with my first child,
> who turned and turned, sick, fretful.
>
> When dawn came I held my hand over the absence of fever,
> over skin which had stopped burning, as if I knew the secrets
> of health and air, as if I understood them

and listened to the silence
and thought, I must have learned that somewhere.[15]

We frequently underestimate ourselves, even projecting onto others the gifts and beauty we cannot find within. How do we rebalance the view we might have of ourselves? Perhaps, like Boland, calling to mind what we have actually done. In analysis, the dreams might even offer narratives or images which, when gently opened, reveal much that is both new and strangely familiar to us. The change that may be needed then may not be real or actual but rather one of re-valuing ourselves. This is perhaps the greatest change of all and often surprises us in its effect. I think the soul enjoys such moments. Maybe it's as if it smiles, if one can say such a thing, and we become lit from within.

It is fair to say that Boland has been conscious throughout her writing of her role as a guide and a forerunner for others, especially, perhaps, women writers. The emergence of a new generation of poets, both men and women, in Ireland in recent years is at least in part a tribute to her influence and generosity.

I have for the purpose of my theme selected only a tiny part and aspect of Boland's work—this concentration inevitably misses the full width and depth of what she has created. It is not just the treasures themselves she offers but also an ongoing reflection of how she found them. For me as an analyst, what makes Boland's work extra special is her ability to highlight and describe the pursuit of a full and creative life. Is it not least what every analyst would wish to offer the people with whom she works? Sometimes it is enough for someone just to be there. Boland captures this by returning to the writer's desk and the solitude which is now somehow different in her poem "Is It Still The Same."

"Is It Still The Same"

young woman who climbs the stairs,
who closes a child's door
who goes to her table
in a room at the back of a house?...
You can see nothing of her, but her head
bent over the page, her hand moving,
moving again, and her hair.
I wrote like that once,

But this is different;
This time, when she looks up, I will be there.[16]

NOTES

1. C. G. Jung, *Collected Works*, tr. R. F. C. Hull (Princeton: Princeton University Press, 1953), vol. 18, para. 1292.

2. Eavan Boland, "The Women," *The Journey & Other Poems* (Manchester, UK: Carcanet Press, 1987).

3. Adrienne Rich, "Planetarium," *Poems Selected and New 1950-1984* (New York: W. W. Norton and Co., 1984), p. 115.

4. Boland, "Woman in Kitchen," *New Collected Poems* (New York: Norton, 2008), p. 109.

5. Boland, "Suburban Woman," *New Collected Poems*, p. 63.

6. Boland, "In the Garden," *New Collected Poems,* p. 106.

7. Boland, "The Unlived Life," *New Collected Poems*, p. 135.

8. Boland, *Object Lessons: The Life of the Woman and the Poet in Our Time* (London: Random House-Vintage, 1996), p. 93.

9. Boland, "Envoi," *New Collected Poems*, p. 150.

10. Boland, "Introduction" to *Object Lessons,* p. 1.

11. Boland, *Object Lessons,* p. 106.

12. Boland, "Night Feed," *New Collected Poems,* p. 92.

13. Boland, "Midnight Flowers," *New Collected Poems*, p. 193.

14. Boland, "Then," *New Collected Poems*, p. 283.

15. Boland, "Inheritance," *Domestic Violence* (Manchester, UK: Carcanet Press Ltd., 2007).

16. Boland, *Against Love Poetry* (New York: Norton, 2001).

Oedipus in an Irish Bog: Seamus Heaney, Freud, and Jung

Editor's Note: Irish poet, writer, and lecturer, Seamus Heaney, was awarded the Nobel Prize in Literature in 1995. Born in April 1939 on a farm near Belfast, Northern Ireland, he currently lives in Dublin. Main collections of his poetry include: *Death of a Naturalist* (1966), *Door into the Dark* (1969), *Wintering Out* (1975), *Field Work* (1979), Station Island (1984), *The Haw Lantern* (1987), *Seeing Things* (1991), *The Spirit Level* (1996), *Electric Light* (2001), and *District and Circle* (2006). Collected editions of his poetry include: *Selected Poems 1965-1975*, *New Selected Poems 1966-1987*, and *Opened Ground: Poems 1966-1996*. His prose works include: *Preoccupations: Selected Prose 1968-1978*, *The Government of the Tongue*, *The Redress of Poetry: Oxford Lectures*, and *Finders Keepers: Selected Prose 1971-2001*. He is married to Marie Heaney, the author of *Over Nine Waves*, a collection of traditional Irish myths and legends.

This article explores Seamus Heaney's controversial use of myth in his poems about preserved ancient bodies found in northern European bogs. It takes as its starting point a minor incident in the relationship

Susan Rowland, Ph.D., is Reader in English and Jungian Studies at the University of Greenwich, UK, and author of *Jung as a Writer* (Routledge, 2005). She was chair of the International Association of Jungian Studies, 2003-2006.

between Sigmund Freud and C. G. Jung about these same bog discoveries. A small disagreement between them proves to turn upon their different attitudes to myth. Here both Freud and Jung illuminate Heaney's later attempt to read ritual and communal violence through myth and sacrifice that seems rooted in the Irish landscape as much as in the collective imagination.

FREUD, JUNG, MYTHS, AND BOGS

In 1909, Sigmund Freud and C. G. Jung were on their way to America when they quarrelled. The spark flared from Jung's mention to Freud of the surprisingly well-preserved bodies that were being discovered in northern European bogs. Jung recalls this episode in *Memories, Dreams, Reflections* (hereinafter "*MDR*") as an attempt on his part to make light conversation.[1] His effort to amuse Freud goes disastrously wrong when the older man faints. Recovering, Freud banishes this topic of conversation with the accusation that Jung harbors a death wish towards him. In the iconography of *MDR*, the failed discussion about bodies in bogs picks up the theme of "mud" which had been introduced previously: Freud begs Jung to remain faithful to *his* [Freud's] psychoanalysis lest it be overwhelmed by "a black tide of mud" of the occult, a dread Jung immediately describes as "mythological."[2]

I would like to suggest that Jung's report of his fascination with bog bodies reveals something prophetic about his own work. Jung says:

> Having read about these peat corpses, I recalled them when we were in Bremen, but, being a bit muddled, confused them with the mummies in the lead cellars of the city. This interest of mine got on Freud's nerves.[3]

Here is an early example of what later became both a creative therapeutic practice and a method of reading history psychologically by drawing in other cultures. Jung's suggestive confusion looks like an embryonic attempt at amplification. An image from the unconscious (preserved dead bodies) is allowed to develop *of itself* a connection to other cultural images such as mummified corpses discovered in the German cellars of Bremen. Even more intimate to Jung's later work is his way of linking cultures and histories by analogy. The ancient bog bodies, thousands of years old from a world and a religion long vanished, are (involuntarily) associated with habits of embalming the dead that may be mysterious, yet are more recent and more directly part of Jung's Europe.

Such musing by Jung anticipates vast swathes of his later writing in *Aion* in which he draws numinous and strange symbols from history to create a portal to the Other for the modern mind.[4] A more precise example of this reaching out to the other through history (time) and different culture (space) is in his "Trickster" essay.[5] Here extended meditation upon the Native American trickster myth becomes a *treatment* for the better psychological health of medieval Europe, which possesses an analogous cultural energy. Modernity is left thinly protected by the toxic emaciated version of the trickster in the shadow. Only history itself, rejuvenated by psychic re-invention, has the narrative and imaginative potency to become the trickster for modernity, as I have argued elsewhere.[6]

To sum up, what Jung reports at the end of his life as a careless failure of tact on his part (mentioning the dead bog bodies to Freud) not only stumbles over Freud's fear of death, likely heightened by Freud's analogous fear of being deposed by Jung, but the incident is also indicative of larger themes. Yet it would be a mistake to ignore Freud's reaction in a reading of this tense moment. For Freud's anxiety cuts through what Jung's inclination to analogy omits, the *difference* between dead bodies in bogs and those in German cellars. Whereas the Germans have mummified their bodies as a deliberate act of preservation, no one can tell whether throwing dead people into bogs has a similar purpose. What is evident, however, is that, unlike the Germans, the bog people were murdered. Historians tend to offer two possible explanations: the bog people were executed as criminals or ritually sacrificed to a fierce earth goddess.

So before leaving the passionate encounter of Jung and Freud over these European mysteries (in more than one sense), we should recall the depth of their response. Faced by what he takes to be a personal eruption of unconscious violence towards him from Jung, Freud faints. His body *speaks* in answer to talk of bog bodies and mummies. Jung, by contrast (he says), involuntarily begins a process of analogy that will, in later writing, become the building of a "personal myth."[7] His therapeutic mythmaking is also collective. For him history feeds the necessarily psychic growth of a personal and cultural shadow.

In this broken exchange between Freud and Jung are the shards of their descent into war. It is personal in the collapse of their elder/younger, father/son confederation as Freud collapses into Jung's arms. He falls, not to be rescued; it is an action ceding momentary defeat. Their conflict concerns interpretation of ritual violence as *personally* Oedipal or collectively/symbolically ritual. Or, to put another way, Freud insists that violence and absorption in death are to be understood as perennial human battles in which myth is the narrative of the individual's attempt to live with unspeakable desires. Jung, of course, in theory granted Freudian psychoanalysis a place in his understanding of unconscious impulses. Yet by contrast, his instinct was towards the accretion of meaning, not its reduction to instincts. Jung wanted to make *more myths* as a way of coming to terms with individual agony in a cultural and historical framework.

SEAMUS HEANEY:
POETRY AND VIOLENCE IN THE NATURE OF IRELAND

It is time to introduce a third culture and a third man who fell into the bog. Seamus Heaney is probably the most famous living Irish poet. He was born in 1939 to an Irish Catholic family in Northern Ireland. At the height of the appalling violence known as the Troubles, he moved with his family to the Irish Republic. Before that move he suffered personal and family experience of the killing and bombing between four armed groups: the British Army (that originally went in to defend the Catholic population, later regarded as aggressor to them), the mainly Protestant Northern Irish Police, the Irish Republican Army (the chief but not the only armed group aiming for a Catholic-united Ireland), and Protestant terrorists. It was at this very terrible period in British and Irish politics that Heaney became fascinated by discoveries of bog bodies. In the astonishingly fertile peat bogs, what was preserved was an image of murder, sacrifice, victimage, and a kind of union with the earth itself that recalls all too painfully an endless war over "opened ground," the title of Heaney's collected poems 1966-1996.[8]

The 1969 poem, "Bogland," marks out this particular land as ripe for inner psychic as well as outer exploration:

> Our pioneers keep striking
> Inwards and downwards.
>
> Every layer they strip
> Seems camped on before.[9]

Later, from 1975, the bog's obscure deeps of nature and human nature are explored even more intensely, particularly in "Bog Queen," "Strange Fruit," "Punishment," "Kinship."[10] Before looking at these poems, however, I want to offer a story that Heaney himself told about the violence in Northern Ireland in those days. This anecdote was part of his 1995 Nobel acceptance speech and is published in *Opened Ground* as "Crediting Poetry."[11]

On a January evening in 1976 a minibus of workers was being driven home in Northern Ireland when it was held up by a group of armed and masked men. The workers were lined up at the side of the road with guns pointing at them. Then one of the masked men said: "Any Catholics among you, step out here."[12] In that group all the workers were Protestants bar one. So all presumed that these were Protestant paramilitaries out to kill a lone Catholic amongst a Protestant workforce. The Catholic man prepared to step out. Before he did so, he felt the Protestant man next to him take his hand. Here was one of his co-workers telling him not to go, we will not betray you, no one need know which religion you are. Yet the man who put out his hand was too late for the Catholic man was in the very act of stepping forward. All at once the Catholic was pulled to one side and the masked men gunned down all the other workers. The presumption had been wrong. It was an IRA gang out to kill Protestants.

Heaney says of this dreadful atrocity that it illustrated for him the choices and possibilities for Ireland in the Troubles: is the future for his country one of collective slaughter or of that touch of the hand that reaches beyond tribal loyalties and their violent sacrifices? The poems of his bog people are one of those places where he tries to explore the deep darkness of the roots of violence in the Irish past, and what might flower from those same bogs. A particular cultural ingredient of this pain is that the notion that the bog people have been sacrificed to a nature goddess is a myth with a bloody history in Irish politics. Irish art has long figured Ireland as a dream woman, who is also herself an aspect of the land as a terrible mother demanding sacrifices. Yeats, with whom Heaney associates himself in "Crediting Poetry," represented Ireland as Cathleen Ni Houlihan, who could appear as old woman, young girl, or goddess, driving young men to fight to the death for her.[13] In "Crediting Poetry" Heaney refers to the side of Yeats that paid tribute to the terrible sorrows of the Civil War. He omitted the aspect of the poet that appeared to celebrate the inspiration of the terrible goddess.[14]

In the poem "Kinship," Heaney handles the bog as more than physical setting with near magical properties of preserving the past. It is wet soggy earth where nature and culture entwine. It evokes language as more than a cultural artifact in the desire to *represent* the world. Rather the digestive and transformative powers of the bog invoke numinous qualities of language suggesting its *continuity* with nature. Heaney seems to summon nature in his poems as that which roots language and gives it numinosity:

> Kinned by the hieroglyphic peat
> on the spreadfield
> to the strangled victim,
> the love nest in the bracken
>
> I step through origins.[15]

Yet, it is particularly in "Kinship" that the infused natural power of words, that vibrant union between earth and poem, is given troubling narrative form in the myth of the goddess. The bog is an "[i]nsatiable bride," sucking down the sword in a terrifying wedding of sexuality and killing. At the end, Heaney records how "we slaughter/ for the common good" while the bog/goddess "swallows/our love and terror."[16]

Recent critics, notably David Kennedy, have observed with disapprobation both Heaney's organicist view of language and Oedipal fantasy in the bog poems.[17] Kennedy takes the conventional critical view that myth always tries to remove literature from its connection to a particular history. Myth in literature is open to criticism when it appears to support or constellate a truth beyond itself, or a logos, as the ancient Greeks put it.[18] Here Kennedy sees the myth of the sacrifice-demanding goddess as effacing the actual histories and ideologies of the power struggle between the British state and the diverse communities in Northern Ireland. He thinks that Heaney has a fantasy of digging a simple historical turh out of the bog and criticizes it on political grounds. In effect, myths of an ancient unknown past can be found possessing a truth of being that can replace unpleasant truths of the present. History can be re-started from imaginary myth. Kennedy says that Heaney is here losing the specific Irish context for a preferred lapse into non-specific myth. The effect of Heaney's myth is to strip away the histories and ideologies informing the present. Heaney's organic language is de-historicizing and de-politicizing.

I have gone into detail of Kennedy's criticism because it goes to the heart of objections to much nature writing, that it uses nature for conservative purposes to evade realities of the discourses of power, and of myth.

Crucially, we are also back in that taut arena of bodily proximity and sharp exchange between Freud and Jung we described earlier. Between Freud's insistence on the Oedipus myth as a personal dynamic with the younger man and Jung's cultural analogies reaching out to myth building, we have Heaney's own ingredients for his vision of Oedipus, in the perverse love for a feminine Ireland that inspires killing. Perhaps among Freud, Jung, Kennedy, and Heaney, we may be able to sort out an-Other *place* for myth, poetry, and even Oedipus.

Myth, Knowledge, and Story

Politically oriented critics object to myth in art because they regard it as limiting meaning to aristocratic narratives that form political or religious or philosophical abstract ideas that work by excluding an Other. So the later poetry of T. S. Eliot adopts mythical narratives explicitly to endorse an exclusive and theocratic version of Christian government. The mythical story of Plato's cave has long been taken to sponsor notions of truth and reality that are expressed as abstract, conceptual, and rational. Such a structuring of truth is characterized by dividing off reason from its Other, whether that other is conceived of as narrative or body or matter or feminine or chaos or sexuality or unconscious and so on. Symptomatically, Plato described a polis best remembered for *excluding* poets.

On the other hand, Plato's banishing of those notable liars, the poets, suggests other possibilities for myth in art. The ancient Greeks themselves contrasted the use of myth as narratives for *logos* with what they called *mythos*. The critic Laurence Coupe has developed this opposition.[19] For the Greeks, logos is the abstract truth that some myths in some contexts, such as Plato's philosophy, can be made to yield. Mythos, on the other hand, stands for myth as ontologically story. Mythos is where the story is the *matter*, the origin and the end of what story may have been and may come to invoke. Myths as mythos do not exclude, do not erect impermeable barriers to the Other, for they are infinitely re-tellable stories of in-corporation. What seems to be other this time is available as the narrative *place* of the next re-telling. Coupe calls this opposition "allegory," for myth used to abstract a doctrine or a truth, and "radical typology," where myth recapitulates as an endless desire for conjunctio with the other.

Given that mythos or radical typology embraces the Other, whether as matter or body etc., I'd like to return the forgiving possibilities of this notion to Heaney's true story of the roadside atrocity. Surely here we do see the two types of myth in the poisoned atmosphere of the Northern Irish Troubles. Those who kill are imprisoned in logos in the sense that they regard the other side as absolutely Other. They do not touch them; only bullets fly. Of course the divided communities are absolutely Other if you regard the stories that shape them, the myths of Irish Catholicism and Protestantism, as capable of allegorically abstracting the two communities from each other. In this world, Catholic and Protestant are discrete entities like concepts. It is the man who reaches out a hand who figures an-other way with myth. His bodily connection with the other is an act of in-corporation that invokes the other, more muted myths of Irish history, of the shared land that Heaney writes of, relationships across the barriers, a shared immersion in nature and bogs that invokes a sense *in the senses* of human nature.

In Christian culture, as I have written elsewhere, abstract logos knowledge goes back to hegemonic readings of Genesis. These situate the Creator as a rational intelligence forming nature as matter *separate* from masculine mind.[20] Man is then formed in the image of this God and teaches a privileging of masculinity as rationality and logos as long as it is split off from (and so making) femininity, unconscious, body and nature. Hence the dualism of mythos and logos, radical typology and allegory. Of course to give the impression that logos simply tends to sponsor terrible violence and mythos produces reconciliation is to fall into the very splitting and dualism that is the problem that this binary enacts and challenges. Logos in our culture stems from a father god, and mythos is a mode of the earth mother whose ways are those of connection and relating as opposed to separation and discrimination. What this binary really teaches us is the necessity of *both*. We need to regard logos and mythos as separate and discrete entities, the properties of separating, connecting, *and* see them as working together, separating then connecting, then separating, etc. In fact, logos and mythos stand for two types of mutually constituting consciousness, both humanly vital when mutually sustaining. They are a consciousness of rational (ego) separateness and also one of learning through relating to unconscious and other as matter, body, etc.

What Heaney's story of Irish violence actually shows is the horrific constellation of extreme and distorted versions of one type of consciousness. Violence here stems from logos myth pursued to absolute structuring of Other, one that *must* be eradicated for the identity of the *same* (Catholic or Protestant) to be maintained. Yet the continuity of terrorist attacks was also a perversion of the mythos of incorporation, when individuals sank themselves in to a story that acted like earth mother's bog in swallowing the self through the body into a token of murderous sacrifice. Divorcing the other, even as the other way of consciousness, is a disaster, as all the myths tell us, even Oedipus.

HEANEY'S MYTH

> I lay waiting
> Between the turf face and the demesne wall[21]

To return to Kennedy's criticism of Heaney's bog poems is to perceive it now as an argument about myth. Kennedy assumes that myth always and inevitably produces a hard kernel of "truth" that is always an ideological truth because of the contamination of story in the first place. I agree that lived in culture no story or myth is without ideology or political *weight*. However, it is the nature of mythos or radical typology to be lived bodily and socially as a flexible, even self-critical ideology. Mythos has to be like this because its very being is to be lived as a possibility that does not foreclose on the Other. So if, as I am arguing, Heaney embraces mythos rather than logos, then his myths of the earth mother as bog construct a space of meaning where it is possible to explore the desires and fears encapsulated in Irish politics *and to criticize* what actions and beliefs are ascribed to them.

Most importantly, Heaney's poetic mythos includes the reader. Mythos provides an interactive field of meaning that reaches out to the reader as in-corporated in the project. We, too, learn separation and connection to the passions and desires invoked in the matter of myth. Kennedy is right that this is an organicist notion of language, about structuring wholes of meaning and reaching out to make a whole with the reader's consciousness. He is wrong, however, to suggest that this means the covert re-inscription of myths of exclusion. No, like Jung, Heaney's wholes have also to figure holes: wholeness is only possible if myth desires, passionately, to enfold also an absence of meaning, for mythos is only mythos when there is space for the other. Heaney's Irish bogs are radical typology versions of myths of sacrifice to the Irish earth. Within this is a critical exploration of violence; criticism made possible by the deeper consciousness evoked by citing what is toxic in allegorical Irish myth and re-siting it through the common earth. The bogs and their culture of the dead are at once the space the communities must share and the history common to both. They are everybody's land and the pre-Christian (so pre-division into Catholic and Protestant) earth mother myth.

If poetry can convert a poisoned logos into mythos and include the reader, psyche and body, in the renewed field of meaning, then poetry is itself a way of healing the community. As Heaney says:

> [T]here are times when a deeper need enters…not only a surprising variation played upon the world, but a retuning of the world itself.[22]

These reflections suggest a return to Freud, Jung, and Oedipus.

OEDIPUS VARIATIONS

One thought on the Freud-Jung encounter in 1909 is that Freud anticipates Heaney by reading his body as enacting the myth of Oedipus, as a story of violent desires between men. Sophocles's Oedipus, who discovers that he has murdered his father and committed incest with his mother, is a myth from which is derived Freud's logos of universal truth of repressed desires of patricide and forbidden sexuality. By emphasizing the violent dimension of the myth, Freud is here peculiarly *Irish* and shows a real flexibility in taking the role of Laius facing a patricidal son. Jung, by contrast, stressed the productive role of the mother in the Oedipus myth. Oedipus's problem is that he has *failed* to overcome what the Sphinx signifies.

> The riddle was, in fact, the trap the Sphinx laid for the unwary wanderer. Overestimating his intellect in a typically masculine way, Oedipus walked right into it, and unknowingly committed the crime of incest. The riddle of the Sphinx was herself—the terrible mother-imago, which Oedipus would not take as a warning.[23]

To Jung, the Sphinx is the originary creative unconscious who remains a terrible devouring presence because Oedipus fails to establish a connection to this maternal creature. His assumption that intellectual triumph solves the problem of the "other" is catastrophic. In effect, Oedipus fails to understand his story *as both types of myth*. He is caught by literal enactment of the Oedipus complex because he does not take the Sphinx as the generative potential for "other" stories, stories of the "other" that she is. Failure to comprehend mythos condemns him to logos. It is true that Oedipus, in Freud's vision, is the one man not to suffer from the Oedipus complex for Oedipus does in life what the complex is supposed to prevent. The Oedipus complex includes an allegorical idea of a life built on literal repression of incestuous desires (Freudian) and also a way of living such desires in stories, narratives enacting love and restraint.

I am suggesting that Freud's vision of the psyche through the Oedipus drama prefers the allegorical in the desire to build concepts out of myth. However, only Oedipus, in this perspective, is condemned to absolute literalism—without connecting to his passions and therefore the possibility of *re-writing the story*. Jung, on the other hand, always emphatically prefers radical typology in the myths we are heir to. So it is the Sphinx, the most inhuman, most "other" player in the narrative who embodies the origin of that most mysterious whole, that has to be also hole, the self. Unlike Freud, Jung's writing itself is made from the tension between knowledge as logos, conceptual as generated from stories of the psyche, and truth as endlessly generative and mysterious because always reaching out to the other in mythos.[24]

Not only does this contrast in styles of knowing, in preference for one or other type of consciousness, divide the two men in their written psychologies, we can also see the acting out of two approaches to Oedipus in the tragic 1909 encounter. Freud is bodily incorporated into the myth as Laius facing a faithless son. By insisting that Jung harbored a death wish toward him, Freud squashes his own bodily action into something as close as possible to the Oedipus myth as Freudian concept. Even though this bodily in-corporation is suggestive of the creative possibilities of mythos, Freud refuses to allow his position in the story as one killed, to be re-imagined as one reborn. Just think what might have been possible to depth psychology if *both Jung and Freud could have been reborn from the bog of the sacrificed bodies?*

> a slimy birth cord
> of bog, had been cut [25]

Jung's reaction to the conversation about bog bodies is indicative of his preference for amplifying myth into radical typology. In particular, it anticipates one method of doing this by cultural analogy: the bog bodies of another culture induce a slip whereby he finds himself talking about mummified corpses found in the cellars of his Europe. This kind of "slip" is what Kennedy criticizes in Heaney because he argues that it always means an ideological wiping out of inconvenient truth. Jung is not immune to this very danger, for example in making generalizations about indigenous tribal cultures and immediately and colonially appropriating them as truths about European origins in "Archaic Man."[26] Kennedy is right that easy switching between past and present can structure allegorical forms of truth that betray the complexities of the Other. My point here about Jung is that his drive towards the unconscious as creative and in part unknowable preserves as what is most prominent his mythical preference for radical typology that does offer a space for the other as Other. His allegorical mishaps when cultural are always resolved in the same text. In "Archaic Man" the western tendency to appropriate through logos is itself deeply criticized through a radical typological vision of the cruel colonialism of white modernity.

Freud and Jung collide because Freud needs Oedipus as myth to be allegorical so that conceptuality can be built into his structure of consciousness. Threaten the allegorical mode as dominant, and you threaten the supremacy of the ego, he thinks. No wonder he regarded Jung with extinguishing horror. Jung needed a vision of death to contain with it the seed of rebirth. He needs the priority of the unconscious as fertile mother who would always feed the ego with an-other story. So Freud's faint could never have been interpreted as just a death wish to Jung. By analogy he brings the dead bodies in bogs *home* to the self of the cultural unconscious. There the dead are dis-covered, dug up from bog and cellar, sprouting many tales. These tales cannot be limited, for that would be to suggest that the unconscious is finally knowable. For Jung, the human unconscious is our umbilical cord to nature: its treatment of life and death is endless.

> Here is the girl's head like
> an exhumed gourd…
> Murdered, forgotten,
> nameless, terrible…[27]

Seamus Heaney is a mythmaker. In using Oedipal myth to make a meaningful connection between murdered bodies in bogs and Irish politics, he is well aware of the dangers of "relating" without its necessary other of "distinguishing." As the more polarized Freud and Jung know, but fail to admit to each other, neither logos nor mythos can exist alone, even if one of them obscures the presence of the other. Simply aiming for connecting and relating, body and unconsciousness, is not to find the loving arms of the earth mother, but rather to regress fatally, to be swallowed up by a bog of unconsciousness. The social equivalent is mindless (literally!) indiscriminate violence. Freud also needs allegorical Oedipus complex to have narrative flexibility in the inscriptions of an individual life. In parallel Jung requires the story telling characterizing of the unconscious to be potent through their mitigation of abstract ideas.

Heaney aims to right the mythical unbalance of the Irish, and to a certain extent, the modern world. Poetry that is in-spired, inspirited, dissolves rigid political allegories and allows the Other to speak its own stories inside us. "Punishment" is a poem about a bog woman that begins by an act of bodily kinship.

> I can feel the tug
> of the halter[28]

Importantly, it ends not with Heaney taking over the story of the sacrificed woman for his own purposes. Rather evoking her makes possible another act of reaching out to victims. Heaney steps back, by first implicitly condemning himself for standing silent when girls in Northern Ireland were tarred and feathered for consorting with British soldiers. These women, while not killed, also have the blackened bodies of the bog victims. The final lines bring Heaney and us back with a shock to the notion of tribal revenge. Heaney ends divided between connection with the contemporary women made possible by the resemblance to the bog body, while still acknowledging the atavistic pull of being part of a tribe in a hostile environment. Crucially, it is not mythical appropriation of the bog or the earth mother. Rather than slippage of modern politics into ancient atrocity, it is Heaney's perception of *difference* between old and new victim that encourages him to feel sympathy and connection outside his tribal loyalties. In a way "Punishment" is a detour from a paralyzed present, via a past where nature and human body are now one, to return to the present with expanded sense of self and the chance of connecting to others. I would suggest that Jung in 1909, moving from bog bodies to bodies in cellars in attempting to converse with a much older man, was trying to embark on the same journey.

So Freud, Jung, and Heaney are fascinated by bog bodies, and their peculiar grip on the imagination leads them to mother earth, the unconscious, the body, and the presence of the past. Bog bodies, image of the ego as submerged in the other, bring forth Oedipus as hero of the primal structure with nature as parents. Heaney is criticized for his Oedipal figuring of the relationship to nature where nature is a devouring mother demanding blood sacrifices. Such a notion is perceptible in Irish political myths demanding that men and women be prepared to die and kill for the land of Ireland. Of course, this take on the story recalls Jung's reading of Oedipus as the dreadful revenge of an unconscious spurned by Oedipus's failure with the Sphinx. In fact, both Freud and Jung on Oedipus stress the need for both earth mother and sky father consciousness. We see it in Freud's insistence on identifying with the father in order to repress the desire for the mother, yet keep the possibility of many stories enacting this dilemma.

Both kinds of consciousness are also present in Jung allowing for a need for paternal discrimination while forging relationship to the unconscious through many stories. To put it simply, Heaney's Oedipus is both Freudian and Jungian. He exhibits a greater emphasis on radical typology in order to woo his readers from their inheritance of the allegorical myths that divide them.

> I stand at the edge of
> centuries
> facing a goddess[29]

Heaney's story of the roadside murders and one touch of the hand is itself a myth when he describes it as a longing for an-Other future for his homeland. Because his Oedipal bog poems *treat* toxic polarized social myths with rejuvenating radical typology, his Oedipus is reborn from his bog-mother. His rebirth offers hope that the Oedipus myth could be, for all of us, a myth of becoming. Oedipus is reborn within us as no longer paralyzed between fear and desire, no longer locked into murderous rage. In Sophocles' play, Oedipus is always demanding answers while unfortunately not listening to what any of the anxious people around him are trying to tell him. He hears nothing until he realizes that he himself is the story he needs to hear. His body and soul are at last reborn in union; the myth consciously as well as unconsciously expressed. Oedipus reborn can hear what the other is trying to tell him. That is why Heaney's poetry makes the bog people speak, without speaking for them.

> *and I rose from the dark*[30]
> (italics mine)

NOTES

1. C. G. Jung, *Memories, Dreams, Reflections* [hereinafter *MDR*] (London: Collins and Routledge & Kegan Paul, 1963), pp. 179-80.

2. *Ibid.*, p. 178.

3. *Ibid.*, pp. 179-80.

4. C. G. Jung, *Collected Works*, trans. R. F. C. Hull (Princeton: Princeton University Press, 1953-91), volume 9ii, *Aion*. All future references to Jung's *Collected Works*, abbreviated to *CW* will be by volume and paragraph number.

5. *CW* 9i § 456-488.

6. Susan Rowland, *Jung as a Writer* (London and New York: Routledge, 2005).

7. *MDR*, pp. 195, 224.

8. Seamus Heaney, *Opened Ground: Poems 1966-1996* (London: Faber & Faber, 1998).

9. Heaney, *Opened Ground*, pp. 41-42.

10. *Ibid.*, pp. 112-126.

11. *Ibid.*, pp. 445-467.

12. *Ibid.*, p. 456.

13. See plays by W. B. Yeats such as "The Countess Cathleen," "Cathleen Ni Houlihan," in *The Collected Plays of W. B. Yeats* (London: Macmillan, 1934).

14. Heaney, *Opened Ground*, pp. 461-464.

15. *Ibid.*, pp. 120-126.

16. *Ibid.*

17. David Kenney, "Mound-dwellers and Mummers: Language and Community in Seamus Heaney's Wintering out," *Irish Studies Review*, 10:3, pp. 303-313.

18. Laurence Coupe, *Myth* (London and New York: Routledge, 1997), pp. 9, 39.

19. *Ibid.*, pp. 100-101.

20. Susan Rowland, "Nature Writing: Jung's Eco-Logic in the Conjunctio of Comedy and Tragedy," *Spring: A Journal of Archetype and Culture*, vol. 7, 2006, pp. 275-97.

21. Heaney, *Opened Ground*, p. 112.

22. *Ibid.*, p. 454.

23. Jung, *CW* 5 § 181.

24. For more on Jung's writing as mythos see Rowland, *Jung as a Writer*.

25. Heaney, *Opened Ground*, p. 114.

26. Jung, *Modern Man in Search of a Soul* (London: Routledge/Ark, 1933), pp. 127-54.

27. Heaney, *Opened Ground*, p. 119.

28. *Ibid.*, pp. 117-118.

29. *Ibid.*, p. 123.

30. *Ibid.*, p. 114.

"The Third Battle of Magh Tuired"
An Excerpt from *Dreamtime*
by John Moriarty

Editor's Note: Spring is honored to publish the following excerpt from *Dreamtime,* a book by renowned Irish philosopher and writer, John Moriarty (1938-2007).

John Moriarty was born in north Kerry in 1938 and educated at Listowel and University College Dublin. He taught English Literature at the University of Manitoba in Canada for six years, returning to Ireland in 1971 where he lived at the foot of Mangerton Mountain in northern County Kerry. He is the author of *Dreamtime* (1994, revised 1999); the trilogy, *Turtle Was Gone a Long Time: Crossing the Kedron* (1996), *Horsehead Nebula Neighing* (1997), and *Anaconda Canoe* (1998); *Nostos,* an autobiography (2001); *Invoking Ireland* (2005, revised 2006); *Night Journey to Buddh Gaia* (2006); *Serious Sounds* (2007); *One Evening in Eden* (2007), a boxed CD collection of his talks, stories, and poetry; and *What the Curlew Knew,* his final book, published posthumously in 2007.

More information about him can be found online at www.johnmoriarty.net.

Spring extends its gratitude to Thomas Moore, a close friend of John Moriarty, for suggesting the publication of his work in *Spring* and for writing the following introductory remarks about him.

The John Moriarty I Knew
by Thomas Moore

In the year 2000 I was getting ready to spend a year with my family in Dublin and was talking with my friend, Christopher Bamford, who has written on Celtic Spirituality. Chris suggested that I look up John Moriarty, an Irish writer who, he said, would be particularly interesting. After settling into Dublin I called John and arranged to meet him at a hotel just off Grafton Street, the pedestrian shopping area of downtown Dublin. We sat in a lounge drinking tea for hours.

John was a big man in those days, with a corona of long, thick, graying hair. He spoke in his native Kerry dialect and musicality, and the words poured out of him. He seemed overstocked with pent-up ideas, images, and plans. But he was not the ambitious sort. His rich language rose up from the imagination in his heart. He was warm, original, and, if I may use the word without any sentimentality, inspired.

I had read some of John's work in what is perhaps his most accessible book, *Dreamtime*. He writes passionately, as though the muse were still whispering in his ear. He uses the colorful language of Greek, Christian, and Irish mythology, all of them so mixed together that they make a subtle, thick texture of imagery. I was surprised in our conversation to see how strong Christian theology was in him. In that, he reminded me of the Renaissance magus I have written about, Marsilio Ficino, who practiced Greek and Hermetic magic and yet was a priest assigned to the cathedral in Florence.

John was truly a bard, in the Irish tradition. He would write with the same torrent of inspiration with which he spoke. When I returned to New Hampshire after the year in Dublin, John would phone, or I'd phone him, and I'd mainly listen as his inspiration poured out of the telephone. In some people such a gush of words would feel like loquaciousness, but in John it was a pleasing flow of images.

When you read John's work, you have to understand that his deep reading of Irish and Greek mythology is in the same vein as his deep reading of Gospel texts. He hears the overtones and undertones that make the mythology come alive and speak to our current concerns. In this he is an archetypalist, appreciating many dimensions of an image at once, eschewing any simplistic one-dimensional approach, avoiding naïve allegory and moralism.

As a writer, John is like James Joyce, creating a thick texture of language, mythology, and broad learning, but his method is different from Joyce's. When he quotes a source, he likes to cite large sections, and he has no compunction about repeating and repeating key phrases, in the manner of a musical form. His work is full of themes and variations, chansons, sonatas, fugues, and madrigals. Occasionally you will come upon a melisma—a long, free-flowing expression of emotion or realization.

I think it's best to read John Moriarty the way you listen to music. Don't look up every obscure reference, but let the sounds and rhythms add dimension to the meaningful sentences you happen to pick up. Allow the repetition to deepen your appreciation for an idea. Go down into the whirlpool of inspiration and come back out with whatever sticks to you.

If ever there were a modern writer who worked according to William Blake's dictum—I am the secretary; the authors are in eternity—it is John Moriarty. And his main theme is close to that: the discovery of eternity in an era when chronological time is "in your face," controlling everything you do, and influencing your reading of events.

In one of his last books, *Invoking Ireland*, John contrasts the spirit of the old gods, the Tuatha Dé Danaan, with the Formorians, who cut down trees and redirected rivers. He lived in the ancient Ireland, but around him prowled the Celtic Tiger, Ireland's fast-track entry into the modern world. Bulldozers are now at work in the valley of Tara, and the Irish are losing some of the ancient Druidic stuff that was alive in John.

I spent Christmas week of 2000 in a hotel in Killarney, not far from John's house. I hadn't met John yet, but every morning I looked out the window to see two mountains covered with snow, looking like the breasts of the earth. Later, John told me how important those "paps" were to him. They are called an Dá Chích Anann, the breasts of Anu, goddess of the earth. John, the deep Christian, lived in the shadows of those paps and wrote out of reverence for them.

In March of 2007 I gave a talk in the city of Limerick and then visited Glenstal Abby, not far away. I then went to Dublin and visited John in The Mater Hospital, which is not far from the Abbey theater. John had had cancer of the colon, the liver, and the lungs. When I got to his room, he was asleep, just having returned from the last hope he had, an experimental procedure to starve the liver tumor. It didn't work. He was thinner now and his hair was short. He looked unusually handsome and healthy. When he woke up, I sat on his bed for over two hours having my last conversation with him. We laughed and discussed theology. John asked me for a blessing. He closed his eyes, and I put my hands on his head and made the sign of the cross over him. He died on June 1, 2007.

"The Third Battle of Magh Tuired"*
from *Dreamtime* by John Moriarty

Hovering in my doorway, darkening it, a scald crow called, once. Her call was a screech, piercing and bald. There was something human in it.

A red man walked through my dreams that night.

It's the Third Battle of Magh Tuired, he said.

Fighting itself in you, he said.

Even his words were red.

I woke. But the dream didn't fade. There was aggression in the room, an aggressive smell of boar badger in it. And that confirmed an impression I had of him. He looked as though it was only occasionally he was human.

Again the next day, in the hills, I saw the scald crow. Eating an afterbirth, a sheep's, she was. And that reminded me of a dream I had :a hag knee deep in a river washing my modern mind: downstream, in pool after pool, the fish died.

It didn't surprise me that I dreamed such a dream. I was often at odds with my modern head. Its modern way of seeing hurt things.

In the end I had no choice. I gave in to the grain of strange growing in me. I came home to my valley.

---

*In Irish mythology, there are accounts of a first and a second battle of Magh Tuired. In the first, the Tuatha De Danann fought the Firbolg. In the second, they fought the Fomorians. Both were fought to decide which of the peoples involved would possess the land of Ireland. Since the three people represented three different states of mind, the issue on both occasions is as much philosophic as economic. — *John Moriarty*

Somedays the blue of the mountains was flush with the mountains. Somedays it was here in my house, it was in my well. Tempted one day, I took off my clothes and I let it clothe me.

I went out into the bogs. It's my ghost shirt I thought, walking in heather. The blue of the mountains is my ghost shirt, and I started dancing, ghost-dancing its mentality out of my mind,

      Ghost-dancing Genesis chapter one verses twenty-
            six and twenty-eight out of it,
        Ghost-dancing Aristotle's principle of non-
          contradiction out of it.
      Ghost-dancing its bubonic perfections out of it.
      Ghost-dancing its Medusa mindset out of it.

Wondering would I die as the fish had died I drank, coming home, from the river.

It didn't kill me.

It was later that day though that the scald crow screeched in my doorway. How piercing it was. How bald. It frightened me back into the discarded sanities of shirt and trousers and socks and boots. The socks size ten. The boots size ten. The laces long enough for a bow knot.

It didn't work. The red man walked through my dreams that night, and in the hills the next day there was no lamb. The sheep had given birth to an afterbirth only.

To ease her udder I milked her morning and evening. Looking into her eyes as she turned to go the last time I milked her, it occurred to me that dominated nature was in trouble.

Meaning also my mind, I said to myself.

Meaning also my mind ….

Meaning also my mind ….

Meaning also my mind … it was like a mantra. Meaning also my mind. I let my farm go back to the wild.

As I imagined it, spores came on every wind. Passing undigested through the gizzards and intestines of blackbirds and thrushes the seeds of hawthorn, bilberry, briar and mountain ash came. Never again, seeking to curb it, would I set fire to furze.

I didn't dream the dream. The dream dreamed me.

My pillow either side of my head was savagely sliced. As a ham might be sliced, as bread might be sliced, sliced inwards from both ends towards my head. The precision and speed of the slicing, the slices

falling sideways away, that was frightful. It was frightful to think that
it wasn't the pillow, it was my head was meant. And I saw no one, no
weapon, no hand. I saw only the slicing. Of two things all day I was
sure. I had ghost-danced myself into trouble. Depths of my psyche
inaccessible to me, hostile to my conscious ambitions for me, had taken
over. By nightfall there was something else I knew. The totemic
protection I had recently sought and found wasn't helping me. It wasn't
helping me now to be dressed in the colours of the scald crow, grey
and black.

Even if the trilobite was my totem, it wouldn't have helped. The
trilobite's jurisdictive writ didn't run deep enough.

I envied Orpheus. He with his music could assuage what was savage
or beastly in him.

I was learning the hard way. I was a paleface. The ghost-dance would
harm, maybe havoc, me. And like it or not, the paschal lamb, a lamb
slain or sliced from before the foundation of the world, that lamb was
my totem.

And the supper of the lamb...

But there was no lamb in the hills that day. The sheep gave birth
to an afterbirth only. And in her form as scald crow, Badhbh, the war
hag, ate it.

Badhbh had come back. She had darkened by doorway.

I recalled her encounter with Cuchulainn:

Cuchulainn beheld at this time a young woman of noble figure coming toward
him, wrapped in garments of many colours.

Who are you? he said.

I am King Buan's daughter, she said, and I have brought you my treasure and
my cattle. I love you because of the great tales I have heard.

You come at a bad time. We no longer flourish here, but famish. I can't attend
to a woman during a struggle like this.

But I might be a help.

It wasn't for a woman's backside I took on this ordeal.

Then I'll hinder, she said. When you are busiest in the fight I'll come against
you. I'll get under your feet in the shape of an eel and trip you in the ford.

That is easier to believe. You are no king's daughter.

But I'll catch and crack your eel's ribs with my toes and you'll carry that mark
forever unless I lift it from you with a blessing.

I'll come in the shape of a grey she-wolf, to stampede the beast into the ford
against you.

Then I'll hurl a sling-stone at you and burst the eye in your head, and you'll carry that mark forever unless I lift it from you with a blessing.

I'll come before you in the form of a hornless red heifer and lead the cattle herd to trample you in the waters, by ford and pool, and you won't know me.

Then I'll hurl a stone at you, he said, and shatter your leg, and you'll carry that mark forever unless I lift it from you with a blessing.

Then she left him.

Red-mouthed Badhbh had screeched in my doorway. I was in trouble.

Cut down to a stump of a head on a stump of a pillow, I was having bad dreams. The deepest lobes, the most clenched lobes, were opening.

On Michaelmas Eve, having quenched my lamp, I took out my baptismal candle and I lit it.

I had always felt there were depths in me my baptism hadn't reached. And even if it did reach them it wouldn't or couldn't aggrandize them into its blessedness. It couldn't or wouldn't beatify them.

It was a calm night, there were no draughts, so it wouldn't gutter.

There was, I imagined, an hour's light left in it.

Lighted at my baptism from the paschal candle, it was therefore a wounded light.

The paschal candle has five wounds in it, four of them spike wounds, one a spear wound. And they are real wounds. They bleed. It's a red religion I've been baptized into.

What can I make of it? Wounded light?

The candle burns. Burns and gutters.

Wounded wax. Wounded wick. Wounded light.

Totemically one with the wounded wax, wounded wick, wounded light. Totemically one with the slain lamb, the lamb sliced wafer-thin from the foundations of the world. What can I make of it?

A Paleface, I'm not able maybe for the religion of the Plains Indians.

A Paleface, a Celt of the Celtic Dreamtime, I'm not able maybe for my own religion.

I'm not able maybe for the dreams that dream me. And as she said she would, here she comes, the hornless red heifer leading her red-horned herd.

The Battle goes on in my guttering house.

It's the ghost-dance of the wounded candle.

It's the ghost-dance of a candle going out.

It's the ghost-dance I so suddenly am in the depths of my mind.
 I am able to ghost-dance.
 I am able to ghost-dance.
 I am able to ghost-dance.
I am ghost-dancing its modern mentality out of my mind.

I am ghost-dancing the forms of my European sensibility and the categories of my European understanding out of my mind.

The forms of my European sensibility and the categories of my European understanding are a Balor's eye in me, and I am dancing it, I am ghost-dancing it, out of sight and out of mind in me.

Ireland and the Timeless Sense of Attachment
An "Enterview" with Thomas Moore

ROBERT S. HENDERSON

THOMAS MOORE was born in Detroit. At 13 he entered the Servite religious order of the Catholic Church in preparation for a life of teaching and ministry. He left the order before being ordained.

He received his Ph.D. in religion from Syracuse University. His many publications include: *The Care of the Soul, The Soul's Religion, The Soul of Sex, Dark Eros, Rituals of the Imagination, The Planets Within, A Blue Fire, Meditations, Dwells in Daily Life, Soulmates, The Re-enchantment of Everyday Life, The Education of the Heart, The Book of Job, Original Self, Dark Nights of the Soul,* and *A Life at Work*.

He and his wife, Joan, live in New Hampshire, with their two children, Siobhan and Abraham.

Robert S. Henderson (RH): I know you have had a long and abiding interest in Ireland. What does Ireland mean to you?

Thomas Moore (TM): My great-grandparents left the town of Thurles in County Tipperary, Ireland in the late 1800's and settled on

Rev. Dr. Robert S. Henderson is a pastoral psychotherapist in Glastonbury, Connecticut. He and his wife, Janis, a psychotherapist, are co-authors of *Living with Jung: "Enterviews" with Jungian Analysts: Volume 1* (Spring Journal Books, 2006). Volumes 2 and 3 are forthcoming, in 2008 and 2009, respectively.

a 125-acre hilly farm in upstate New York. I spent most of the summers of my childhood on that farm with my Irish aunts and uncles.

When I was nineteen, I was living in a religious order that had its monastic school of philosophy in Northern Ireland so I lived in County Tyrone for two years, traveling to many parts of Ireland and getting to know the people very well. In particular, the Director of the National Gallery, Thomas McGreevy, in Dublin took me under his wing and gave me a personal education. He was an intimate of James Joyce, Samuel Beckett, W. B. Yeats, D. H. Lawrence, and many other writers and artists. His friendship was precious to me. Whenever I would go to see him at the National Gallery I would pass through a secret doorway to his private office and sit by the fire with him. Later we would go for high tea at the Shelbourne Hotel a few blocks away, passing by the home of Oscar Wilde. You might say that I got into Ireland by the back door. I have made many visits to Ireland since then, too many to count, and my family and I lived there for a year, while our two children went to an Irish school.

I have lectured throughout Ireland about spirituality and soul, and, even as I write, tomorrow I'm off to the Irish seacoast of County Clare, a favorite holiday spot for me and my family. Americans tend to think of the Irish as super-friendly and quaint. I know them as extraordinarily intelligent, tough, and visionary. They are far ahead of us in so many ways, and generally they love America and Americans. My good friend John Moriarty, who I think was Ireland's best living writer (he died just a few months ago),* has often told me of his love for America.

The Irish are sophisticated about the world. They travel widely. My wife's family members all speak Irish and French fluently and are engaged in many forms of cultural advancement. In many ways America is a more conservative country, obsessed with itself rather than, like the Irish, intellectually engaged with the rest of the world.

The Irish have great compassion for the people of the world. They are generally forward-looking and progressive. They're always asking me how Americans can be so religiously naïve and politically self-absorbed. The Irish are inexplicably gifted with words. I love to go to a Dublin launch of a new book and hear raucous discussions filling the room in Irish and English. There are so many poets, so many people

---

* *Editor's Note*: "The Third Battle of Magh Tuired," an excerpt from John Moriarty's book *Dreamtime*, with an introduction by Thomas Moore, precedes this interview.

who love poetry, that it is no wonder that this little country has produced such writers as Joyce, Beckett, and Brian Friel, to mention only a few, in a relatively short time. But people on the street are poets, too. I have found the cab drivers more literate and full of wit than most university professors I've known.

It isn't easy living in Ireland. People drink with enviable social grace, but far too much. They drive their little roads recklessly and have no patience for pedestrians. They can be bullies and super-patriots and highly opinionated moralists. Feminism in Ireland is aggressive, and the country is both highly religious and defiantly secular. The country is plagued by murders, sexual abuse, and slaughter on the roads. It doesn't know what to do with those seeking asylum within its green borders.

When we lived there for a year, my wife, a serious artist, placed an exhibit of her paintings in the immigration offices where we had to register as aliens not long before. In the middle of her beautiful installation, I brought her lunch and watched as she deftly fought with a high-placed police officer who tried to bully her off the premises. So here is my first description of Ireland. I'll try to get more subtle as our conversation continues.

(**RH**): What is it about John Moriarty that touches you so much?

(**TM**): I met John Moriarty eight years ago. We met in a hotel in Dublin and talked for a longer time than either of us had at our disposal. I think John is the greatest living Irish writer for a number of reasons. He knows his theology and mythology very well and sees them deep in his own life and in our culture without the usual distance people bring to such an enterprise. He is both pagan and Christian deep in his soul, and his imagination just flows with his knowledge. A telephone call from him is a remarkable thing. I'll never forget the call I received from him just after September 11, 2001. He talked of Moby Dick as the central myth of America and kept repeating, "God Bless America."

John both practices his theology and explores it intellectually and artistically. He writes like a bard, repeating one phrase after another. He speaks and writes musically. He is more "integrated" in this sense than Joyce and more explicit than Beckett, and yet he is very much in their tradition.

I have been trying to condense his 750-page autobiography entitled *Nostos,* or *Homecoming,* but to cut any of his words is to do an injustice to him. Still, I hope to have a condensation available soon, with an introduction and appreciation.

John takes an image, such as the "Kedron ravine" through which, according to the Gospels, Jesus passed on his way to the Mount of Olives where he prepared for his execution, and he sees a huge, powerful image there—a passage through the depths we all have to endure on our way toward the realization of our destiny.

John is a singing poet, a rare echo of the figure in Greece and in Ireland who once told the mysteries of human life. When John talks or writes he is clearly possessed by a muse. Maybe this is what I find so appealing in him. He allows himself to be possessed for his theological art. In this, he is more of an artist than many a clever painter or writer who aims at self-expression and is merely proud of his ideas. John is blissfully possessed and writes out of the full vigor of his imagination. Let me quote a passage from *Nostos*:

> Jesus went all the way down and stood Grand Canyon deep in the world karma. He didn't only stand there of course. From within his own depths he was willing to be Caotlicuized. Hindus think of Vishnu as Vishvarupa, as containing with himself all forms, all creatures, all creation. It is redemptive that Jesus is Vishvaiurupa. It is redemptive that Jesus is Vishvaguga, that he is all Grand Canyon strata, that he is all Grand Canyon ages...In Gethsemane, Jesus went aside three times to pray. We are told that the first time he went aside he fell on his face praying. Presumably, he fell on his face on each of the other occasions also. The first time he fell into the depths of the Kainozoic, the second time he feel into the depths of the Mesozoic, the third time he fell into the depths of the Paleozoic. Next day he staggered and fell three times under his cross. Burdened by the world karma, he Vishvarupa, he Vishvaguga, fell redemptive into the same three depths, and that we can now think of as the Harrowing of Hell, as the harrowing of our individual and collective hell. And D. H. Lawrence believed that without such a harrowing, no new cosmic age can emerge. (p. 605)

This tiny piece shows John's tunefulness and his outstanding ability to drawn on many mythological sources to go deep into his theological intuition. This, I believe, is the model for theology of the future. Not competitive, not selective, not dogmatic, not superficial, but profound and of world proportions.

On June 1st of this year, 2007, John Moriarty died at his home in County Kerry, Ireland. I had an opportunity to visit John in The Mater Hospital in Dublin in March, minutes after the last treatment he had that we hoped might halt his cancer. But he had a large tumor and the procedure didn't work. We had a rousing conversation, as I sat on his bed and we laughed and talked theology.

John was a maverick in a land of mavericks. He had a rich personality and a multi-leveled way of talking even in ordinary conversation. I have to say that I never had an ordinary conversation with him in the seven years I knew him. When I was back home in New Hampshire, he would call and launch into a monologue that was as full of mythology, theology, and literature as long and as rich as his books are. His writing can be daunting, as he combines Greek myth, ancient Irish literature and lore, Christian mythology (he treats the Gospels as myth in the deepest sense), and his own biography. His book *Nostos* and the more recent *Night Journey to Buddha Gaia* follow this pattern.

In some ways I see John Moriarty's writing as being right on the heels of Joyce and Beckett. Joyce compressed mythology into a literary display of brilliance that stirs the intellect to life for its sheer joy and exuberance. Beckett also weaves myth and theology into his very different, darker, and spare plays and novels. John writes as one who lives his mythology.

In my first conversation with John, in a hotel just off Grafton Street in Dublin, I was surprised at John's devotedness to Christianity, though it was certainly of the Celtic slant. Just before his death, he was creating a hedge school in Kerry. When he spoke of it, he was more passionate than ever about building a monastic community for the twenty-first century, restoring the Irish heritage of learning and a spiritual, community life. A hedge school, by the way, was the makeshift learning center that took place behind hedgerows, when the English held Ireland and forbade education to the Irish. So there was an element of subversiveness in John's idea of the new monastery.

John was a highly spiritual man, as well as a mythologist of the human condition. In *Nostos* he says, "Exposure to hell calls for far less restructuring of the psyche and self than does exposure to heaven."

In another recent book, *Invoking Ireland*, he calls on the Irish to recover the sense of the sacred that is in their past, rather than convert to modernist values that are becoming stronger in an economically vibrant Ireland. He refers to ancient tales of a battle between the Tuatha Dé Danann, the god-fearing spirits that shaped Ireland in its beginnings, and the Fomorians, who cut down the forests, built towers on the land, and re-routed rivers. John saw a new ascendancy of Fomorians, not only in Ireland, of course, but across the world.

He titled a section of *Invoking Ireland* "Orpheus in Ireland," a good description of John himself. A few lines from this section will give you a taste of John's vision and style:

> Sinking down into the music common to all things, that all things are composed of, Orpheus was symphonic, more, he was homeo-phonic, with all things as, in turn, were all things, snake and lion, with him. In this wise he was able for the world more or less than he found it. At ease with the animal in himself, animals in the world around him were at ease with him.

I can't bear the thought of a world without John's voice, so warm, passionate, and inspired, speaking for the Tuatha Dé Danann and for a similar sensibility in the Gospels; so literate and profound and musical. You can hear his voice on his web site johnmoriarty.com, but the recordings there give you only a taste of a man through whom the gods spoke with rare clarity and resonance.

(RH): When I think of Ireland, I think of many things, including struggle. I have often wondered if it is the struggle in the Irish people that has lended itself to the vast array of creativity that is apparent in their writings and music. Have you found this to be true, and if so, how do you understand the relationship between their struggle and creativity?

(TM): A non-Irish reader should understand that Ireland has its own unique personality which sets it apart from other countries. It is also far unlike popular images, especially those you get from the movies. I have lived in Ireland for three full years and visited many times. My impression is that the Irish are an extremely sophisticated, intelligent, and progressive people. They travel a great deal and are well informed about what is happening in the world. They are also unusually interested in poetry and literature and have special gifts in these areas. At the same time, they have struggled for most of their existence against those who wanted to oppress them. They have tried to fight back, but perhaps their best response has been to educate their young people. During English oppression, for example, they created the subversive hedge schools, which I mentioned earlier, for this purpose.

Today you see the results of their emphasis on education. The Irish are attractive to global corporations in need of highly educated and intelligent people for sophisticated technology and personal qualities for business transactions. The result is the "Celtic Tiger," an impressive economic renewal that strikes you as soon as you land in the country. One down side of this economic boom is a rush into a post-modern future without sufficient care for the past—learning about the past and maintaining what the Irish call the "antiquities," or archeological remains of the earliest cultural artifacts. Currently, the valley of Tara, one of the most sacred centers of Irish spirituality, is threatened with road development. Farmers, too, often regard interest in archeology as an extravagant sentimentality and destroy precious monuments.

The Irish remember their struggles in the past and honor their heroes. In Dublin, you can still see bullet holes in the General Post Office in the center of town on O'Connell Street which Irish republicans seized in the 1916 Easter Rising to proclaim the Irish Republic. Contemporary artists remember "the famine," emigration, and old styles of living. The Irish have no interest in romanticizing or going back to the old ways. They have taken to the advantages of modern life quickly and don't want to surrender them.

(RH): What does Ireland and its history, people, and stories have to teach someone interested in Jungian psychology?

(TM): Jungian psychology is interested in mythology and archaic images for conveying archetypal patterns that structure human lives everywhere. Jungians might especially appreciate Ireland because its mythology is rich and largely untapped. Even today you can find people keeping up age-old traditions such as preserving fairy forts and piously visiting holy wells. A map shows mountains, springs, and valleys all named for mythological and legendary stories going far back into history. For example, I remember one rather insignificant hill named "Cúchulainn's chair" for the great Irish legendary hero. One problem for visitors is that a thorough understanding of Irish mythology requires at least some acquaintance with the Irish language.

In many instances Irish literature keeps alive the old mythology, as in the writing of Yeats, Joyce, and John Moriarty. Personally, I find Irish theater today written and performed with a level of excellence I have seen nowhere else. One evening last year I attended a performance at the Abbey Theater in Dublin. Afterwards, a playwright and a director discussed theological aspects of drama that would strongly appeal to a Jungian audience and at a level unsurpassed in any psychological or academic meeting I have ever attended. I have also found fascinating experimental theater at "The Fringe," a city-wide display of theater performed in small venues every autumn. I have also enjoyed readings from Joyce's writings in the Martello Tower in Sandycove, the setting of the opening scenes of his *Ulysses*. I suspect that Jungians visiting Ireland and willing to go beyond the obvious resources would find their imagination expanded by Irish mythology and culture.

(**RH**): Music has been important to Ireland and if I recall correctly, you were thinking once of making music your profession. What is it about music that has made it so important to you and to the Irish people?

(**TM**): I was nineteen and had only been in Ireland a few weeks when I was invited to play the piano at a *ceili*, a lively local gathering for music and dancing held at a nearby town. I remember playing so many turns of a jig or reel that my fingers became numb.

Irish music is either fast and spirited or full of pathos. Americans sometimes think of Irish music as being the sentimental ballads, such as "Danny Boy" or "When Irish Eyes Are Smiling." But in Ireland, you hear "airs," as they say, that are rooted deep in the heart and full of solid feeling. It isn't unusual for me to be at dinner with relatives where they sing many of the old "airs" in Irish around the table. I also have a friend who sings *sean-nós*, the old style that sounds like the old Irish flutes but with the added pathos of the human voice.

My daughter Siobhán went to school for a year in Ireland when she was seven and picked up the special lilt of the singing voice typical of Ireland. She continues lessons in singing and performs now with local American groups who keep up the *ceili* tradition. She now wants to go back to Doolin, the little village by the sea that is one of the centers of Irish music and where she has listened to folk singing many times, and sing there.

Another memorable experience for me was to spend a summer producing a CD of Christmas music in the Irish style. I worked elbow to elbow with Johnny Cunningham, a wonderful Scottish fiddler who, sadly, died four years ago. Johnny knew many Irish musicians, the best of them, and gathered them in a studio on 53rd Street in New York, where we overdubbed and invented in a burst of creativity, nothing written down, everything improvised and all done in a serious but hilarious atmosphere. I'm very proud of that CD, even though the recording company eventually shelved it.

Irish musicians that I've worked with don't like to speak of "Celtic" music. I think they find the word romanticized and overused. They are also often fiercely devoted to real Irish music and not the Hollywood type sometimes shown in the movies. But that is also true of Ireland in general. It is a far different country from that caricatured in commercials and films.

Irish music, with its lighting-fast fiddles and flutes, seems to emerge from the sprite-like "little people" who populate fairy forts and remote wells, and the heart-wringing slow airs rise up out of the remote, gray rocky shores. The place itself exudes a musicality that you hear in the lilt of everyday conversations. Some Irish music, like the landscape and the ancient monuments, echoes a constant spirit of the place's timeless sense of attachment to place and people.

(**RH**): What are a couple of times when you were visiting Ireland that left a mark on your soul?

(**TM**): I could narrate a history of my relationship with Ireland with memories of pubs I've visited: A young girl dancing with smart precision in a packed pub in Doolin; watching fiddlers and pipers over two or three hours file into a pub in an old part of Dublin and playing with great spirit and skill; meeting actors, directors, writers, and poets in a bright modern pub in Dalkey; going regularly with a friend to a very out-of-the-way historic pub on the outskirts of Dublin.

I also could tell the story according to the geography of the country. Ireland is small, but each town and area seems packed with history and natural interest. Three holy wells come to mind: one, near a castle ruins outside Dingle, where we baptized our children; another on a hillside in Connemara next to a fairy fort; and a third in the Burren of County Clare, still used daily by local people. Visiting the monastic beehive stone huts on the coast of Kerry, with a view to the mysterious island of Skellig Michael; spending a summer holiday in my twenties on the haunting coast of Donegal; walking the unearthly landscape of County Clare; playing Irish football in the shadow of a castle ruin in the northern county of Tyrone.

The most significant memory of Ireland I have involves a story I've told many times. I was living in a Catholic religious community in the North. I was young and on a quest for a spiritual identity and for knowledge. I arrived in Ireland with the idea of picking up a piece of Irish art. As a quasi-monk, I had no money, but I thought I'd find a way. So, I wrote to the public relations department of the National Gallery in Dublin. There was no such department then, but I received a letter from the distinguished director of the gallery, Thomas M. McGreevy, who I mentioned at the beginning of our interview. He was a poet and spent considerable time in Paris.

McGreevy played a special fatherly role for many painters and writers. He was especially important in the life of James Joyce and his wife Nora. He had had several intense friendships, as with W. B. Yeats, Jack Yeats, T. S. Eliot, D. H. Lawrence, Wallace Stevens, and, when I met him, with Samuel Beckett. He was one of the most important people in Beckett's life.

McGreevy invited me to Dublin, and I visited him several times at the Gallery. He would sit, smoking, with a shawl over his shoulders, in front of a small fireplace in a room behind the director's office and tell me story after story of his many friendships. Later, he wrote me a letter telling me that my apprenticeship with him had given him fresh vitality and meaning, while for my part I received a precious education and became profoundly attached to Ireland.

One day McGreevy told me that he and Beckett were going to Venice for an exhibition of Irish art. "Sam," knowing about me from McGreevy, asked that I come along. I was living a strict monastic-style life at the time, and my prior wouldn't give me permission. I wasn't ready to leave the religious order yet, and so I missed the opportunity to be with Beckett and McGreevy.

One day McGreevy and I were walking along Merrion Square, where today in the park you can see an outrageous image of Oscar Wilde, who had lived across the road. We were heading for the Shelbourne Hotel and four o'clock tea. A tall, gaunt man, who was quite disheveled and ragged, approached us. I didn't know what to expect. He introduced himself and then recited McGreevy's poem "Red Hugh O'Donnell" there on the street. McGreevy was very moved, and the event affected me deeply. I learned something about what it meant to be a cultured person and beheld one of the secret beauties of Ireland: its abiding esteem for poetry and poets.

THE CELTIC TIGER

What need you, being come to sense,
But fumble in a greasy till
And add the halfpence to the pence
And prayer to shivering prayer, until
You have dried marrow from the bone;
For men were born to pray and save:
Romantic Ireland's dead and gone,
It's with O'Leary in the grave.

—W. B. Yeats, September 1913[1]

Since moving to Ireland in 2001, I have found it to be a dynamic and fascinating place to live, with a very rich culture. However it is not a country without its problems. The increases in economic prosperity and living standards achieved here during the Celtic Tiger years have also been accompanied by major increases in alcoholism, drug use, crime, violence, and housing costs, and unwelcome climate

Hugh McGovern is a clinical psychologist in the Irish health service. He has a Ph.D. in Clinical Psychology with emphasis in Depth Psychology from Pacifica Graduate Institute, and an M.A. degree in Psychology from the State University of West Georgia. He wrote his doctoral dissertation on Jung and Nietzsche. He is also a member of The Psychological Society of Ireland, the Irish Analytical Psychology Association, and the Yeats Society Sligo.

changes. On the basis of my experiences as a clinical psychologist and immigrant here over the past seven years (and having been raised in an Irish Canadian family), I would like to make the following observations.

As many readers may already know, the Celtic Tiger refers to the period of rapid economic growth and prosperity that has occurred over the past decade in Ireland and ended within the past year. During this time the Republic of Ireland has enjoyed unprecedented economic expansion, has become one of the wealthiest countries in the world (at least in material terms), and has undergone a profound and far-reaching transformation. This transformation is still influencing Irish political, economic, religious, artistic, social, and other institutions, as well as the lives of everyone living here. In recent months, however, the "Tiger" has been tamed to a large extent, apparently as a result of recent economic developments including a slowdown in the Irish housing market, a loss of international competitiveness following high wages and other costs, and the recent global credit crunch. Nonetheless, the Celtic Tiger has undoubtedly led to an improved quality of life for many people in Ireland, which has been a most welcome development after previous years of high unemployment, poverty, and emigration. There has been another remarkable development in Ireland as well—the achievement of a genuine peace in the North, where Catholic and Protestant leaders have managed to put aside their political differences and form a unity government which has been functioning quite effectively since its inception last May.

Among the negative aspects of the Celtic Tiger, however, are a major increase in arrests for illegal drug offenses, a number of recent high profile deaths of young Irish people from cocaine overdoses, increasing rates of alcohol consumption and public order offenses, and some brutal murders carried out by rival drug gangs in Dublin and Limerick, which have included the killing of some innocent bystanders who might have served as witnesses. Furthermore, the suicide rate (particularly among young men) has become an increasingly serious problem, and as a further tragedy, hundreds of people are dying on Irish roads in car accidents each year. Hence this "Tiger" has its dark aspects, and these are becoming more apparent almost daily now.

Regrettably the emphasis on financial gain and material wealth that has characterized the Celtic Tiger years appears to have been accompanied by a corresponding loss of psychological connection for many Irish people to their cultural roots, with which they have historically had very strong ties (in part due to Ireland's history of foreign invasion). This loss of connection also appears to have included a widespread abandonment by many people of both pagan and Christian mythological and spiritual traditions—which have long been a major source of inspiration for Ireland's renowned artistic, literary, musical, and poetic legacy. It would further appear that many Irish people today are functioning psychologically within the myth of modern Western capitalism. Hence they tend to see themselves largely as consumers of material goods, often produced by corporations, rather than as citizens or individuals. Indeed many seem more interested in going to shopping malls or the pub on Sundays than in attending Church, which they used to do in very large numbers. The Catholic Church, which was once a dominant institution in Irish life, has lost much of its influence in recent years, partly due to a number of scandals involving sexual abuse of children by some of its priests. As in many other Western countries, there has also been a shift of emphasis from religious and community issues toward more secular and individual concerns—along with an apparent loss of connection to the Celtic and Christian traditions. This loss is less evident in many rural areas, where religious and folk traditions are still alive and well to an extent today.

John Moriarty, an Irish philosopher and mystic who died last June, emphasizes that modern Ireland needs to maintain its links with its pagan and Christian past.* In his words, there is a great need "to bring Oisin and Patrick together."[2] He further maintains that the Tuatha De Danaan, ancient gods said to inhabit Ireland and guarantee the fertility of its land, have been supplanted in the modern Irish psyche by the Fomorians, mythical invaders or shadow selves whom the Irish are constantly in danger of becoming. According to him, the Tuatha and the Fomorians are:

> two peoples who have chosen two different ways of being in the world. The Fomorians have chosen to shape nature to suit them. Surrendering to it, the Tuatha De Danaan have chosen to let nature shape them to suit it. Our way is now wholly Fomorian. It isn't working, or rather, it has proved to be utterly disastrous.[3]

Editor's Note: For more about John Moriarty, see in this issue "The Third Battle of Magh Tuired," an excerpt from John Moriarty's book *Dreamtime*, with an introduction by Thomas Moore, as well as Robert Henderson's interview with Thomas Moore.

Moriarty also believed that Balor, the Celtic god of death and king of the Fomorians, had infiltrated or obscured the perception of modern Irish people with his evil eye. In Irish mythology one of Balor's eyes becomes infected with poison concocted by the Druids, and this eye becomes so destructive to the world that it has to be covered with a nine-layered lid. Moriarty believes that the lifting of this lid, as recorded in the *Cath Mag Tuiread* (one of Ireland's oldest books), is a key event which has driven much of Irish history. In today's Ireland:

> it is the modern economic eye. Its lid lifted from it in the seventeenth century, it is destroying our planet.[4]

His book *Invoking Ireland* also addresses the question of how, working from within their own cultural traditions, the Irish people might reconstitute themselves to offset the negative effects of recent years. While this is clearly a topic of major importance, it is beyond the scope of this essay.

It is perhaps largely due to this modern economic "eye" and the myth of capitalism which is so prevalent in Ireland today that the wealth generated in the Celtic Tiger years has not been equally distributed. A recent newspaper article reported that many areas of the country are struggling economically.[5] In the Midlands and Southeast, for example, people are earning significantly less than in other regions. In the same article, one economist warned that some areas are in danger of being left behind permanently, unless they receive more government investment soon. A recent EU survey reported in the same newspaper found that approximately 7% of the population are living in poverty, and a further 17% are at risk of poverty.[6] At the same time, there are reportedly 33,000 millionaires in Ireland today. Another survey by a major Irish bank found that one percent of the population owns 20% of Ireland's wealth, and five percent have 40% of its wealth.[7] Hence it would seem that the financial gains of the Celtic Tiger years have benefited those fortunate to receive them, while bypassing many others who have not been so fortunate.

Like all tigers then, the Celtic Tiger appears to be a predator, and thus it has been strong, cruel, instinctive, and savage at times. The tiger, a predatory animal, can function psychologically as a symbol of the power and danger of uncontrolled desires. Ireland's economic "Tiger" has been a creator of much wealth for property developers, banks, businesses, and some individuals here, yet it has also been a destroyer for some others who have not been blessed to participate in the spoils of its financial hunt. There are no tigers in Irish mythology to the best of my knowledge, perhaps since tigers are not native to Ireland. Hence the Irish people may well be largely collectively unaware of its symbolic significance. In retrospect it would probably have been wiser for Ireland to have adopted a much kinder animal as an emblem of the Republic's economic boom—one more willing to share the spoils of its wealth with those being left behind today, one less environmentally destructive to the country's beautiful landscape, and one more suited to former Irish prime minister Eamonn de Valera's vision for Ireland as "the home of a people who valued material wealth only as a basis for right living."[8]

In closing I would like to emphasize that while this essay focuses mainly on the Celtic Tiger's shadow aspects, I have been fortunate to enjoy a very good life and meet many fine people since emigrating to Ireland seven years ago. I am also happy to report that the "Tiger" has had relatively little impact on my personal circumstances (apart from the high cost of housing, which is now decreasing after rising by more than 300 percent). I can also recommend Ireland as a fascinating and beautiful place to come for a short or long stay.

NOTES

1. W. B. Yeats, *The Poems*, ed. Daniel Albright (London: J. M. Dent and Sons, 1991), p. 159.

2. John Moriarty, *Invoking Ireland* (Dublin: Lilliput Press, 2005), p. 217.

3. *Ibid.*, p. 7.

4. *Ibid.*, p. 229.

5. Isabel Hayes, "Rural Ireland 'in Danger of Being Left Behind,'" in *The Sunday Tribune,* December 9, 2007.

6. Michael Clifford, "Role Model for a Generation Living on Borrowed Time," in *The Sunday Tribune*, December 9, 2007.

7. *Ibid.*

8. Eamonn de Valera, St. Patrick's Day Address, March 17, 1943.

I would like to acknowledge the scholarly assistance of Ms. Stella Mew with this paper for her proofreading and helpful suggestions. — Hugh McGovern

A Visual Translation of Brian Merriman's "The Midnight Court" by Pauline Bewick

In this issue, *Spring* is honored to feature the artwork of Pauline Bewick, one of Ireland's leading contemporary artists. Her painting, *The Owl*, appears on our front cover. Here we present her recently completed and exhibited visual translation of the well-known poem, "The Midnight Court," by the 18th-century Irish poet Brian Merriman. Bewick's *Visual Translation of "The Midnight Court"* consists of a series of eleven paintings based on selected couplets taken from an English translation of the poem's original Irish text by Prof. Kieran R. Byrne, Director of the Waterford Institute of Technology, Waterford, Ireland. The introductory material was complied from various sources, but is based largely on notes written by Prof. Byrne for the catalogue for the *Visual Translation*'s exhibition premiere in 2007, and we thank Prof. Byrne for granting permission to reproduce his material here. Also included in the introductory material is an edited version of an interview with Bewick by Nina Finn-Kelcey on the process she went through in creating the visual translation. Pauline Bewick very kindly provided a brief explanatory note for each of the eleven paintings and these appear under their respective paintings.

Pauline Bewick: A Brief Biography

Pauline Bewick was born in Northumberland, England, and grew up on a small farm in County Kerry, Ireland. She began painting at the age of two, and has enjoyed a prolific career as an artist spanning seven decades. Her vivid paintings are featured in galleries and collections worldwide. She has also written and illustrated several books, including *The South Seas and a Box of Paints* (Art Books Int., 1996), an account of her two years spent with the Cook Island Maori people on the Pacific islands. Pauline's biography, *Pauline Bewick, Painting a Life* (Wolfhound Press, 1985; new edition 2001) was written by Dr. James White, art historian and former Director of the National Gallery of Ireland.

In 2006, to mark her 70th birthday, Pauline donated a collection of 500 works, known as the Seven Ages, Kerry Collection and Waterford Collection, to the Irish State, received on behalf on the State by President Mary McAleese. These works are now on permanent display to the public at the Waterford Institute of Technology and at Library Place, Killorglin, County Kerry. A third part of this collection, known as the travelling collection, will be shown worldwide starting at the Galway Arts Festival, July 2008.

For more information about Pauline Bewick and her work, please see her website, www.paulinebewick.com.

ABOUT "THE MIDNIGHT COURT" BY BRIAN MERRIMAN AND THE VISUAL TRANSLATION BY PAULINE BEWICK

Brian Merriman (c. 1747-1805) was a poet and scholar who composed one of the great poems of Ireland, "The Midnight Court," which met with instant acclaim. It is arranged in four parts and addresses a number of major themes that had been part of a wider critical discourse across Europe since medieval times and even earlier: the regeneration of the population, priestly celibacy, free love, and male and female sexual angst. Around these themes the poem weaves its colorful tapestry.

A comic epic of just over 1000 lines, the poem is a burlesque variant of the Irish *aisling* tradition of dream-vision poetry. In it, the poet-narrator falls asleep beside the waters of Loch Grainey, a lake in County Clare, and dreams of a fairy court ruled by a figure named Aoibheal. The court has set itself the task of trying Irish men for their crime of not populating the countryside sufficiently. Two figures, a *sheebhean*— a beautiful woman who is a traditional figure in Irish Gaelic poetry—and a cuckolded old man, give evidence from their personal experiences. In the process, the man argues that bastards (such, perhaps, as Merriman himself) can grow to be healthy members of society without married parents, so illegitimacy should not be considered a blemish on one's character. In turn, the woman argues that because there are so few eligible men in Ireland, members of the clergy should be allowed to marry. The court's judgement is to allow women to seize upon any man of age 21 or older and beat him until he submits to being married; older unmarried men are to be treated even more harshly. The poet is summarily seized by the court's bailiff and awakens just in time to escape punishment.

In early 2007, Pauline Bewick was commissioned to create a visual translation of Prof. Kieran Byrne's English version of the Merriman's original Irish text. The *Visual Translation of "The Midnight Court"* was successfully completed and exhibited for the first time at The Shelbourne Hotel in Dublin on November 14, 2007. The exhibition will go on tour in Europe commencing in Paris in May 2008, and then throughout the U.S. in 2009.

Pauline Bewick's visual translation, in eleven pieces, carries the mastery and genius of "The Midnight Court" readily. Clearly, as an artist she is a disciple of Merriman, and dogma holds no fear for her. She conveys the plot and themes of the poem with all of the persuasiveness and conviction for which her art is known. Merriman, with his unique idiom, his mixture of mischief and mirth, naturally attracted her. Like Merriman, she has the ability to startle and surprise, reflecting shade and emphasis to encompass the poetic emotional experience of fear, sensuality, fantasy, and impish gaiety of life. The geography of the poem; its inhabitants; their customs, charms, and dwellings; the plants and animals—all are to be found in Bewick's translation, meshed with the double ironies characteristic of the Merriman genre. The wit of her line, the colour and abandon of her interpretation match Merriman's play on words in that uniquely harlequin way.

Her visual translation of "The Midnight Court" shows Pauline Bewick in her most glorious form, eloquent and expansive.

NINA FINN-KELCEY'S INTEVIEW WITH PAULINE BEWICK

NFK: Once you had accepted the commission, how did you begin the creative process?

PB: Shiny, witty, and so alive, Kieran Byrne put the idea of a visual translation to me, saying, "You of all people could do it"—and I knew he was right. From the very start he trusted me. Years ago I had read "The Midnight Court," and the title had led me to thinking of courting at midnight! And in a way, maybe that's the idea?

Inspiration can be so elusive, so I immediately started sketching ideas into my small sketchbook. I let the excited air drop into my pen and scribbled the first sketches. Yes, they had what I wanted. I then traced the best parts and took them to an architect's office in Dublin and had them enlarged onto tracing paper, size 41 x 50 inches. Back in Kerry, I transferred them down with graphite paper onto the thick Arches paper. Taking a brush, I painted them in sepia acrylic, bleeding the sepia lines to create shadows, spraying water with a garden spray-bottle to bleed the sepia where I wanted it to go, tilting the paper to direct it and blotting where I wanted it to stop. All this in a sort of frenzy.

I canceled lots of events and found it hard to sleep the nights through with the buzz of what was happening.

In order to keep continuity throughout the paintings, it was important that I should do them more or less all at the same time. Keeping in mind that the sun rises at the start of the poem and then we go through the night of the court scene until the sun rises the next day, when the poem ends. Pat (my husband) and I read the poem through together about a dozen times, in order to gather who was saying what. Merriman is not straightforward. His rollicking style is deceptive. The undercurrents are numerous and Professor Byrne's help with his translation was essential.

I did not want to dress the people in the costumes of 1780, so I kept them timeless by leaving them nude with the exception of the courtroom scene.

NFK: Did you draw inspiration from the area in which the poem was set?

PB: Yes. Although the time of year when I started was not July, the month in which the poem is set, I needed to see the location. Pat and I drove to Clare and stayed in Dromoland Castle, driving on the next day to Lough Grainy. There I got the atmosphere from the lake, reeds, swans and the "curve of the river." I did sketches and two pastel paintings near the Merriman stone plaque at Caher. The Slieve Aughty mountains were not easy to find! We eventually drove up the hill and there they were.

We went to the small village of Feakle and had lunch at Pepper's Pub. We met the owner, Gary Pepper, an inspiring man who took us to meet Brian McMahon at the post office, who in turn showed us an old photograph of the now-demolished church that stood in the graveyard and was perhaps the setting of the courtroom. We entered the graveyard and met four people who had just buried their mother the day before. We talked together amongst the gravestones and beside the secret grave of Biddy Early, the well-known witch. One of the family members, Tim Moloney, quoted couplet after couplet in Irish of "The Midnight Court" and answered questions on places, etc.

When we got home with the information on this trip, I started the process in earnest. When eight paintings were done, I realized we needed ten. When ten were done, Kieran Byrne felt that the collection needed one more, a raunchy one. I decided to set this scene not in a shebeen, or pub, but out on the bog road, and painted a scene of rollicking and frolicking, perhaps the time of conception of the illegitimate baby born to the old stager's bride on their wedding night.

In order to keep a balance between painting and illustration, I did not throw in everything mentioned in Merriman's text—for example, in the baby scene he mentioned sweet cakes, the old hags smoking pipes, a churn of milk, the midwife, and the priest. I represented all that with a turf fire in the background. My fear all the way through these paintings was that the excitement would go away and that another idea would take over. However, all was well on one of the most exciting series of paintings that I have ever done.

When it came time to consider the framing of the paintings, I decided to ask the master carpenter Luc Racine, who has made frames for me before. This time I asked him for 8-inch wide oak. The artist and sculptor, Alan Hall, had carved lettering for the Kerry Seven Ages Collection [a retrospective exhibition of Pauline's work—premiered Nov. 2006], which made him a good choice for this project. Each frame was engraved with the couplets taken from Merriman's poem and was then gilded in gold.

NFK: What did you think of the poem itself?

PB: At first reading I resented that the women should flog the men, but on second thoughts, we do have our own way of punishing men, a more subliminal way, which a man might interpret as "flogging," men being more straightforward in their thinking, women more subtle. So I had to keep in mind that this poem was written by a man. I find it hard to know what Merriman really thought about women. The scene where the *sheebhean* wails and cries, pleading that she is beautiful and has tried many pishogues [incantations, magic spells] but still can't attract a man, she reminds me a little of Molly Bloom in the last chapter of *Ulysses*. Like Molly Bloom, she indulges in her comeliness, but I can find no hint as to what Merriman thinks of such a woman.

He does talk of women gossiping and he talks of women throwing themselves around in ditches for any man who wants to have them. And then he talks of the Queen of Craglee, with her intelligence and dignity, who takes the side of the women. There is no sympathy from the queen towards the man who wants to "play around." Yet Merriman puts into the mouth of the old stager the words about illegitimate children being stronger, having been conceived in passion without the chains of marriage. Personally, I agree with the old stager that we should not be restrained within a marriage, and he may well have a point that children born from high passion may be stronger. "A pulp of a pup you ever did see, healthy and hardy in every degree."

Merriman talks of the vitality being bled out of Ireland at the time, a thing continued until recently, but now the bright ones stay in Ireland—hence the Celtic Tiger. In Merriman's day, the wild geese created wines, and the further I have traveled the more I have come across the Irish diaspora. For instance, on the Tahitian island of Moorea, we met a fisherman, black and fat, and his name was O'Connor. In Samoa, Holly, Poppy [Bewick's daughters], and I were painting, when along the road walked two men in Lavalava, one a pure Polynesian and the other an Irishman talking at the top of his voice in a Cork accent. He was a schoolteacher over there.

The human need for possessions, such as a farm or land, cows to milk, barley growing and all that it represents, such as fine shoes, jewelery, fine silks, and cambric aprons—perhaps this is why the female wants to tie the knot and keep a strong man on the farm to mind her children and the land. The man escaping from these restraints in his wildest wishes would like to sow his seed wherever he roams. Merriman's criticism of the church and priesthood stems from the restraint that families put on a son by forcing him to enter the priesthood. Unlike other interpreters of Merriman, especially Merriman scholars, I think Merriman's appreciation of nature is huge. Women can have unrestrained and hilarious enjoyment in total sexual freedom to the same extent as men, but it trips them up should they conceive. It is the woman who has to look after the baby.

A Visual Translation of "The Midnight Court"[†]

1

For often I walked by the curve of the river
On the plains where the morning dew crystals the heather

Painting 1: The scenery around Lough Grainy, where poet Brian Merriman strolled each day and where he was inspired to write "The Midnight Court." The painting also represents the place in the poem where the poet sat down, fell asleep, and began to dream about the Midnight Court.

[†]All images in this series are courtesy of Pauline Bewick.

2

Making for me on the rim of the bay
A fiery brute in wild array

Painting 2: The poet feels the ground trembling beneath him as he
sleeps, and a witch rides in on the dark storm clouds demanding that
he wake up and attend the Midnight Court.

3

Sparking spectacular alight with flame
Shimmering beauty with its doors ornate

Painting 3: Aoibhail, Queen of Munster, presiding over the Midnight Court.

4

Fixed in her stare with fire in her eye
With temper and pain she began to cry

Painting 4: A young woman pleads on behalf of the women of Ireland
that the men folk of Ireland are impotent and lazy.

5

On the farmyard o'er I scattered seed
And a cabbage beneath my head I'd leave

Painting 5: The young lady dreams of a man to love her and take her as his wife.

6

At once leaping up nimbly and fiercely
A cagey old stager bitter and wistful

Painting 6: An old man speaks for the men of Ireland, asserting that
the women are too demanding and raunchy and would be more suited
to working in the fields.

7

Flat on the road and nothing to shield her
With a mob from the bog and Doorus around her

Painting 7: A scene showing that the women of Ireland should be entitled to grab any man, from the clergy or otherwise, over the age of 21 and force him to marry and procreate.

8

A pulp of a pup that you ever did see
Healthy and hardy in every degree

Painting 8: This painting represents a healthy young child born out of
wedlock.

9

Set free together, as nature ordained
From loving and coupling, lets not be restrained

Painting 9: This painting represents the idea that nature ordained that all living things should be free and people, including the clergy, should be allowed to make love at will.

10

Put into action and fill us with glee
The punishment set by the Queen of Craglee

Painting 10: Queen Aoibhail of Munster decides in favor of the women
of Ireland and sentences the offenders to a death by hanging.

11

Then I awoke from my dream and rubbed clear my eye
And in one bounden leap, of my fear I was free

Painting 11: Merriman awakes from his dream and leaps up into the air realizing that he is free.

WATER—A REFLECTION ON ASPECTS OF LIVING IN MODERN IRELAND

EILEEN BOYLE

INTRODUCTION

As this article lived and worked itself in me during the early months, I was striving for an Apollonian mode of communication which would deliver a clear portrait of modern-day Ireland. However, when I allowed it, what really wanted to emerge was the following, rather mercurial, piece which dips into a variety of puddles and comes up with some questions for the soul.

THE RECENT PAST—SOME PERSONAL EXPERIENCES

A few days after being asked to write for this issue of *Spring*, I woke up in Santa Maria, California, having just attended the Nature & Human Nature Conference in Santa Barbara. In that stage between sleep and waking, I had the impression that I was surrounded by water—waterfalls, streams, rivers, sea, and waves, all flowing vigorously

Eileen Boyle works as a counselor in a city center college of further education in Dublin. She is currently co-ordinating the college's green ecology program. She is a graduate of Trinity College, Dublin, University College, Dublin and holds a Master's Degree in Transpersonal Arts and Practice from University of Chichester. Eileen lives in Dublin with her husband John and son Rory.

and with a great variety of sounds. In this dreamy state I asked what this meant, and the answer I got back was "Write about Ireland through water." I was surprised to then wake up in a dry bed, but the sensation stays with me. The overriding sense I had, and still have, is of how we attempt to imprison water. That substance which is in essence so free. I have been caring for this live idea/quest ever since and have tried to work with it and to remain open and true to any ideas coming through it and through my subsequent research into water.

The first images that came to me were of my childhood, 1950s and early 60s in rural Ireland. The well on our farm, the lovely daffodils surrounding the well and framing the worn pathway to that watery hole. The stone steps down to the platform where one put in the bucket and drew up the water. I also remembered the adults' warnings of danger and the rule that we children should not go there alone. I accompanied the grown-ups and was fascinated by the drop down to the dark, small pool below. Our lives depended so strongly on that precious source, I sometimes feared that it might dry up.

In fact, until shortly before my birth, two families living even more remotely off the beaten track than we did came each day to get their drinking water from our well. The great effort of carrying large buckets of water such long distances seemed astonishing to me as a child, as I knew their abandoned homesteads were surrounded by water—drains, bogs, and bog holes.

In addition to the well, we had a few barrels collecting rain water from the roof, and of course there were small streams from which the animals drank at shallow places we called "*mairnings*." During very hot summer days we were allowed to go there and splash, paddle, and catch pinkeens (small fish) in jam jars.

During my early years we had no flush toilet and no water on tap. We were bathed in an iron tub in front of the open fire. This family event took place in our main room, the kitchen our only heated room. First, adequate water had to be heated over the fire, then came the bathing and the drying of us children. When I was 10 in 1960, there were five adults and eight children living in our house.

Slowly "modernization" came, and the well was covered over but not redundant, as a pump and pipes now took spring water into our house. The main reason for the change was safety. Persisting in my imagination, that well, covered up and almost forgotten, remains the heart or living center of my childhood peasant holding.

Modern Living

The Construction Tsunami

Am I unique in observing that Ireland today seems like one big building site? Our luscious countryside is disappearing overnight and motorways, housing estates, and satellite towns are spreading over the landscape. My concern is for the irreversible damage that this unboundaried "human progress" is causing to our beautiful island and to all its non-human inhabitants as well as to the earth. As for water, Kim Wilkie states that homes are the biggest users of water in the UK and reminds us that "Germans manage to live perfectly comfortable lives while consuming a third less water than the English."[1] I use the English example as figures are not available in the Irish context because our water is not metered. However, our Environmental Protection Agency estimates that each household in Ireland consumes approximately 300 liters of water each day, while 1.1 billion people, 17% of the global population, do not have access to clean water.[2] To me, one thing is certain, the more houses, the more water used, especially since in our forging ahead without reflection, we equip these houses with several "en suites" and bathrooms. This allows us to capture and store more and more water in tanks and pipes awaiting our turning of the tap…water at our service—being just another free resource to be plundered, consumed, and imprisoned.

However, while we may not recognize it, water has not remained an entirely passive actor in our story. In Spring 2007 the nation was shocked to learn of serious and large scale water contamination caused by an outbreak of cryptosporidium in the Galway region affecting one of our fastest growing urban areas. Cryptosporidium, is a "microscopic parasitic bug," encased in a cocoon-like hard structure called an oocyst. When ingested by humans, it attaches itself to the intestines and begins to replicate. The body reacts, causing diarrhea and severe cramps which can last for at least a week in healthy people. Young children and those with weakened immune systems are at much greater risk, and the infection can become extremely serious, causing death in the most extreme cases. The source of the two damaging strains of the bug, parvum and hominis, are animal and human waste.[3] Raw sewage and lack of adequate treatment facilities, combined with other sources of pollution like overdevelopment and deteriorating farming practices, have all contributed to the water contamination problem in this region.[4]

Questions emerging from the above reflection are:

> 1. Have the recent building boom and the "Celtic Tiger" really brought fulfillment and tranquility to our lives?
>
> 2. Are we Irish just a nation corrupt with greed after our "success" story, or is there any way that we can slow down this "tsunami" and restore our consumption of resources to a manageable, unexploitative, and earth-respecting stream?
>
> 3. Can we Irish become more reflective and begin to see water as co-performer in the theater of life?

It has become apparent that many people all over the country are experiencing a shortage of clean drinking water. For example, as recently as October 12, 2007 the morning news headlines reported that one in five homes was supplied with water from polluted sources.[5] SWAN (Ireland's Sustainable Water Network) lists among the main sources of pollution in Ireland: discharges from municipal sewage treatment works, effluent from septic tanks, and runoff from "hard surfaces," e.g., roads, streets, car parks.[6]

We seem so addicted to this patriarchal mode of trying to control nature for our own purposes—which has turned our fertile island into a building site—that we are blind to the consequences of our actions, even when these are obvious, i.e., affecting our health and being well documented in published reports. New motorways are springing up and yet the traffic is rarely flowing. Mothers drive their children to school and childcare protected from the rain drops in large jeeps more suited to off road conditions than to the narrow streets of the sprawling new suburbs.

New-Wave Holidays

Most Irish families now aim for three holidays (vacations) per year. This has widespread environmental consequences and leaves a huge carbon footprint, including: multiple flights, westernized resorts, and the maintenance and continual updating of amenities in massive, corporate amusement water parks. This, even in countries where the local population does not have access to adequate clean drinking water. In addition, back home, our dermatology clinics are filled with those suffering the results of sun damage to their fair skin which is more suited to the now-despised cloudy and overcast Irish weather.

Ireland is generally regarded as a green, verdant, lush, watery place surrounded by powerful sea waves, with many lakes, rivers, streams, and sacred wells. On the one hand we pride ourselves in living in such a lush and green place, and yet we consider rain, the very source of the verdure, to be a national hassle, complaining as it pours down from the sky. The rain prevents us being like "the continentals" with whose ways we are so familiar, having spent so many holidays outside our own country. We too want to eat outdoors and sip wine on balmy evenings, or be like the Americans who populate our television screens barbecuing and sitting around the pool. We seem addicted to "sunshine," or to the notion of uninterrupted sun, and it seems to me that the national mood actually swings with changes in our weather, being much more sensitive to that than to significant happenings reported in the news.

Not so long ago, Irish people were lucky to have one holiday per year, and in those days they went to one of our beauty spots to be outdoors and "to take the waters," swimming and bathing in the sea, lakes, and rivers; going to a natural spa; or visiting a holy well on appointed days. It is no longer popular or cool to holiday in Ireland— except for the short breaks. Then, only hotels with state-of-the-art amenities are acceptable—people must have facilities and entertainment whatever the cost and must be protected from the "hardship" of the outdoors as soon a drop of rain falls. In contrast to this, Ginette Paris in her book *Pagan Meditations*[7] recognizes the therapeutic effects and benefits of being close to or working in and with water, especially the pure, running waters of rivers and lakes associated with Artemis.

My questions here are:

1. How we can relearn to honor and enjoy fresh, pure water?

2. Can we embrace rain as a balancing feminine characteristic in our communal unconscious?

3. Could we allow the the maternal waters to teach us to be more who we are—with our wet, green, soft, poetic, and story-loving

natures—and stop us trying to be more like other cultures and climates?

Gaston Bachelard in his book *Water and Dreams* invites us to "see how profoundly *maternal* the waters are. Water swells seeds and causes springs to gush forth. Water is a substance that we see everywhere springing up and increasing. The spring is an irresistible birth, a *continuous* birth. The unconscious that loves such great images is forever marked by them."[8]

Therapy as a Life-Buoy

The new affluence and increased disposable income allow people to go to therapy, as well as to beauty clinics and day spas.

"Dissolved hearts," as described by Carl Jung,[9] and fluid egos are not welcome in this economic climate where hard sell and concrete blocks are the foundation stones of the boom. People find that they need the seclusion of the therapy room to reflect on their lives, which are growing increasingly complex and stressful and which are not necessarily being experienced as more fulfilling.

Living in modern Ireland with its new "wealth" and caught in improved economics, people struggle to stay afloat, which seems to be the price our opportunities demand. Many clients in therapy do not feel content with their lives. In fact, they are very confused because now they have access to money which they previously had believed would offer "the solution" to their problems. Materialism and consumerism are rampant in Ireland and resemble "dis-eases" and obsessions.

It could be suggested that the increased interest and involvement in therapy in Ireland reflects our geographic location. Hence, we are caught between the English approach and American models. The European influence in this area is very recent. There is often a sense of people remaining in consumerist mode, "buying solutions" or "paying for time and space," as they become able to afford this now-acceptable luxury. Here, in therapy, people can pour out their stories and woes and have their watery eyes and dissolved states accepted.

A second aspect of this is the explosion of therapy and psychology training courses, which are in great and increasing demand by both young graduates and people changing careers in mid-life. Those in this latter group often put themselves under huge financial pressures to participate in these very expensive training programs. The training programs are often quite narrowly focused and concentrate on skill development and theory rather than encouraging reflection on stories and images. Courses are often advertized as being inclusive of "spirituality," which seems to have wide appeal especially for people who are changing careers and who want to get away from the rat race. Yet, when qualified, the majority of new therapists find themselves caught in the very commercial environment of the Celtic Tiger from which they apparently were trying to escape.

Here I am left asking:

> 1. Does the new reliance on therapy in Ireland, which often neglects soul and encourages normative and ego-centered development, actually contribute to the perpetuation of the construction tsunami and the new-wave holidays described in the preceding sections?

> 2. What is the Irish psyche—personal and communal—seeking in this "crazy" pursuit of a career which has become idealized?

Thomas Moore calls for us "to recover (our) innocence."[10] He wisely calls on individuals and societies to find ways to wash away our impurities, guilt, and pollution and become more tranquil, which he says is an essential ingredient for human life. As I understand it, Moore and others of us who invite soul into psychotherapy are attempting to work with clients in a way which challenges some of the capitalist and post-modern values of consumerism and domination.

CONCLUSION

It is important for me to clarify that my focus is not for a move backwards to the "good old times." I shared my own early experiences because they contrast so strongly with today's situation. In the Artemisian sense, I had the opportunity to taste fresh spring water as well as experience the advantages and disadvantages of living with wild water in more primitive conditions. My plea is that we find ways to allow water to regain its purity, life, and zest.

I leave you with a joyful, spontaneous experience I was fortunate enough to observe: Anya is a 22-month-old girl who lived in a Russian hospital for her first year of life, having been abandoned by her mother at birth. She spent 9 months on a cot in an orphanage where her basic needs were met, but where she received no affection or stimulation. She was recently adopted by an Irish couple and arrived to our rainy Irish summer. Anya had never been outdoors, much less in nature, so for her the experience of a garden, plants, and trees is paradise. I observe her finding the open door and dashing out on her new-found legs (walking is also new for her). Watching for destruction to the lush plants with the eye of a gardener, I am surprised to find that Anya, with unusual gentleness for a young child, dips her fingers into the little pools of water on each leaf and flower and then washes her face over and over with the fresh rain water.

NOTES

1. Resurgence No. 241, p. 18.

2. "Treating our Water," Environmental Protection Agency, *Science and Technology in Action*, 2nd edition, 2006.

3. Liam Reid, "Coming to a tap near you, "*Irish Times*, Weekend, 14.04.2007.

4. *Ibid.*

5. *Newstalk News Headlines*, 12th October, 2007.

6. SWAN Sustainable Water Network, Irish Water Quality, Threats to Ireland's Waters, Main Pollution Threats, p. 1 (of 3) http://www.swanireland.ie/page.php.

7. Ginette Paris, *Pagan Meditations* (Woodstock, CT: Spring Publications, 1995), pp. 110-113.

8. Gaston Bachelard, *Water and Dreams: An Essay on the Imagination of Matter*, trans. Edith R. Farrell (Dallas: The Pegasus Foundation, The Dallas Institute of Humanities and Culture, 1982), p. 14.

9. C. G. Jung, quoted in Thomas Moore, *Dark Nights of the Soul: A Guide to Finding Your Way Through Life's Ordeals* (London: Piatkus, 2004), p. 61.

10. *Ibid.*, pp. 61-65.

A Sense of Place[1]

KLAUS OTTMANN

> Where are we at all? and whenabouts in the name of space?
>
> —James Joyce, *Finnegans Wake*

In his *Preschool for Aesthetics* (1804), the German Romantic writer Jean Paul (Johann Paul Friedrich Richter) defined true poetic spirit as follows:

> Every novel must accommodate a universal spirit, which, without hampering the free flow of movement, like God vis-à-vis free mankind, will stealthily draw the historical whole together and toward a *single* goal, just as according to Boyle every true structure must respond in a particular tone; a merely historical novel is only a story.[2]

Ireland (and Irish art) seems deeply rooted in a collective historical experience and has long been defined by *difference,* geographically as well

Klaus Ottmann is Editor-in-Chief of Spring Publications and an adjunct curator of the Parrish Art Museum in Southampton, New York. He is the author of *Thought Through My Eyes: Writings on Art, 1977-2006* (Putnam, CT.: Spring Publications, 2006), *The Genius Decision: The Extraordinary and the Postmodern Condition* (Putnam, CT: Spring Publications, 2004), and *The Essential Mark Rothko* (New York: Harry N. Abrams, 2003). In 2006, Ottmann translated Gershom Scholem's book *Alchemy and Kabbalah* into English (Putnam, CT: Spring Publications, 2006). His most recent curatorial projects include *Open E V+ A 2007: A Sense of Place,* an international survey of contemporary art held citywide in Limerick, Ireland (March - May 2007) and *Still Points of the Turning World,* SITE Santa Fe's Sixth International Biennial (July 2006 - January 2007). His website is: www.klausottmann.net.

culturally: the colonialists versus the colonists; the North versus the Republic; Irish (Gaelic) versus English; Catholicism vs. Protestantism. What unifies these differences with respect to a universal Irish spirit is a strong sense of *Place*.

For art to be experienced or observed, it has to be emplaced—put in place, however temporarily. Irish art and culture is entrenched in one place, one history, and one culture, yet it now has to embrace diversity within its borders. It must inevitably focus on the dialectic of emplacement and displacement. The poet Seamus Heaney speaks of the "two often contradictory demands" under which Irish poets labor: "To be faithful to the collective historical experience and to be true to the recognitions of the emerging self." According to Heaney, the two ways in which a place is known—one is the lived and illiterate; the other, learned and literate—co-exist "in a conscious and unconscious tension" in the artistic sensibility.

Today Ireland is no longer an insular, postcolonial community with an ingrained distrust of strangers, but a modern global society that is as much defined by its history as it is by its new affinity with the European Union and openness to the world at large.

In the works of Irish painters Tony Gunning and Eithna Joyce a certain urgency is evident that is prompted by the newfound affluence of the Irish economy and its impact on the land. While Gunning's colorful paintings depict mostly scenes of urbanization and alienation, Joyce's delicate canvases celebrate the poetry of nature and the simple life. Neither artist, however, contents himself or herself with a Romantic mythologizing of peasant life in the tradition of "colonial" Irish landscape painting. Rather, both artists show us a *damaged* idyll. Joyce uses, in her own words, "a mixture of realistic and abstract images to create a tension within the picture, mirroring the current tensions we find between man and nature." In *Ardour* (Fig. 1, p. 225), she divides a rural landscape into two canvases framed side by side. On the left, a telegraph pole rise above the ink-drawn horizon line, which continues over both canvases. The lines from the telegraph pole, drawn in ink, extend from the "spoiled" half of the landscape into the bucolic, unspoiled half. Both sides are further distinguished by different overlaid abstract patterns, stripes in the left frame and dots in the right. The use of abstract patterns, the drawn ink lines, and the fissure created by the two adjacent canvases lend a conceptual, ironic dimension to her painting.

Similarly, Tony Gunning's realist observations on the impact of economic prosperity on the Irish landscape reflect a growing concern with the urbanization and materialization of modern life. His style is reminiscent of the "primitive" yet decidedly modernist canvases of the French Post-Impressionist painter Henri Rousseau (1844-1910), who, like Gunning, was entirely self-taught and thus had created for himself a unique style of his own. Like Rousseau's, the vivid colors in Gunning's paintings are flat and uniformly distributed, a technique that keeps them isolated from each other. And incidentally, just as Rousseau took up painting seriously only in his late 40s, after retiring from his job at the toll collector's office in Paris (thus his sobriquet *Le Douanier*, "the customs officer"), Gunning entered artistic life relatively late, after retiring in 2000 from the Office of the Revenue Commissioners, the Irish government agency responsible for customs and taxation. But unlike Rousseau's imaginative and, later, surreal landscapes, Gunning's arresting land- and urbanscapes have a social-realist undertone that belies their "naïve" painting style. One of his most remarkable paintings, *Lay-Bye* (2006) (Fig. 2, p. 225) depicts a discarded couch and a broken chair that is missing one leg and is standing on a small rug in front of the couch. Abandoned on an idyllic Irish lay-bye near a green and rocky coastline, it is a reminder of the fragility of a society that was once deeply emplaced and isolated and is now a formidable force in a global economics. Here the worn, displaced couch becomes a symbol for the increasing displacement of the Irish *soul*.

In his most recent series of paintings, Gunning conjures up this displacement of the Irish soul felicitously with depictions of generic shopping malls and urban situations (Figs. 3, 4, and 5, pp. 226-228).

WHO'S AFRAID OF LOCAL ART?

When I was asked to curate the 2007 edition of Ireland's only annual international exhibition of contemporary art in Limerick, the theme of Place was an obvious choice. Long poverty-stricken, politically oppressed, and largely isolated from the world, Ireland has now grown into the most affluent country in the European Union. Its three airports have become major hubs for European and international airlines, and the rise of the euro and fall of the American dollar have transformed Ireland into a global society, whose members are as much at home in the shops in New York's Time Warner Center as they are on Grafton Street in Dublin.

Yet Ireland still manifests a strong sense of place; for instance, most of its food is locally produced and proudly identified as such on restaurant menus throughout Ireland: lamb from Roscommon; fresh oysters from the shore of County Clare; salmon from the River Shannon; potatoes from Tipperary.

Like other international annuals or biennials of contemporary art, such as the Venice Biennale, the Whitney Biennial in New York, or the SITE Santa Fe Biennial, Limerick's *e v+ a* (*exhibition of visual+ art*), now in its 32nd year, is curated each year by a different, single, invited curator of international standing and presents the work of Irish and international contemporary artists. Unlike them, however, *e v+ a* (the plus sign is meant to call attention to the fact that art engages and integrates all the senses, not mainly or only the visual sense), alternates between two distinct formats: the traditional "invited" format, in which each curator selects the artists at his or her discretion based on his or her curatorial vision and personal preferences, and, every alternate year, the "open" format, in which the artists are chosen by the curator from proposals submitted by artists. The "open" format is usually shunned in the curatorial world, since it is thought to exclude what has been sanctioned by the art market and museum worlds as "good art" and opens the exhibition to the much-dreaded "local artist."

"Local art" is a dirty word in the art world, especially in the U.S., where the art market is concentrated in New York and Los Angeles, and up-and-coming artists are more or less forced to move to one of these two cities to be recognized as serious artists. In many European countries, such as Germany or Italy, this negative notion of local artists does not exist, since there are no distinct art centers, or, as in the case of Paris, such centers no longer have the same centralized importance as they did in the past.

With increasing globalization, the art market, which at the beginning of the 20th century was centered in only two cities, Paris and New York, now encompasses Beijing and Shanghai, London, Dubai, Berlin, Mexico City, and Mumbai. While globalization can benefit local situations (in this case, artists working in geographical regions previously ignored by curators, critics, and galleries), it can also dilute local traditions. And since these newly discovered regions often do not yet have a critical structure in place (art magazines, contemporary art museums), these global markets are mostly driven by art fairs, auction houses, and galleries from New York or London. A case in point is the proliferation of contemporary Chinese art that is currently flooding the art world—a phenomenon that has almost no support from critics or curators but has become one of the major exports of the Chinese economy (almost on par with the sale of arms to the Sudanese regime that is committing genocide in Darfur). Moreover, most of the works by these new Chinese artists, which are too numerous to keep track of, even for longtime art professionals like myself, seem to have little to do with Chinese traditions; instead, many just seem to be copying 1960s American pop art. Last year, at SITE Santa Fe, an alternative exhibition space that hosts the only international biennial of contemporary art in the United States, I was joined (as the curator of the 2006 SITE Santa Fe biennial) by other previous curators on a panel whose subject was "global art." I decided to play devil's advocate and stated that "globalism is the death of art" and that art needs "place." One of my esteemed colleagues, the critic and curator Dave Hickey, immediately assumed that I was talking about "local artists" and dismissed my pronouncement with the assertion that "good" art does not need a place. He confused the notion of "global" with "universal." Of course, "good" art has to have a universal appeal that transcends its specific, localized origins. However, art cannot have universal appeal without being local. In fact, the more local it is, that is, the more it is "in its place," the more "global" art becomes (in a transcendent sense). Or, in the language of archetypal psychology, art needs to be ensouled. Much of the Chinese contemporary art that is entering the global art market appears to be "emptied of soul"—it is mere commodity, and having no roots in local traditions, it is out of place without ever being in place.

The new buzzword in economics is "glocalism," which is defined by CERFE, an Italian economics and social science research organization, as "a social process that is especially evident in cities where it consists of the concurrent drives toward globalization and localization ... [as a] diffused social action ... that can be interpreted as a kind of ideal and cultural movement oriented towards linking the benefits of globalization to local situations, and toward governing globalization also through local situations."[3] No one speaks yet of "glocal art";

perhaps it sounds too uncomfortably close to "local art" to be embraced by art professionals.

For me, the experience of working, in Limerick, with an exhibition model that is open to local art on an international scale has been highly rewarding. I ended up selecting 32 artists, of which 18 were of Irish descent, The remaining 14 artists were from the United Kingdom, continental Europe, Canada, and the United States (all chosen from submitted proposals). For three months, from March 29 through June 24, 2007, the place (the city of Limerick and the traditional and non-traditional venues chosen by me and the artists) became the limit and the condition of all the art and related events, where the artistic sensibilities of those at home and those displaced co-existed in a conscious and unconscious tension.

NOTES

[1] This essay has been adapted from the catalogue essay for the 2007 ev+ a exhibition of visual art in Limerick, Ireland.

[2] Timothy J. Casey, ed., *Jean Paul: A Reader,* trans. Erika Casey (Baltimore and London: The Johns Hopkins University Press, 1992), p. 262.

[3] <http://www.scu.edu/sts/nexus/summer2003/KochSavirArticle .cfm> (accessed May 13, 2008).

Fig. 1: Eithna Joyce, *Ardour* (2006); oil and ink on canvas. (Image courtesy of the artist.)

Fig. 2: Tony Gunning, *Lay-Bye* (2006); acrylic on linen. (Image courtesy of the artist.)

Fig. 3: Tony Gunning, *Shopping Mall* (2007). (Image courtesy of the artist.)

Fig. 4: Tony Gunning, *Clone Street* (2007). (Image courtesy of the artist.)

Fig. 5: Tony Gunning. *Coffee Shop* (2007). (Image courtesy of the artist.)

Irish Americans:
Longing for Home

THE IRISH AMERICAN PSYCHE

MAUREEN MURDOCK

I had lost not only a place but the past that goes with it and, with it, the clues from which to construct a present self.

—Eavan Boland[1]

For years I dreamed the same dream from time to time: a whitewashed thatched roof cottage on a gentle incline, a woman in a light blue dress sitting in a rocking chair in front of the hearth, a black iron kettle hanging over the fire. She stares out the window at a body of water. She is waiting for someone to return from the sea.

During my first visit to Ireland in 1975 I kept looking for the thatched cottage of my dreams. Certainly there were many of them on the Aran Isles, in Kerry, and Dingle, but I couldn't find my cottage; it felt like it was located northwest, somewhere near Clifden. In 1990 I returned to Ireland with my daughter, Heather, and her friend, Holly, and told them about my dream. We stayed in Clifden for several days, but I saw no cottage that felt familiar. The day we left Clifden, on our return drive east to Newgrange, Holly pestered me to find my cottage.

Maureen Murdock is a depth psychotherapist in private practice in Santa Barbara and was Core Faculty in the MA Counseling Psychology Program at Pacifica Graduate Institute. She is the author of the best-selling book, *The Heroine's Journey*, as well as the newly revised *Fathers' Daughters: Breaking the Ties that Bind*; *Unreliable Truth: On Memoir and Memory*; *Spinning Inward: Using Guided Imagery with Children*; and *The Heroine's Journey Workbook*. Her books have been translated into over a dozen languages.

"We can't leave until we find it," she insisted. Surprised and pleased that she was willing to entertain my dream, I took a back road out of Clifden. About five miles after we had left the main road, I took an abrupt right up a small narrow lane where there was an old, abandoned, graying white-washed cottage sitting in the middle of the bog. It didn't have a thatched roof; the tin roof was rusting, but it called to me.

Paying more attention to the cottage than the road, I drove the car into a ditch and got stuck. As we walked around the car looking for a way to get it out from the mud, a man in a battered station wagon came down the lane and told us the nearest tow truck was at the gas station back in Clifden. I thanked him and stared at the ruin of the cottage that stood on a slight incline up the lane from the ditch.

"Let's go check it out," said Holly. "Maybe it's your cottage."

"No," I said, "it can't be. There's no water around here."

"Let's go anyway," the two girls said excitedly, "before we have to hike back into town to get a tow."

We trudged across the mucky bog and crossed the threshold into the house. It was clear the cottage had not been occupied in decades. It was in complete disrepair; there was no door, no glass in the windows, and the walls were cracked. The room we entered had a hearth on the right, the remains of an iron pot hanging from a hook. I walked to the hearth and the hairs at the back of my neck began to tingle.

Holly called from the left side of the room.

"Come here and look at what I found." I went into a small adjoining room, which perhaps had been a bedroom, to find Holly looking out the open space where a window had once been. There in the distance was water. Not the ocean but a body of water we had not seen from the road. Chills ran down my spine.

Jung, Freud, and other psychoanalytic theorists believed that individuals are destined to act out apocalyptic themes of ancient history that are handed down from generation to generation through not only the institutions of society, but in the collective unconscious. The Irish are great dreamers and value fantasy, the unseen realms, and the wisdom of the land. It was no "accident" that I drove into the ditch that day; the cottage of my dreams wanted to be found.

At the core of the Irish American story is the longing for home and the unresolved questions related to loss, place, and identity. During the Great Hunger (1845-49), the population of Ireland was reduced from 8 million to 5 million people and everywhere there was death, starvation, and forced emigration. It was the worst catastrophe in western Europe in the 19th century. 1.2 million people lay dead in less than five years and 2 million more emigrated to the U.S. during the next decade. The scale of flight from Ireland in coffin ships to America was unprecedented in the history of international migration. Other groups who left eastern Europe thought of themselves as immigrants, but the Irish considered themselves "exiles," cut off by English landlords from their land and communities.[2] The departure, the leaving, and the sorrow of never going back "home" and the piece of the self that was lost in that forced departure is still embedded in the Irish American psyche.

Does the woman in my dream wait for those who have left to return or does the dreamer long to return to the homeland?

For those who have been forced to leave home, the archetypal theme of longing for home, Paradise Lost, never really dissipates. It is inherited by the next generation and the next.

> From what we know of trauma now, it's clear that both those who stayed in Ireland and those who left, never to return to their homeland, were marked emotionally and psychologically, and that inheritance has to have marked their children and grandchildren.[3]

Although I am 4 generations removed from my relatives who fled Ireland in 1846, I still long for that elusive metaphor, home.

EMIGRATION

> Exile, like memory, may be a place of hope and delusion. But there are rules of light there and principles of darkness, something like a tunnel, in fact. The further you go in, the less you see, the more you know your location by a brute absence of destination.

> —Eavan Boland[4]

Emigration became the organizing principle of Irish American society in the mid to late 19th century and into the 20th century up through the 1950's. Instead of assimilating like other immigrant groups, the Irish in America stayed Irish.[5] Because they did not *choose* to emigrate, they continued to keep alive their memories of life "that used to be" in their imagination. Through song and poetry they constructed a new immigrant self that was divided between the idyllic past and the difficult attempt to survive in a hostile present.

They left an agrarian culture and plunged into the fastest industrializing society in the world. Facing punishing cultural economic pressures and discrimination by the primarily Protestant Anglo-Saxon society in which they found themselves, they regrouped primarily around the Catholic Church, tied together in local parishes which helped them view the urban world as small and parish-sized.[6] The Church became the center of Irish Catholic life with its network of schools, hospitals, and social service agencies. The Church offered community, respectability, and hope, but unfortunately, it was also sexually repressive, intellectually narrow, moralistic, and rigid. The priests demanded absolute obedience.

More than any other ethnic group, Irish Americans struggled with their sense of sin and guilt, even for sins they had not committed. They internalized the "myth of badness," convinced that no matter how hard they tried to be good, they would fail. Because the priests convinced them of their "original sin," they held human nature to be evil and believed they should suffer for their sins.[7] Sex was considered dangerous and any form of physical tenderness, affection, or intimacy was to be avoided. I noticed every time my third generation Irish American father tried to hug my third generation Irish American mother in the kitchen in front of me and my sister, she pushed him away. This repression of emotions and physical contact is deeply encoded in the Irish American psyche.

In their quest for respectability in a primarily WASP society, the Irish adopted the American values of upward mobility, progress, and the pressure to achieve. Irish immigrant women usually were young and unmarried and had no recourse but to find immediate work in factories and as maids. Household labor was difficult, poorly paid, and sometimes so degrading that most "native born Americans" simply refused to do it, but it gave them food and a place to live. In 1850, three-quarters of Irish immigrant women were employed as domestic servants in Protestant homes, and as late as 1900, 60% of Irish-born women were maids serving food in Boston's Back Bay or polishing windows in Fifth Avenue homes.[8]

Along with the wages they earned in wealthy homes, they learned what sort of books, music, and manners belonged in a respectable family's home—and, more significantly, just how much an education could buy. Culture and respectability became important to them. Irish American men worked as laborers building railroads, bridges, and canals, or gravitated toward urban occupations such as priests, firemen, policemen, and in civil service. The women were more responsible and thrifty than their male counterparts; they saved their money and sent it home to help their parents or for passage for their siblings to emigrate. "They also contributed a significant amount of their income to the Church building a network of charitable and educational institutions."[9]

There was a great emphasis on education by Irish American immigrants for daughters as well as for sons. The second generation of Irish American females did not work as maids but became secretaries, teachers, and nurses who entered the white-collar world a generation before their brothers did. Girls often stayed in school longer than their brothers. They got involved in the labor movement, focused on political action by organizing strikes of working men and teachers. They created and staffed the largest network of women's colleges in the nation. Many of our current women politicians, including Speaker of the House of Representatives, Nancy Pelosi, are graduates of these women's Catholic colleges and universities.

CULTURAL AMNESIA

But all of this striving for upward mobility came at a price. The Irish American immigrants suffered from collective amnesia. They did their best to forget the poverty, the oppression, and the famine of the past.[10]

It became a matter of survival for the Irish American to wipe out the memory of The Great Hunger. There were no famine stories told or memorials built for over one hundred years. Garrett O'Connor, an Irish-born Los Angeles psychiatrist, attributes this collective amnesia to what he calls "malignant shame."[11] O'Connor theorizes that where there is prolonged political or governmental abuse of an entire population, in this case, the Irish by British colonization, malignant shame (low self-esteem, misperceptions of cultural inferiority, and suppression of feelings) is internalized by the culture and passed on to subsequent generations. In Ireland, the Irish were deprived by the British of their language, education, and skills that were transportable to the New World. For years, Irish Americans suffered bigotry and were consistently met with "No Irish need apply" signs and representations of themselves as simian invaders. O'Connor attributes the Irish American Catholic self-misperception of personal and cultural inferiority to this cultural oppression and has identified self-denigration, contempt for authority, and lack of self-confidence as enduring traits.

"The Irish are great talkers and storytellers, but they prefer silence to speech when it comes to the realm of emotions."[12] While Irish Americans are celebrated for being willing to display their emotions through fictional characters in poetry, drama, literature, and song, they are not skilled at revealing their true feelings in intimate relationships. The Irish are known for their wit, not for their ability to communicate what's really going on, although compulsive talking to oneself or others is readily accepted because of its unique capacity to suffocate emotion.

And the religious and cultural ethic of Irish Catholicism stresses silent suffering. If you're Irish, you're supposed to grin and bear it. You're told that suffering will make you a better person. You're encouraged to get over it. Stoicism is admired. Confession is available, but you are never persuaded to seek help to deal with the deeper issues of cultural dissonance that displacement from one's homeland engenders.[13]

Because they were exiled, the Irish often deal with feelings of hurt, loss, disappointment, or conflict by shunning. "Simply cutting off a family member by not speaking or writing is a common pattern in Irish and Irish American families."[14] I experienced this myself when I came home pregnant as a graduating senior from college. I knew my parents would be upset by my unwed pregnancy; it confirmed all of my mother's fears about sin and sexuality and flew in the face of her quest for respectability. But when my future husband and I announced to my parents that we were going to get married in the church, my mother declared, "Not in *this* parish, you're not."

She not only refused to allow us to marry in our home parish in New Jersey but she arranged to have us married out of state, in New York City, where her friends would not witness her disgrace. It is not unusual for the Irish American to make every effort to avoid drawing attention to themselves if deviant behavior is involved (witness the cover-up of the sexual abuse of hundreds of thousands of children at the hands of Irish Catholic priests). At the time, I did not have the term "shunning" to understand my mother's Irish American cultural way of dealing with shame, but she refused to have anything to do with my husband or me until after our son was born seven months later. Psychological exile runs deep in the Irish American psyche.

EMOTIONAL INHERITANCE

Dickinson College professor, Sharon O'Brien, has written a brilliant memoir about emotional inheritance and the depression many Irish Americans experience, entitled *The Family Silver*. She examines the lives of her Irish American relatives, particularly her father, sister, and herself, and suggests that the American values of upward mobility, progress, and individuality carried a double-edged sword, creating both desire and depression in generations of her family members. She suggests that not only do we bear a genetic inheritance from our forebears, but we inherit our ancestors' emotional histories, particularly their unexpressed stories of exile, grief, and yearning.

Many who achieved success in this country did so at the risk of losing their families. "Who do you think you are?" is a common Irish American phrase reserved for those who better themselves through education and professional achievement. The underlying message, of course, is "Stay where you belong." In spite of the fact that Irish American Catholics have been among the best educated and wealthiest people in the country since the mid-1960s, there seems to be an almost atavistic need to downplay their success. "Don't go getting a swelled head" or "Don't get above yourself" are other Irish-American phrases batted around in the house of my childhood in the 1950s and 1960s.

Yes, we were encouraged to succeed but only to a certain degree. This created what author Pete Hamill has called the "green ceiling," where one could be successful but success had limits. "To have an ambition beyond the cops and the firemen was to be guilty of the sin of pride. It meant you didn't accept your lot in life."[15]

Frank Mc Court, the author of *Angela's Ashes*, also speaks to this self-deferential tone of the Irish American:

> The Irish were ashamed of themselves when they got here. They dropped the O's and the Mc's from their names. They were so busy hanging on, and then prospering and coming right up against the establishment, they lost sight of themselves.[16]

Dr. O'Connor suggests that conditions such as alcoholism, depression, child abuse, suicide, ruined marriages, and unfulfilled dreams come from the malignant shame inherited from our forebears. Devious conniving, shunning, interpersonal treachery, and secret delight at the misfortunes of others are contemporary reminders of family power struggles for property and tribal land grabs inherited from ancestors who barely survived colonial rule. Family political struggles became a breeding ground for generations of Irish American politicians.

Because the Irish had no facility in expressing their inner feelings, Irish Americans drank to relieve their pain and sorrow. They drank because they were homesick, lonely, disoriented, disconnected from home. They drank to show their group identity, their Irish nationalism, what made them different from other ethnic groups.[17] According to social scientist Richard Stivers, who studied Irish American drinking patterns in *A Hair of the Dog: Irish Drinking and American Stereotype*, drinking became part of the long tradition of Irish male bonding in the late nineteenth century as a symbol of masculine identity in a defeated society.

In the years after the Famine, men began drinking heavily and routinely in what Stivers calls "bachelor groups." These groups fulfilled important economic and religious functions in Irish society, keeping young men and women apart. The Church, obsessed with preventing sexual "sin," condoned this custom because it kept the men in the pub, off-limits to females. The focus was on sports, storytelling, humor, poetry, song, and the pleasures of tearing one another apart.[18]

Unfortunately, the more they drank, the more they became problem drinkers. Irish Americans were at a high risk for developing alcoholism because heavy drinking ran in their families and was tolerated, if not expected and encouraged, in Irish social settings, particularly weddings and wakes. While Irish American men were more likely to drink than their female counterparts, Irish American women drank more than any other ethnic group.[19] Alcohol masked their depression and anxiety or allowed it to explode.

There is a paradoxical nature to the Irish American psyche. The saying goes: "The Great Gaels of Ireland are the men that God made mad, for all their wars are merry, and all their songs are sad."[20] Humor, charm, and loyalty coexist with pessimism, envy, and blame. A strong urge to resist authority and engage in conflict is tempered by a stronger need to appease it. A constant need for approval is frustrated by a chronic fear of judgment.

> Irish Americans have become justly known for their wit, courage, good humor and generosity, their imagination, sense of higher purpose and legendary capacity to triumph over adversity, which has enabled them to attain unprecedented distinction in business, politics, law, medicine, religion, the theater, and the arts.[21]

Finally, I would like to return to the image of my dream. If the dreamer is indeed longing for home, it is a theme constantly repeated by the women in my mother-line. My grandmother's mother McGuire emigrated from Ireland to New York with her husband, son, and three little girls, but she and her husband died within months of their arrival. At age three, my grandmother waited on the curb for her mother to return home, refusing to budge despite her sisters' entreaties. An orphan, she survived on the streets of Manhattan mothered by her older sister, Maime.

When she married my grandfather Dunn, they moved into a house in Rego Park, Queens, where she put up lace curtains in the windows, a picture of the Sacred Heart in her living room, and a statue of Mary in her front yard. She felt like a queen in her domain. Years later, as my grandfather's income increased and his position as a men's club manager grew in prestige, he tried to entice her to move from Rego Park to Long Island, another enclave of Irish Americans. "I'm not leaving my home," she declared and true to her word, she didn't budge until a couple of years before her death at 101.

My mother and father moved from Queens to the suburbs of Bergen County, New Jersey, as many third generation Irish Americans did, but my mother always regretted being displaced from her home parish. She went along with my father's desire to build bigger and bigger houses as his New York advertising agency flourished, but in her last year, suffering from Alzheimer's disease, she repeatedly walked to their front door and cried, "I want to go *home*. Take me *home*."

At the time I suspected that, as a devout Catholic, she was referring to heaven, but now I think her longing for home was an ancestral longing—for a place where she belonged, a place she could reclaim her self. A place where she would no longer feel displaced. It has been over 150 years since my ancestors were thrown out of their homes in Ireland, but many of us still carry that sense of displacement in our psyches.[22] I, too, long for home, a place to put down roots, a place to belong, a piece of the earth to call my own. The woman in the bog house still lives within me.

NOTES

1. Eavan Boland, *Object Lessons* (New York: W. W. Norton & Company, 1995), p. 56.

2. Sharon O'Brien, *The Family Silver: A Memoir of Depression and Inheritance* (Chicago: The University of Chicago Press, 2004), p. 80.

3. *Ibid.*

4. Boland, *Object Lessons*, p. 46.

5. Peter Quinn, *Looking for Jimmy: Search for Irish America* (Woodstock & New York: Overlook Press, 2007).

6. *Ibid.*

7. Monica McGoldrick, "Irish Families," in *Ethnicity and Family Therapy,* Monica McGoldrick, John K. Pearce, and Joseph Giordano, eds. (New York: The Guilford Press, 1982), p. 313.

8. Maureen Dezell, *Irish America: Coming into Clover* (New York: Anchor Books, 2002), p. 91.

9. Quinn, *Looking for Jimmy*, p. 278.

10. *Ibid.*, p. 48.

11. Garrett O'Connor, M.D., "Recognizing and Healing Malignant Shame: A Statement about the Urgent Need for Psychological and Spiritual Recover from the Effects of Colonialization in Ireland," unpublished manuscript, June 6, 1995.

12. O'Brien, *Family Silver*, p. 34.

13. *Ibid.*, p. 159.

14. *Ibid.*, p. 34.

15. Quoted in Dezell, *Irish America*, p. 81.

16. Dezell, *Irish America*, p. 85.

17. *Ibid.*, p. 123.

18. *Ibid.*, p. 122.

19. *Ibid.*, p. 133.

20. McGoldrick, "Irish Families," p. 310.

21. O'Connor, "Recognizing and Healing Malignant Shame."

22. With many thanks to Hillary Flynn, Director of Crossroads, An Irish American Festival, for her thoughts about displacement and the Irish American psyche. From a conversation on 9/14/07.

A Leprechaun Tree Grows in Orange County: Glimmers of an Irish-American Childhood

MAURA CONLON-McIVOR

I grew up on the border of Los Angeles and Orange Counties, not far from those celebrated, cultural spindles of the collective imagination: Disneyland and Hollywood. But by the age of six, the center of my imaginal world revolved around another dazzling site: the apricot tree in our backyard. Every spring I'd gaze up to its branches, waiting for the arrival of its miniscule, green buds. Once spotting them, I'd run into the house yelping, "The leprechauns are coming!" Children are attuned to nature's fecundity. For me, something magical simmered here, a mystical transubstantiation upon the leafing branches. The budding "leprechauns" were tricksters and evoked my childhood pleasure of deep connection to the place I knew my ancestors came from: a fabled island called Ireland.

But in 1960s Los Angeles, nobody spoke of his or her ancestral homeland. Other topics beckoned: The Vietnam War, Bobby Kennedy, the L. A. Dodgers. California unrolled its new interstate freeway system,

Maura Conlon-McIvor, Ph.D., is a journalist, radio announcer, and author of *She's All Eyes: Memoirs of an Irish-American Daughter*, a *Los Angeles Times* bestseller published by TimeWarner, which has been adapted for stage and had its world premier debut in 2007. Maura travels often to Ireland where she holds dual citizenship.

like a carpet, through the arid, sage fields sixty yards from our quiet, suburban street. In those fields my older brother Michael and his friends used to play, unfettered, huddled around their "serpent tree" where soon the roaring 605 and 405 freeways would commingle.

Dreamy California held layers of complexities palpable when my Irish-born grandmother, Mary, visited from New York. Armed with a strong Clare accent, she'd snort under her pale, perspiring skin: "What a damned desert, this place!" One visit she slipped me an illustrated picture book of Ireland (which I still have). She'd never speak of the country from which she sailed as a teenage girl no matter how many questions I asked. I'd have to settle for clues: the fruited leprechauns, her book of shillelaghs and four leaf clovers, and my name, Maura, which—as I would explain for most of my childhood—is Irish for Mary. Like the green leprechauns clinging to their spring branch, my Irishness and I were fused.

That faraway and even dreamier place called Ireland was iconified within the lush surroundings of our local church, St. Hedwigs, in Los Alamitos; the parish lawns were textured like moist linen and lined by endless rows of roses. The pastor, Father Quinn (who, as rumor had it, spent a fortune on those roses), spoke with aristocratic gravitas, his Irish accent much less musical than those of the nuns who ran our elementary school. Sr. Mary Ita, my fourth grade teacher, told me about her niece, named Mary O'Connor, who lived in County Limavady in Northern Ireland. She arranged for Mary and me to become pen pals. I prized Mary's letters filled with lovely Irish penmanship that arrived in the blue, tissue-thin envelope marked *aero mail*. We were Irish girls living on opposite sides of the world!

Such are the early images of an Irish-American childhood—and the rumblings of a quest for identity—as launched in suburban southern California. On a conscious level, these images—the people, their accents—all passed under the radar like the sunrays quietly infiltrating our skins. The letters between County Limavady and Orange County ceased after a few years. I pictured Mary in a wet country perhaps not far from all the bombs in Belfast. How do I tell her about our trips to Disneyland or our backyard pool parties complete with piñata? I knew we lived in a privileged world. Privileged in that we were absolved from any explicit past: Prosperous California tipped to the future. We could settle upon nothing eternal for nothing could settle for long. We had the San Andreas Fault to prove it. No fairy forts, no stone monuments would last here. California was *post*-time.

At some point, I stopped visiting the leprechaun tree. My parents removed it to build a cement patio for my younger siblings' tricycles. But some impression from the tree was not lost—its green fuse tapped a curiosity within. Years later, when wandering the hills of Ireland, the memory of the apricot tree returned. I wondered why I felt such an affinity for those "leprechauns" when "Ireland" had been long synonymous for me with absence of story? Even as I write this essay, I have a dream of my long-deceased mother saying, "You proclaimed 'the leprechauns are coming' with such joy!" Was it just myself attuned to our unconscious Irishness? Was the tree a song of nature beckoning me to discover some deeper story?

Such search for identity—identity being code for how we belong to the world—contravenes the logical matriculations of our conscious days. Virginia Woolf writes of time's "orderly and military progress" and how that

> there is always deep below it, even when we arrive punctually at
> the appointed time with our…polite formalities, a rushing stream
> of broken dreams, nursery rhymes, street cries, half-finished
> sentences and sights.[1]

My leprechaun tree, my "half-finished sight," kept me running between garden and house to announce new life—to proclaim that I was part of something larger than myself, something mysterious and beautiful.

These first images of childhood reveal themselves as soulful harbingers within thin spaces. These *thin spaces*—a Celtic notion denoting the place of connection between the local, material world and the liminal, eternal one—represent an epistemological pivot in how we belong to cosmos, in how the ground of the world opens up to us— beginning early in our lives. Bachelard calls psyche's early landscape the *first time* wherein the revelation of images hold for us—in eternal fashion—intense, psychological values. Such images move us from the "precisions of the social memory" as we return to a "cosmic memory," which is the very memory of "our belonging to the world."[2] We experience the *first time* in *thin spaces*.

Thus as I came of age, I sensed at a deeper level that my Irish inheritance had everything to do with how I belonged to the world.

In eighth grade I was voted "Most Quiet Girl" in my Catholic school. Why should I be anything other than quiet—there were no stories about Ireland, nor about our people, passed down on either side of my family. The silence felt angry, like some ghostly ocean, its waves crashing, scattering pieces of memory I couldn't yet decode. From my corner bedroom window, I'd watch my father—a stoic special agent for the FBI—put out the trash for the evening then cast a shepherd's glance up the street as if searching for his tardy flock. He seemed always to be waiting for something. Another time he admitted to having a conversation with a bumblebee as he strung the Christmas lights on our house. Under the glare of the California sun, we were all living in the borderlands, in the thin spaces, waiting. We just didn't know it.

* * * *

My mother's brother, Fr. Ed Hogan, a Catholic priest, invited me to travel with him to Ireland in the winter of my eighteenth year. He would lead a retreat in County Tipperary, where some of our relations lived, and research further our Hogan family genealogy. On the chilly night when we boarded the plane, I thought of my father and my mother who'd never been before to our ancestral homeland. I thought of old Father Quinn and his roses and the Irish nuns and their long-gone wimples. I thought of my thick-brogued grandmother. I thought of my long-lost pen pal Mary O'Connor. All of them I'd packed into my Samsonite suitcase as if we were sailing to the moon. When I landed in Ireland, my relations in firm embrace looked at me and said, "Welcome Home." I understood "welcome"—but *"home?!"*

Home was 6000 miles away—30 miles from Hollywood, 10 miles from Disneyland, 5 yards from the old leprechaun tree—or was it? Soon I met girls in the local village who had the same name—Maura. Close by I found St. Conlan's Road. The men, wearing tweed jackets and pea caps, had the same ruddy complexions as my father. I saw women with the exotic, almond shape of my mother's eyes. Still, I knew so little about these people, this place that all but one of my ancestors fled because of famine or poverty. I wanted to understand how I belonged—so I did what you do in places of silence, the thin spaces. I returned to the image: I became as the leprechaun tree, feeling my rootedness in this soil fed by the lost stories of my ancestors.

In my Ireland journal of 1978, I write:

> Raindrops/Ireland becomes the flying spades of a waterfall/
> seeking a midnight puddle to rest their wetness upon/buds
> secretly opening up to receive/a message from this womb-sent rain.

Then on another page:

> Whatever you love in life, always be at peace with yourself to
> pursue that freedom and feel that love. Always notice the sky
> and her belongings, always notice the water and her reflections.
> This way you see almost everything. Finally see into your self
> and find the mirror of your people.

During that first trip to Ireland, I witnessed the roll of donkey carts and the spread of quaint thatched roofs. One of my elderly relatives still had the thatch, living in an old cottage where a peat-burning stove provided the only heat—never quite enough in the dead of an Irish winter. We visited another elderly cousin, Queenie, who pulled out an accordion and led us in songs sweet and sad. Then we drove out to rural West Clare to visit my grandmother's youngest sister, Johanna. She still lived on the family homestead where my grandmother was born and raised. Driving on small, winding roads, we asked many farmers if they knew the McMahons of Mullagh. They all did, pointing toward the next helpful landmark along the way. How different this was: people stitched to a place.

The winds howled and the rain fell in perpetual drizzle and the cows hunched toward the grass. My great aunt, her red hair peppered with gray, opened the door as if she were gazing out to the nearby Atlantic watching ships disappear into the horizon. Her eyes then refocused, for this time, one ship was coming home. Aunt Johanna looked at me with the same waiting eyes of my father, as if she'd been waiting a hundred years, as if she had known me forever. In some way, I felt she had and that I had known her. I could barely understand her English, the vowels and consonants bound to their own Irish swirls. But in hearing the warmth of her voice, the mechanization of words seemed ancillary. She stared at the photos I brought of my family in California. I told her about my mother, Mary, my father, Joseph (her nephew), and about my four siblings. I knew I was finding a lost piece of home or, perhaps, a spindle.

* * * *

Stateside the old conversation remained: "Don't you dare ask me about that damned country, do you hear?" My Irish grandmother, who'd worked in New York as a seamstress, said this holding a needle, but it may as well have been a knife. I tried to understand the source of her pathos—that she had to leave Ireland or that she had no desire to ever return. Perhaps it was the Irish koan, the double bind—damned if you stay and damned if you go—that led to this waiting station disconnected from story or place. The base metals underlying this waiting station remained untouched, the soul's *prima materia* not worked. The resulting trauma of not knowing how one belonged to the world manifested as the great waiting—but waiting for what? If place has vanished and with it story, what happens to one's narrative? It waits underground, in darkness, praying for re-emergence, for a spot of soil to nudge so life can begin anew.

The great waiting masks the costs of exile when spirit is closely aligned with land. The historian Kerby Miller writes of the Catholic, Gaelic-speaking Irish and their reluctance to emigrate. According to Solnit, Miller cites "their profound attachment to place; a language in which the word for going abroad translates as *exile*, a literature in which all departures from one's country of origin were regarded as tragic exile."[3] The silence of the exiled Irish transmogrifies into a shield—protecting psyche from viewing her un-protected ruins; the silence harbors the displaced as well as psyche's longing for place. It is the double bind: eternally waiting while not knowing what it is you're waiting for.

Stateside alights another irony: many of the sons of these Irish Catholic emigrants found work—as did my father—as special agents for the FBI. J. Edgar Hoover, himself a Protestant, is said to have recruited at the Catholic colleges knowing these men grew up on the meat and potatoes of hierarchal rigidity and obedience. These silent Irish Catholic sons of silent Irish Catholic mothers entered an occupation where secrecy was the *sine qua non*. Solnit writes, "Trauma is inherited as silence, a silence it may take generations to hear."[4] It would be the next generation—my generation—who would say enough to the secrecy...enough to the wait. We would dig past the genealogical charts and venture down into psyche's bogs. We would sniff for the stories long buried, the poems etched on skeletons. We would re-claim the thin spaces. Life would begin anew.

* * * *

I returned to Ireland after I had graduated from college and visited my great Aunt Johanna. I decided to surprise her with no advance warning of my arrival. When she answered the door, her shock collapsed into flitting anger: "Why the hell didn't you tell me you were coming— I would have killed a goose." We settled in for tea and sandwiches. My great aunt examined my photos, inquiring how close to Hollywood we lived. Then before I could pull out my notebook and ask carefully planned questions about our ancestors, my aunt blurted with visceral concern: "And *who* do you think it was that killed J.R.?" *Dallas,* the wildly popular American television show, had come to Mullagh, Ireland, and she wanted to know everything. I realized then I'd have to find the buried stories elsewhere.

I started reading the Irish authors—Joyce, Yeats, Wilde, Synge— looking for clues into that forlorn condition of waiting, or as Seamus Deane writes, that "specifically Irish form of nostalgia." This nostalgia, he continues, "was consistently directed towards a past so deeply buried that it was not recoverable except as sentiment."[5] Yes, that sentiment— the faraway look in my grandmother's eyes and in my father's eyes: that sentiment courting me in my own quest for identity. I wondered what might lighten the epistemological darkness. What if I broke with tradition and started to tell stories, investigate other peoples' stories— perhaps I might have my own stories to tell. This was my way of beginning to nudge that soil.

I moved to New York City to work as a writer and editor and also to be closer to my extended Irish-American relations. I hoped to uncover more clues about our family but found instead more of that impenetrable sentiment. And so: a new threshold. I enrolled in graduate school in North Carolina and for my thesis wrote on two modern Irish poets. In 1987, I traveled to Ireland and met with Medbh McGuckian in Belfast and Eavan Boland in Dublin. I hoped to uncover the lost voices of the women—the stories of the relational, the human heart, of the hearth. I dove into the old silence so long associated with the Irish that it bordered on the neurotically romantic, finding there the primal timbres of the quest to belong.

McGuckian's poetry was complex and richly coded. Her use of metaphor and contraction and expansion of movement illuminated the culturally specific, psychological entanglement of anima and animus.

Boland's lyric poetry challenged the omission of women from Ireland's literary canon. Each was carving space with language and in so doing generating new ground, nudging fertile soil for psyche's reflection—for psyche's "possibilizing"—psyche the animal naming the image. "The animal heart directly intends, senses, and responds as a unitary whole," writes James Hillman.[6] Something whole was being lifted up—the feminine heart claiming its own wilderness such that it had room to roam. Their story was my story—I felt the longing for a renewed epistemological grounding, for permission of expression, for the radical acceptance of delight when one finally can call psyche "home."

* * * *

I recall a conversation with Irish-born journalist and author, Claire Dunne, who tells me how in 17th-century Ireland, when the old Gaelic order began to crumble, "war on harpists and their instruments peaked with Elizabeth I edicting death on them."[7] She notes how Cromwell destroyed their harps, and how people were forced to hide their musical instruments in the bogs, if nowhere else. I realized how hiding one's harp is synonymous with hiding one's soul. The great waiting ends when one doesn't have to hide anymore. In years to come, I would tell my own story, write my own memoir exposing the journey of how I learned to belong to the world.

I dream that from the ancient Irish bogs emerged an apricot tree on the other side of the world, in Los Alamitos, California to be specific, beckoning a young girl with a Gaelic name to prance around its trunk and proclaim the "leprechauns" are coming! Bachelard writes of loving things "intimately, for themselves, with the slowness of the feminine, that is what leads us to the labyrinth of the intimate nature of things."[8] With the slowness of the feminine…that is how I discovered an intimacy with cosmos which is my Irishness. I notice the sky and her belongings, the water and her reflections. I see into a self who dances and have found the mirror of my people.

NOTES

1. Virginia Woolf, *The Waves* (London: Hogarth Press, 1931), quoted in Jay Griffiths, *A Sideways Look at Time* (New York: Tarcher Putnam, 1999), p. 32.

2. Gaston Bachelard, *The Poetics of Reverie, Childhood, Language and Cosmos* (Boston: Beacon Press, 1971), p. 117.

3. Kerby Miller, quoted in Rebecca Solnit. *Migrations: Some Passages in Ireland* (New York: Verso, 1997), p. 52.

4. Rebecca Solnit, *Migrations,* p. 49.

5. Seamus Deane, *Celtic Revivals* (Winston-Salem: Wake Forest University Press, 1985), p. 14.

6. James Hillman, *The Thought of the Heart and the Soul of the World* (Woodstock, CT: Spring Publications, 1982), p. 15.

7. Claire Dunne, personal conversation, February, 2004.

8. Bachelard, *Poetics of Reverie*, p. 31.

Mystic Faces, History's Traces: Joseph Campbell, Irish Mystic

DENNIS PATRICK SLATTERY

The Sufi mystic al-Hallaj said the same thing, 'I and my Beloved are one,' and he too was crucified. This is the mystical realization: you and that divine immortal being of beings of which you are a particle, are one.

—Joseph Campbell, *Mythic Worlds, Modern Words:*
Joseph Campbell on the Art of James Joyce[1]

Each reader of Joseph Campbell's enormous body of work comes to it seeking what one needs, desires, hopes for, or, in some instances, may not expect. I thought that what was going to be the big magnet for me was what Campbell had discerned about myth. To my surprise, I stayed for lunch, to feast on the mystical quality of his thought, disposition, and insights. That is my topic of exploration

Dennis Patrick Slattery, Ph.D., is Core Faculty, Mythological Studies at Pacifica Graduate Institute, and has been teaching for forty years. He has authored or co-edited twelve books, including: *Harvesting Darkness: Essays on Literature, Film, Myth, and Culture*; *The Wounded Body: Remembering the Markings of Flesh*; *Grace in the Desert*; and, most recently, *Varieties of Mythic Experience: Essays on Psyche, Religion and Culture* (Daimon-Verlag, 2008), co-edited with Glen Slater.

for this essay. But I also choose to write about him for several reasons that link us, beyond our passion for underlining books as a form of meditation. "Kindred souls" is too kitschy for my tastes; and yet ....

Both the Campbell and the Slattery clans have their origins in County Mayo on the western terrain of southern Ireland. As individuals in those clans, both Campbell and I love to explore that interstitial space that lies moist and shadowy between the realms of spirit, poetry, the depth psychology of C. G. Jung, myth, and history. Moreover, we share a love of teaching (I am in my 39th year in the classroom); a sense of humor which shields us from taking ourselves too seriously; a love of language's lyric and metaphoric inflections; a desire to migrate ideas hatched in our reading and teaching to the wider cultural landscape; an openness to travel and to other cultural habits of mind and behavior; a belief, explicit or more subtle, that some deep relationship obtains between the mystic and the poet. To this last venue, Joseph Campbell was both.

Campbell added immeasurably to the conversation on world mythology; his major strength as I understand him, is as a magnificent synthesizer, a harvester of ideas through narrative agglutination. His ability to sum up, to sniff out relationships, to intuit analogies, to create metaphorical bridges between what appear to be disparate cultural expressions, is remarkable, especially when added to his own original insights, adroitly affirmed with both conviction and grace. So often have I gazed at his neat, thin, and sharply-penciled hand on yellow legal pads of his work in the Joseph Campbell Archives housed at Pacifica Graduate Institute. He had adopted the habit of summarizing a book in neat bullet points on yellow paper. The curator for the Archives, Richard Buchen, told my students and me that when Campbell finished a book, he would summarize it in one page, a compressed distillation of many pages of neatly-inscribed notes. It is as if he compressed in order to better comprehend what he had read. Compression and comprehension went hand in hand with his thin silver metal ruler, the instrument he used with fidelity during his meditation exercises. It is safely housed in a glass case in the Archives, reminding one of a crown jewel under glass, or a sliver of the true cross on eternal display for pilgrims to gaze on with reverence and awe.

His own roots are no less compressed. His grandfather, Charles, the Larsens' biography of Campbell informs us, sailed from County

Mayo during the three years (1845-47) in which the potato crop failed. Charles married and had three children: Mary, Rebecca, and Charles William, who will become Joseph Campbell's father.[2] Reflecting later on his family's heritage and their living in Boston, Joseph Campbell said that "being an Irish Catholic in Boston or New York in those days ... was 'to be neither fish nor fowl.'"[3]

Early in 1928, when he is 24, his biographers relate, Campbell makes his first sojourn to Ireland. His initial quips about his impressions reflect the vernacular speaking that he would be known for throughout his life: "Ireland was a funny little dream," and "My trip to Ireland was a riot."[4] Much later, and now accompanied by his wife, Jean, the two travel to Ireland in 1957 so he can trace, with great relish, the sacred geography of Joyce's *Finnegans Wake*, and "to follow the course of the hearse in the *Wake*."[5] The land of his heritage takes on a mythopoetic hue as Campbell tracks Joyce's mystical, dreamy novel, which was published 4 May, 1939.[6] Five years later, Campbell, along with Henry Morton Robinson, publishes *The Skeleton Key to Finnegans Wake* in 1944, which remained for years the only extensive guide to such an innovative and enigmatic fictional labyrinth stewing language, myth, history, and pure Irish genius.

Readers of Campbell would not be surprised to learn that Joyce's dream work captured the imagination of the budding mythologist, for the novel carries both a mythos and a mystical linguistic landscape that I believe lies at the heart of Campbell's inclinations as a writer and as a person. To that sensibility, or way of being conscious to and in the world, I wish to devote the remainder of this essay. I hope to reveal some of the lineaments of this propensity for the mystical in and through his involvement with the mythical. Indeed, like Thomas Merton or the Anglican priest, Bede Griffiths, or C. G. Jung, Campbell is both a synthesizer and a unifier of large sweeps of history and culture. His delight lies largely in seeking and discovering patterns inherent in the human soul that find expression in world mythologies and religious traditions, literary patterns, and rituals worldwide. His landscape of exploration is global, finding within it inflected (one of his favorite words) local customs and mores of behavior and thought. To that extent, he is an inheritor of a tradition of work begun in 1934 when Maud Bodkin wrote her classic work, *Archetypal Patterns in Poetry,* that she hoped would further unite the studies of "psychology and imaginative literature."[7] Freud and Jung were her two priests of the imagination in this innovative project.

Perhaps a salient place to begin is with an observation of Campbell's in *Oriental Mythology*, the second volume of his magnum opus, *The Masks of God*. Largely in this study, but not exclusively, he practices his own form of cultural and mythological yoga, by which I mean to point to the origin of that word, which Campbell obliges by stating: "The Indian term *yoga* is derived from the Sanskrit verbal root *yuj*, 'to link, join, or unite,' which is related etymologically to 'yoke,' a yoke of oxen, and is in sense analogous to the word 'religion' (Latin *re-ligio*), 'to link back, or bind.'"[8] I sense that Campbell is perhaps one of the most astute and persistently practicing yogis in that his work sustains this quality of "linking back," of sensing analogies where someone else might see only differentiation, separation, even alienation. His work reveals to me the writer's intense desire to burst through "the illusion of duality, [which] is the trick of *maya*. 'Thou art that' (*tat tvam asi*) is the proper thought for the first step to wisdom." By collapsing the *I* of myself into the *Thou* of the other, dualism is usurped, a linking is established, and a consciousness of wholeness is achieved. Herein lies the heart beat of Campbell's life work as I understand it.

Moreover, something else is roiling about in the early pages of this volume. He wishes at the same time to further "the basic difference between the Oriental and Occidental approaches to the cultivation of the soul,"[9] a distinction I wish to link back to throughout this essay. Campbell designs it this way:

> ... [S]piritual maturity, as understood in the modern Occident, requires a differentiation of *ego* from *id*, whereas in the Orient, throughout the history at least of every teaching that has stemmed from India, ego (*aham-kara*: 'the making of the sound 'I') is impugned as the principle of libidinous delusion, to be dissolved.[10]

What I wish the reader to note in the above distinction is the place of history in the making of such a constant position derived from India and to hold that for a moment, to be linked to an observation Campbell delineates a few pages later. Ever a storyteller, he deploys narratives themselves to press home an observation or an insight. In relating the story of the "Buddha-to-be," the prince Gautama Shakyamuni, he follows him on his quest wherein the young man "seeks the knowledge that should release all beings from sorrow"[11] until he reaches the still point of the revolving universe, which, Campbell observes, "is described here in mythological terms, lest it should be taken for a physical place to be sought somewhere on earth. For its location is psychological."[12] He continues by affirming that this point is one of balance and equilibrium, and more importantly, it is "in the mind from which the universe can be perfectly regarded: the still-standing point of disengagement around which all things turn."[13]

I find these statements by him in relatively close succession to be marrying several important stems of thought: history, spiritual awakening, mythology, and psychology. Blended together in Campbell's lifelong studies, these disciplines, together with his passion for wisdom embodied in multiple, but primarily Western, literary traditions, comprise the mythic mystic that is this unique student of world mythologies. In addition, his citation above is cautionary, and one he tirelessly repeated throughout his life: mistaking the vehicle of an image for the tenor of its reality to which it points. This confusion, I sense, occurs when the condition of mind is literal rather than contemplative, as he reminds us in speaking of the image of the Promised Land: "Its connotation—that is, its real meaning—however, is of a spiritual place in the heart that can only be entered by contemplation."[14]

I refer the reader back to Campbell's distinction above that "the supporting point of the universe" within Shakyamuni's quest is described in mythological terms "lest it should be taken for a physical place." Here is a pivot point of contention for Campbell: to mistake, as he will say later, the finger pointing at the moon, for the moon itself; in the postmodern lingo of literary criticism, to mistake the signifier for the thing signified. To do so is to commit a cardinal mythological transgression: to take the metaphor literally, or to mistake the symbol for what is now to be understood symbolically, or to take the figure for the ground. A more accurate and engaging interpretation derails at just this juncture of switching the tracks.

THE ENERGY OF MYTH AND MYSTICISM

When literalism deflects the symbolic order of awareness, the mythic life dissociates and collapses; when it does, the mystical element of awareness, which I believe is the end of Campbell's own pilgrimage towards understanding, evaporates as blue haze. I say this because of another refrain he uses in several of his writings: first, he suggests, is the literal stories that comprise the myth; but if that mythos is alive and vibrant, animated by symbols, then it serves the culture and the individual through "four fundamental functions: the mystical, the cosmological, the sociological and the psychological."[15] Embedded in all of these functions, it seems to me, is the symbol, which Campbell defines in another context as "an energy-evoking and directing agent. When given a meaning, either corporeal or spiritual, it serves for the engagement of the energy to itself."[16] The mythical, therefore, driven by the energies of the symbol, is then that point midway between the sensate world and the mystical realm of being, a path on which Campbell as mystic and monk is always tending as the goal of the journey. Artists themselves, he believes, are an essential part of the hero mythos, for they are called, he asserts, "to cast the new images of mythology. That is, they provide the contemporary metaphors that allow us to realize the transcendent, infinite and abundant nature of being as it is."[17] Culturally, we might best look to the artists to restrain us from becoming so overly denotative in our interpretative projects that we lose the connotative ground that artists insist we see by means of as eternal analogies of Being.

He phrases it slightly differently when in conversation with Michael Toms, who interviewed Campbell over a ten-year period, beginning in 1975. In this conversation, Campbell recalls another insight from the East: "Another lesson in Buddhism is if you see the Buddha coming down the road, run away. Because if you concretize the divine in any fixed image and say 'There it is' you're off course."[18] Toms suggests "We're really talking about the Great Mystery, the ineffable" to which Campbell replies: "That's what we're talking about. It's exciting to talk about it."[19] In their continued discussion the archetype of the Waste Land edges into the conversation. For Campbell it is a powerful and perduring image, in part because it depicts the life of so many people. He pushes the idea of the Wasteland into the psychological and spiritual condition to which it refers:

> The moment the life process stops, it starts drying up; and the whole sense of myth is finding the courage to follow the process. ... [T]hat's what hell is: the place of people who could

not yield their ego system to allow the grace of a transpersonal power to move them. [20]

In his own manner and style, the mythologist taps into the source and place of energy that I believe underlies all of his writings: the energy wellspring is the transcendent unknowable to which the powers of metaphor lead one. Kant outlines "a simple formula for the proper reading of a metaphysical symbol."[21] In the four-part schema—a is to b as c is to x—what intrigued Campbell is that "x represents a quantity that is not only unknown but absolutely unknowable—which is to say, metaphysical."[22] However, metaphor carries in its vital organs a source of energy that has the capacity to lead one to the ungraspable x.

In an Irish context, this very energy has been called *Dana*, named after the Tuatha De Danann, whom Frank MacEowen refers to as ancient "earth-loving people in the Celtic past" who embodied "a tradition beneath the traditions, an undercurrent simmering and churning beneath what is called 'Celtic' or 'Druid' tradition."[23] They were a people intimate with the force and energy "of the spiral powers of the earth and spirit."[24] MacEowen's own travels in Ireland attuned him to the "primordial power" that he believes inhabits the swirl of the spiral, a spiralic life force or principle of power.

Now without "going Celtic" in these musings, I do want to insist that there is a correlation and communion between myth, mysticism, mystery, and energy, what in another context the British biologist Rupert Sheldrake, whose work was familiar to and quoted by Campbell, calls morphogenetic fields and which the former calls the mythogenetic zone: "And the mythogenetic zone, [is] the primary region of origin of the myths ...."[25] wherein energy coagulates and folds back on itself. I suggest that the spiral is the motion of myth in this more precise way: my reading of Campbell aggravates two questions that spiral back on one another: (1) In what ways is myth historical? (2) In what ways is history mythic? Might it be that myth is: the inner sleeve of history?[26] Might history be the informing temporal agent of what is beyond time, space, and causality? To press further: how does myth, which explores, discovers, and voices the timeless and the transcendent, or at the very least, lead a soul to this space?

He outlines the first function of myth in the face of affirming, negating, or reforming the world as it is, as that force that arouses "in the mind a sense of awe before this situation through one of three ways of participating in it."[27] For my purposes in this essay, the first function is most essential, for Campbell regards it "as the essentially religious function of mythology—that is, the mystical function" by which the individual comes into direct contact "with the mystery of being."[28]

In her simple but powerful abridged version of a more staggering study of Mysticism, Evelyn Underhill writes of the ordinary man of common sense: he orders and arranges his world to "reducible little squares,"[29] which are static and safe elements to guide his sense of the real. But on the other side, she affirms that the neat and orderly patterns of the woven work "are short ends, clumsy joins and patches; all of these disturb my simple philosophy."[30] Behind the manicured hedges of my ordered world of appearances, where I would place the historical self's reality, is another, more confusing, and very differently arranged landscape of myth. The mythical and the mystical are both in the fabric of reality, but backside. This backside of things is the realm of Campbell's exploration and the texture of his design as mystically situated explorer of the inherent mystery embroidered in all that is.

"To give up one's own comfortably upholstered universe" is the task of the artist, the poet, and the mystic, Underhill further affirms, and it puts one closer to the animals, in that, like animals, "the mystic and the poet strive for a directness of apprehension which we have lost. The terrier gets and responds to the real smell, not a notion or a name."[31] That "real smell" one arrives at through the imaginal act of contemplation Underhill describes as "the essential activity of all artists," one which embodies "a virginal outlook on all things, a celestial power of communion with veritable life, when sensation is freed from the tyranny of thought."[32] Perhaps, to push the analogy one more waltzing step, W. B. Yeats writes, in one of the most formidable works on "Ireland's mystical and spiritual tradition," *Mythologies*, that before he can be initiated into the tradition of alchemy, he must learn the complex steps of "a magical dance, *for rhythm was the wheel of Eternity*, on which alone the transient and accidental could be broken, and the spirit set free."[33] The mystic, the poet, and the animal participate in this eternal round of the rhythm of life itself. My offering is that Joseph Campbell, in his own bodily vitality, his love of and player of music, his gourmet appetite, his love of the geishas, participated in such an elegant and exuberant energy flow of the universe.

Now there are dozens of definitions and descriptions of the mystic. I am suggesting here, however, that what unites in the soul of Joseph Campbell are the complementary impulses of mythologist, poet, mystic, and historian, wrapped in the psychological cellophane or gossamer of depth psychology as outlined and promoted by C. G. Jung. Recursivity, coil and recoil, spiraling, retrieval, deepening, a love of metaphor and its necessity, the folding back of energy and patterns of consciousness both individually and collectively—all these are skeins working in bits and "joins" on the backside of Campbell's marvelously polished prose studies of myth.

JOURNEYING AND JOURNALING INTO DESTINY

I base the above proposition in part on two of his works that, to date, have not been widely read or discussed, but which make up the qualitative backdrop of his inflections towards the mystical. Both *Baksheesh and Brahman* as well as *Sake and Satori* are the extended and often neatly polished journals of Campbell he kept during his year-long pilgrimage around the world in 1954-55 at the age of 50. In that journey, a spiraling of sorts around the globe, he not only discovered and settled on his life work; he also came to inhabit a certain *habitus* of mind, an exuberance of body and a *gravitas* of spirit that molted into the mystic he became through a favorite pastime of his: brooding. He writes for instance on Wednesday, September 8, 1954 in Amarnath, India as he travels to a temple by car with friends: "During the drive I had time to brood a bit more on the Indian problem."[34]

One reads in these early journal entries the growth and further sophistication of an analogical imagination, one which discerns relationship, connectedness and commonality through the clear sharp eyes of differentiation; he learns to envision a Oneness foraging amongst the Many. Multiplicity in India breeds in Campbell a vision of an underlying Unity, a pattern of exploration that he would continue to sharpen for the rest of his days. Two pages, 22-23, are illustrations of his thought processes, his listings—he adored lists and used them everywhere as compressed ordering principles!—as a way of seeing in history, in memory, patterns of mythic presences. And then, in a slight lifting of the veil that accompanies one of Campbell's fictional heroes, Stephen Dedalus, as he walks the strand in Joyce's *A Portrait of the Artist as a Young Man*, and suffers in one unplanned knee-buckling instant what Joyce referred to as "esthetic arrest," Campbell offers this poetic, even lyric, description of an analogous emotional moment:

> Last evening, during our boat ride, I saw a woman standing alone, in one of those canal-vistas, and she seemed to me to be linked to nature in the way of these people, that is to say, linked to nature by being linked to a principle beyond nature, through a ritual attitude, something very different from the romantic return to nature and intuition of God through nature.[35]

Being related both *to* and *beyond* at the same instant is the heart thump of mysticial experience and Campbell's participation in it. These two italicized prepositions are as well mythic propositions of one connected to and transcendent of the material world. For Campbell, a mystical sense is: (1) esthetic; (2) mythic; (3) historical; (4) poetic; (5) depth psychological. In his fine chapter on Joyce's *A Portrait of the Artist,* Campbell draws a dramatic comparison between Dante's beholding Beatrice Portinari in the streets of 14th-century Florence and Stephen's coming upon the woman on the strand that sparks or ignites an instant of "esthetic arrest."[36]

> It is an eternal moment. … What he sees is not simply a lovely girl, but a ray of light of eternity. It opens his third eye (his inward eye); the world drops back a dimension; his life is now committed to this seizure.[37]

Stephen's version of bliss is carved out for him in this crux, or crossroad, of time and eternity made possible and poignant by the intrusion of beauty into the querulous quotidian. Esthetics, mimesis, myth, and the mystical congeal in his imagination in an instant. My thesis is that just such a sensibility was also Campbell's guiding shaman in his mature work, which gave a decidedly mystical cast to his thought and writing.

But one more ingredient is necessary at such a rich juncture of mystery and matter: the *sublime.* Continuing with the image and nature of beauty that Joyce outlines in the spirit of Thomistic theory in *Portrait,* Campbell rests on the quality of radiance that accompanies esthetic arrest: If it's a radiance that doesn't overwhelm you, we call it beauty. But if the radiance so diminishes your ego that you are in an almost transcendent rapture, this is the sublime. What renders the sublime is immense space or immense power. What such a moment of transcendence that expands immediately and forcefully one's orbit of awareness leads to is "a beautiful accord"... the "enchantment of the heart."[38] Discovery, recognition, rapture, release, rejoicing—the properties of such an encounter in and through the material world is an experience that preoccupied Campbell as he searched with abandon through world mythologies for this moment in human consciousness.

Such an experience of the sublime, moreover, is not alien to another of Campbell's trenchant interests: history itself in its relation to myth. We gain an inkling of such import for him in the philosopher Schopenhauer's insight into the unfolding of a human life. His essay, "An Apparent Intention in the Fate of the Individual," outlines how so many people and events we encounter in the pilgrimage of our lives seem gratuitous, accidental, haphazard as we live through them: "Then you get on in your sixties or seventies and look back, your life looks like a well-planned novel with a coherent theme. Things have happened, you realize, in an appropriate way."[39] Structure and coherence replace the chance quality of those events seen from an angle of the present; now, recollected in a backward gaze, one sees pattern, accord, coherence, theme, congruence, relevance where before there was a chaotic array of incidents and characters with no interior design.

I would push Campbell's idea of a novel taking shape in one's life here into a little lower layer. What one discovers is the mytho-poetic character of one's being in its temporal becoming, arrangement, order, and coherence; and contrary to Schopenhauer's question: Who wrote all of these? Which answer is: "You did."[40] I would entertain the possibility of more hands at the writing desk of one's life than one's own inscribing self. In addition, Campbell's example from Schopenhauer suggests some further reveries on one's personal memories, a larger mythic pattern embracing it, and a discovery of the unique—OK, novel—*mythos* that one has been spinning out of herself. Memory, history, mythos, and an awareness of some patterning accord between them is as well another corridor of the mystical sense that Campbell's work engages. I assert this last point because I believe it underlines another of his observations expressed earlier in the same volume in a discussion with an audience after he has lectured on Joyce's fiction.

Campbell returns to one of his most heat-generating themes: the nature of God: "God isn't a fact. God is a symbol. As soon as you interpret God as a fact, you are off the beam. ... As I have said, deities in mythological systems are personifications of energies." And then just below, he continues: "But where I have used the word *God*, let us simply say *Brahman*, a neuter noun that refers past itself to the mystery of the total energy of life."[41] His focus on energy is bedrock to his theory and function of the hero outlined so fully in *The Hero with a Thousand Faces* that brought mythic discourse back into high fashion. That is, the hero appears at those moments of crisis in culture when the energy flow between the macrocosm and the microcosm has ceased movement.

The hero's task, which s/he must first hear, then heed by giving up self for a higher achievement, is to restore the flow of the life energy between the cosmos and the collective as well as individual psyche. He observes early in the study: "for the hero as the incarnation of God is himself the navel of the world, the umbilical point through which the energies of eternity break into time."[42] A successful, if you will, heroic quest is, as Campbell asserts, "the unlocking and release again of the flow of life into the body of the world. The miracle of this flow may be represented in physical terms as a circulation of food substance, dynamically as a streaming of energy, or spiritually as a manifestation of grace."[43]

My own reading here is that the energy field or principle is the goal and source of all understanding of mythic thought and sense. I believe it worthy to notice as well that the hero is not *in relation to* God but shares that same *identity as* God. The terms of relation and identity is another staple Campbell motif in his writings; to be incarnated as God elevates the soul of the hero and the heroic potential that resides, most often sleeping in a coiled state, but surfacing in one's dream life, within every individual. In addition, these essential energy fields reveal the deepest patterns in human life and were discerned by Campbell, in important moments, during his year-long pilgrimage in 1954-55, to which I now wish to return.

DISTANCE AND DISCERNMENT

Before we leave India with Campbell and travel to southeast Asia, we should pause for a moment to listen to how this trip released in him a full grasp of his life's work. Much akin to James Joyce, who chose finally to exit Ireland in order to write about her, so did Campbell feel a necessity to leave his normal life and work in order to discern in what direction it needed to develop. Early on in his Indian sojourn, he comes to this recognition:

> What I am to study is definitely here: folk religion, with its roots in the deep past; aristocratic religion, represented in the ruins of the temple art of India; the phenomenon of the sadhu— past, present, future. ... Moreover, it is just possible that there maybe someone in all of this from whom I may wish to learn something fundamental. [44]

His experiences in India develop two complementary impulses in him: one is the power of the human spirit amongst oppressive poverty to remain serene, content, and spiritually rich; the second is the increasing value of Western consciousness that he thirsts to step back into with greater enthusiasm:

> The hope, the immediate teacher of the modern world is the West. The main problems of the modern world are functions of the Western style of life and thought. The most significant approach to the modern problems, therefore, must be via the modern Western psyche—and most emphatically, via the modern American psyche. [45]

His expression here is prologue to a profound awakening in his life's trajectory, delineated in the following manner:

> This realization has moved me to dissolve my earlier thoughts of a series of works on Oriental religion and legend ... and to plan to concentrate on the legendary mythological themes of the West .... [46]

Later, and closer to his time of returning to America, Campbell in Kyoto, Japan suffers both a disillusionment with his proposed projects that were to occupy him for decades, as well as incisive clarity about his life's professional design. Startled by an essay he reads in *Time* on 9 May 1955 by C. S. Lewis in an inaugural lecture as Medieval Studies scholar delivered at Cambridge, Campbell is stunned by Lewis's announcing "a new archetypal image" into history: that of old machines "being superceded by new and better ones."[47] This replacement addresses a larger archetype, which seems the real emphasis of Lewis's address, namely, the impulse to constantly attain new goods and provisions rather than conserve what we have as "the cardinal business of life, would most shock and bewilder [our ancestors] .... I conclude that it is the greatest change in the history of Western man ...."[48] Acquisition and consumption are the new archetypal patterns of being that, Lewis asserts, will and may have already replaced conserving and sustaining as patterns of behavior in the West.

His insights draw Campbell up short to evaluate his own projects. Here he draws a parallel with Buddhism's idea that "'All is without a self' would seem to me to go along very well with the idea of the discarded machines (though not, indeed, with that of striving for goods we have never yet had)."[49] He descends into disillusionment with the Oriental way of thought and life, it seems to me, preferring instead to retrench his future work in historical and philological scholarship— "let's not then try to read our own reactions back into Oriental context."[50] Lewis's making evident a new archetypal pattern emerging in the West persuades Campbell to shy away from his earlier epic plan: "All of this implies great warnings and danger signals for me in the work ahead on my *Basic Mythologies of Mankind*,"[51] works that will eventually materialize into the multi-volume *The Masks of God*.

In addition, his shifting mythology is accompanied by a reassessed methodology in typical Campbell fashion, a series of items drawn up in a crisp, succinct list:

> 1. Beginning from the beginning, I am to follow motifs objectively and historically. Also, I am to record interpretations objectively and historically, on the basis of contemporary texts.[52]

The list is too involved to duplicate here, except for this final item in it which is a colossal shift in the way Campbell would conduct his studies, now that he has absorbed experientially the worlds of India, Southeast Asia, and Japan. My own belief is that without this year-long journey he would not have arrived at what follows, or at least not so early as he did to pursue it with sucesss and which is finally orchestrated by Bill Moyers and him in *The Power of Myth,* the most ubiquitous of all he wrote and created for television.

> 3. The historical milestone represented is that of the recognition of the actual unity of human culture (the diffusion and parallelism of myths). ... The time has come for a global, rather than provincial, history of the images of thought.[53]

These words comprise his big picture, his grand design, and his epic vision. He ends his list with a promise to adhere to the little picture:

5. Make no great cross-cultural leaps, and even within a given culture, do not try to harmonize what philosophers of that culture itself have not harmonized. Stick to the historical perspectives and all will emerge of itself. [54]

Already familiar with and highly influenced by Oswald Spengler's *Decline of the West* when he wrote *Hero*, Campbell seems to be aligning himself in a moment of great resolve with Spengler's sense of history, who himself wrote of "the metaphysically exhausted soil of the West."[55] What Spengler proposed, and Campbell assumes the mantel of, is a morphological grasp of history in which one discovers "from a morphological angle, disparate events will take on under examination 'deep uniformities.'"[56]

The symbol and the archetype are, for Spengler, categories of understanding so that "the whole of mythological religions and artistic thought ... constitutes the essence and kernel of all history."[57] Spengler assists Campbell in blending the disciplines of psychology, religion, mythology, and artistic expressions into a palimpsest and a palette from which he will paint for himself a new inflection of the mythopoetic imagination given fullest commerce in History.[58]

HISTORY AND PSYCHIC ENERGY

I wish to devote the last pages of this article to Campbell's sustained interest in psychic and spiritual energy that flows from earth, individual, culture outward to the wider cosmos and back again, as a spiralic loop that world mythologies give voice to in ritual, rites of passage, narratives, and other forms of incarnate expression. Not to be overlooked or reduced here as well is Campbell's own explorations and love of the smallest forms of life, the seedling and budding plant given elegant display in volume II, Part 2: *The Way of the Seeded Earth*, comprising a section of *The Historical Atlas of World Mythology*,[59] his love and study of *The Way of the Animal Powers*,[60] as well as his decades-long colloquy with Body Worker, Stanley Keleman in *Myth and the Body*.[61] I showcase these works especially at this point because, as a mystic engaged in the transcendent oneness of creation, Campbell is, as many mystical expressions confirm, deeply rooted in the material imagination, the seedlings, as it were, of a mystical fullness.

I have written elsewhere that "psychic and spiritual energy, though not divorced from matter but actually inhering within it, within Mother Earth, seems to be one of Campbell's perennial and abiding concerns."[62] My sense is that the principle of energy as a life force derived both from his study of world mythologies as well as his abiding study of C. G. Jung's work, especially, I suspect, Jung's powerful essay, "On Psychic Energy," a centerpiece of his *Structure and Dynamics of the Psyche.* [63] Yet this energy is materially-inflected, ubiquitous, and links spirit, psyche, and cosmos. Consider his early insight in *Animal Powers*: where he says that poets and artists today are present in large measure

> to perform the work of the first and second functions of a mythology by recognizing through the veil of nature ... the radiance, terrible yet gentle, of the dark, unspeakable light beyond, and through their words and images to reveal the sense of the vast silence that is the ground of us all and of all beings. [64]

Campbell refers here to the first function of a mythology: "to awaken and maintain in the individual a sense of wonder and participation in the mystery of this finally inscrutable universe;"[65] the second "is to fill every particle and quarter of the current cosmological image with its measure of this mystical import."[66] Myths, therefore, are both current to a culture or a people as well as providing a current of energy flow through the grounded gravity of silence, itself an energy field embodied in image.

Furthermore, the body for Campbell is no small player in this cosmic drama of mythic sustenance. He reminds us, for instance, in *The Flight of the Wild Gander* that "myths are the texts of the rites of passage"[67] having their origins in the energies of the organs of the body, both in conflict and in complement to one another. He furthers this idea in *The Power of Myth*: "the archetypes of the unconscious are manifestations of the organs of the body and their powers. Archetypes are biologically grounded ...."[68] Musing on this same idea in another context, I wrote:

> A renewed or revisioned mythos might then include an ability to reimagine the relation of spirit, body and earth in a constant but benevolent dialogic tension between the body's interiority and the world's matter, mediated by the social customs that comprise a specific historical time and place.[69]

To leap another step forward in pursuing this energy trail that snakes through his writings, especially the later ones, in *The Inner Reaches of Outer Space* Campbell observes that "the energy by which the body is pervaded is the same as that which illuminates the world and maintains alive all being, the two breaths being the same."[70]

Such a unitary vision of a comprehensive design of the world's interior and exterior natures he inherited, at least in seedling form, from Ananda K. Coomaraswamy, whom Campbell observes of his thought: he "could maintain that the metaphysical principles symbolized in India in the dreamlike imagery of myth are implicit in mythology everywhere"[71] and goes on to quote from Coomaraswamy's own writing, in which he affirms "an underlying spiritual unity of the human race:"[72] "… the various cultures of mankind are no more than the dialects of one and the same spiritual language."[73]

I have not attempted nor wanted to put sack cloth and ashes or even a crisp Cistercian garment on Joseph Campbell and dress him up in what he is not. However, this contemplative extrovert returns repeatedly to the grand synthesis or design of a world *monomyth*, a term he inherited from James Joyce, that attends and informs his exploration of myth with a decidedly spiritual cast and one which highlights Jung's inspiration of the *unus mundus*. Furthermore, there exists in his prose a coiled, or if I may return to the spiral image here as I bring this brief excursus to completion, energy structure: it folds back, remembers itself, loops back through history and sees by way of analogy the power of myth's presence in the world psyche. Campbell continually intuits a secret harmony between the human being embodied and, as he writes, forms of the macrocosm that are given voice and substance by the miraculous imaginal power of metaphor, what he affirmed repeatedly as "the native tongue of myth."[74]

Images of mythology are all metaphorical of a reality that can only be intuited, never known, Campbell suggests further in the work that I believe most deeply grooves the prominence of metaphor: that the universe might best be imagined as "a living being in the image of a great mother, within whose womb all the worlds, both of life and death, had their existence."[75] Analogy, or an analogical imagination, rests squarely here: "the human body is a duplicate, in miniature, of that macrocosmic form. Throughout the whole a secret harmony holds sway.

It is the function of mythology and relevant rites to make this macro-microcosmic insight known to us ...."[76]

The images of myth are metaphors, symbolic at the same time of vital energies that traverse the cosmos through and into the individual, through the mesocosm of particular and specific cultural and tribal customs. A deep and thick relationship attends such an energy flow, or even energy transfer system, wherein mythic images carry both intellectual, historical, and affective powers to guide the psyche as they direct psychic energy. That Campbell intuited, then traced these divine powers of presence and their capacity to ignite in ritual remembrance is a sign, to me, of his monkish and mystically inflected imagination.

In a discussion on "Earthrise: The Dawning of a New Spiritual Awareness" appended at the back of his book, *Thou Art That*, he sounds the final note, for this exploration anyway, about myth's elaborate design:

> Campbell: Myth has many functions. The first we might term mystical, in that myth makes a connection between our waking consciousness and the whole mystery of the universe. That is its cosmological function ....[77]

Let's leave him there, beaming, in fine company, nested deep in dialogue, as if he were in an Irish pub in Kinvara or Dublin, thinking once more about the place of the imagination in mythic pilgrimaging. A mythic icon for the extraverted soul, Campbell was also a devout solitary: brooding over his studies, musing over his spiraling sentences that often go on for the better part of a hefty paragraph with seemingly inexhaustible rhetorical vitality, he never tired of thinking through myth to the mystical. His energy transported him to the image of the Earthrise, a spectacular photo taken from the moon. That image, he pondered, is the great cosmic bumper sticker to usher in a new mythos, where so many of the borderlines drawn by human fear and fatigue are suddenly dissolved, leaving only the blurred edges of oceans and land, clouds, and wind patterns, and a human imagination to revel at their mysterious design, their sacred narrative, their trenchant moment in a cosmic story, still unfolding, still enfolding and willing to embrace us all.

NOTES

1. Joseph Campbell, *Mythic Worlds, Modern Words: Joseph Campbell on the Art of James Joyce,* ed. Edmund L. Epstein (Novato, CA: New World Library, 2003), p. 71.

2. Stephen and Robin Larsen, *Joseph Campbell: A Fire in the Mind. The Authorized Biography* (Rochester, VT: Inner Traditions, 2002), p. 6.

3. *Ibid.,* p. 7.

4. *Ibid.,* p. 95.

5. *Ibid.,* p. 433.

6. Joseph Campbell, *A Skeleton Key to Finnegans Wake. Unlocking James Joyce's Masterwork,* ed. Edmund L. Epstein (Novato, CA: New World Library, 2005), p. xiii.

7. Maud Bodkin, *Archetypal Patterns in Poetry: Psychological Studies of Imagination* (London: Oxford University Press, 1965), p. v.

8. Joseph Campbell, *Oriental Mythology. The Masks of God* (New York: Viking Press, 1962), p. 13.

9. *Ibid.,* p. 15.

10. *Ibid.*

11. *Ibid.,* p. 17.

12. *Ibid.*

13. *Ibid.*

14. Joseph Campbell, *Thou Art That: Transforming Religious Metaphor*, ed. Eugene Kennedy (Novato, CA: New World Library, 2001), p. 7.

15. Joseph Campbell, *Pathways to Bliss: Mythology and Personal Transformation* (Novato, CA: New World Library, 2004), p. 25.

16. Joseph Campbell, *The Flight of the Wild Gander: Explorations in the Mythological Dimension* (Novato, CA: New World Library, 2001), p. 143.

17. Campbell, *Thou Art That*, p. 6.

18. Michael Toms, *An Open Life: Joseph Campbell in Conversation with Michael Toms,* ed. John M. Maher and Dennie Briggs (Burdet, NY: Larson Publications, 1988), p. 66.

19. *Ibid.*

20. *Ibid.,* p. 67.

21. Campbell, *Flight*, p. 50.

22. *Ibid.*, p. 51.

23. Frank MacEowen, *The Spiral of Memory and Belonging: A Celtic Path of Soul and Kinship* (Novato, CA: New World Library, 2004), p. 27. Another image to explore in relation to the Celtic spiral is that of the coiled Kundalini serpent depicted with such majesty in *The Inner Reaches* (p. 56) which as symbol of "an original knowledge" in its 3.5 spiralic turns, suggests a primordial disposition of psyche.

24. *Ibid.*, p. 28.

25. Campbell, *Flight*, p. 78.

26. I presented this talk, "What's Up History's Inner Sleeve? Myth and the Fabric of Culture," at a Symposium entitled *Myth, Memory and Culture,* jointly sponsored by The Dallas Institute of Humanities and Culture under the direction of Dr. J. Larry Allums and Pacifica Graduate Institute, May 11-12, 2007 in Dallas, Texas.

27. Campbell, *Thou Art That*, p. 3.

28. *Ibid.*

29. Evelyn Underhill, *Practical Mysticism and Abba* (New York: Dutton, 1914), p. 19.

30. *Ibid.*, p. 30.

31. *Ibid.*, p. 27.

32. *Ibid.*, p. 28.

33. William Butler Yeats, *Mythologies* (New York: Touchstone Books, Simon and Schuster, 1998), p. 286 (my italics).

34. Joseph Campbell, *Baksheesh and Brahman: Asian Journals— India,* ed. Robin and Stephen Larsen (Novato, CA: New World Library, 1995), p. 22.

35. *Ibid.*, pp. 22-23.

36. Campbell, *Mythic Worlds*, p. 36.

37. *Ibid.*, p. 19.

38. *Ibid.*, p. 23.

39. *Ibid.*, p. 286.

40. *Ibid.*, p. 286.

41. *Ibid.*, p. 275.

42. Joseph Campbell, *The Hero With a Thousand Faces,* Bollingen Series XVII (Princeton, NJ: Princeton University Press, 1973), p. 49.

43. *Ibid.*, p. 40.

44. Campbell, *Baksheesh,* p. 23.

45. *Ibid.*, p. 165.

46. *Ibid.*, p. 165.

47. Joseph Campbell, *Sake and Satori: Asian Journals—Japan,* ed. David Kudler (Novato, CA: New World Library, 2002), p. 102.

48. *Ibid.*

49. *Ibid.*

50. *Ibid.*, p. 103.

51. *Ibid.*

52. *Ibid.*

53. *Ibid.*

54. *Ibid.*

55. Oswald Spengler, "Form and Actuality," Vol. One. *The Decline of the West,* trans. Charles Francis Atkinson (New York: Knopf, 1948), p. 5.

56. *Ibid.*, p. 6.

57. *Ibid.*, p. 7.

58. Of course I am bypassing the other earlier pilgrimage Campbell inaugurated during the years 1927-28, as Richard Tarnas writes, "to study in Paris and Munich, where he first encountered the work of Freud, Jung, Joyce, Mann and Picasso and conceived his understanding of the mythic foundations of human experience." *Cosmos and Psyche: Intimations of a New World Order* (New York: Viking Press, 2006), p. 331. Nor am I developing the cosmic conjunctions that Tarnas' magisterial study of cosmos' influence on psyche in history develops so eloquently and thoroughly.

59. Joseph Campbell, *The Way of the Seeded Earth.* Vol. 2. Part 2: *Mythologies of the Primitive Planters: The Northern Americans. Historical Atlas of World Mythology* (New York: Harper and Row, n.d.).

60. Joseph Campbell, *The Way of the Animal Powers.* Vol 1. *Historical Atlas of World Mythology* (Alfred Van Der Marck Editions. London: Summerfield Press, 1983).

61. Stanley Keleman, *Myth and the Body: A Colloquy with Joseph Campbell* (Berkeley, CA: Center Press, 1999).

62. Dennis Patrick Slattery, "What's Up History's Inner Sleeve? Myth and the Fabric of Culture." Presented at a conference: "Myth, Memory and Culture," at The Dallas Institute of Humanities and Culture, Dallas, Texas. May 11-12, 2007.

63. C. G. Jung, *The Collected Works* (Bollingen Series XX), ed. Sir Herbert Read, Michael Fordham, *et. al* (New York: Pantheon Books, 1960), § 1-130.

64. Campbell, *Animal Powers*, p. 10.

65. *Ibid.*, p. 8.

66. *Ibid.*

67. Campbell, *Flight*, p. 34.

68. Joseph Campbell, *The Power of Myth,* ed. Betty Sue Flowers (New York: Doubleday, 1988), p. 68.

69. Dennis Patrick Slattery, "The Myth of Nature and the Nature of Myth: Becoming Transparent to Transcendence," *The International Journal of Transpersonal Studies,* 2005, vol. 24. 29-38. Reprinted in *Harvesting Darkness: Essays on Literature, Myth, Film and Culture* (New York: iUniverse, 2006), pp. 288-310.

70. Joseph Campbell, *The Inner Reaches of Outer Space: Metaphor as Myth and as Religion* (Novato, CA: New World Library, 2003), p. 41.

71. *Ibid.*, p. 34.

72. *Ibid.*

73. *Ibid.*

74. Campbell, *Thou Art That*, p. 45.

75. *Ibid.*

76. *Ibid.*

77. *Ibid.*, p. 102.

JUNGIANA

TRANSLATING JUNG'S SEMINAR ON CHILDREN'S DREAMS: AN "ENTERVIEW" WITH ERNST FALZEDER

ROBERT S. HENDERSON

ERNST FALZEDER is the translator of *Children's Dreams: Notes from the Seminar given in 1936-40* by C. G. Jung, which was recently published by Princeton University Press as part of the Philemon Series. Ernst was the main editor of the Freud-Ferenczi correspondence (3 Volumes, Harvard University Press, 1993-2000) and the complete Freud-Abraham correspondence (London: Karnac, 2002), as well as the author of about 200 publications on the history, theory, and technique of psychoanalysis. He lives in Austria where he is a lecturer at the University of Innsbruck, and also works as an author, editor, translator, and ski instructor.

Rev. Dr. Robert S. Henderson is a pastoral psychotherapist in Glastonbury, Connecticut. He and his wife, Janis, a psychotherapist, are co-authors of *Living with Jung: "Enterviews" with Jungian Analysts: Volume 1* (Spring Journal Books, 2006). Volumes 2 and 3 are forthcoming, in 2008 and 2009, respectively.

Robert S. Henderson (RH): What led you as a Freud scholar to become interested in Jung and his work?

Ernst Falzeder (EF): First of all, I have never been *not* interested in Jung. His impact on 20th-century culture and thinking in general, and on psychiatry, psychology, psychotherapy, religious studies, the East/West dialogue, etc., in particular, has been so great that anyone studying these topics should take his contributions into account. My own research has never been exclusively focused on Freud, but I have also studied other major figures of the psychoanalytic movement, such as Sandor Ferenczi, Otto Rank, Karl Abraham, and Alfred Adler, for example, who made major contributions to psychoanalytic theory and technique.

The longer I researched the intellectual history of psychoanalysis, the clearer it became that—as in the case of the afore-mentioned analysts—Jung's pioneering role, too, has not sufficiently been acknowledged in psychoanalytic circles. Many of his earlier contributions have been incorporated into psychoanalytic thinking without acknowledging their origins. So this was my starting point.

Over the past years, largely due to the excellent work done by Sonu Shamdasani, I have more and more come to see Jung less from a psychoanalytic point of view, but as a figure in his own right whose encounter with Freud and psychoanalysis was only an interlude, although a very important one, in his own development. Such was my situation when Sonu asked me, a few years ago, whether I would be willing to translate Jung's seminars on children's dreams into English, a project undertaken by the Philemon Foundation.

In retrospect, this seems to have been a turning point, in that I began—had to begin, as a matter of fact—studying Jung in depth, so as to be able to make an informed and correct translation. One thing led to another, and now I find that I am becoming more and more immersed in various Jung projects. I find it exciting to discover and explore the incredible wealth of still unpublished Jung materials, a situation that is quite different to that in Freud studies. By now we know so much about Freud, nearly all of the texts not published during his lifetime are now accessible in archives, including his letters, and the most important materials have been published, or will be published in the near future.

For the past decades, I have spent much of my time contributing to this, for instance, as the chief editor of the Freud-Ferenczi correspondence and as the editor of the Freud-Abraham correspondence. The situation is completely different in Jung's case, however, and I find it absolutely crucial that the complete body of his work and of his writing, including his correspondence, be made available. I do not say this as a devout Jungian, but as an intellectual historian.

Whatever one may think about Jung's theories, it is a fact that key texts of his have not been published so far, or only in a truncated form. Only when we have the *Complete Works of Jung*, as opposed to the *Collected Works*, will we be able to really follow the development of his thinking, and will it be possible for his ideas to receive a fair and informed evaluation in the marketplace of ideas. This is what the Philemon Foundation set out to do, and I am very glad I can be part of this important project.

RH: What will be going on 50 years from now regarding Jung's legacy?

EF: Who knows? Not even God knows the future, as Freud once jokingly remarked (Jung might disagree). In this age of ongoing destruction of the planet Earth it is also quite uncertain if this question will matter at all 50 years from now. But, if it should, I think that whatever may or may not remain of his specific ideas and concepts, of Jungian teaching or training institutions, of journals, etc., to me there seems to be no doubt that Jung does and will continue to occupy an important place in intellectual history. A certain kind of psychology is not, and will never be, a cumulative science, namely, the kind of psychology that employs an approach that investigates the psyche and the soul from "within," that meets it on its own ground, so to speak, and thus has to rely on self-observation and introspection.

I certainly do not underestimate the value of a psychology whose goal is to obtain quantifiable data on the basis of observing behavior from "without." Just think of Jung's word association test, or the groundbreaking studies in developmental psychology made possible by the observation of mother-infant interaction or separation. But it is evident that this approach has its limits.

If we want to have a psychology that has not completely lost its research object, namely, the soul and the psyche, this has to be complemented, in my view, by an approach that investigates human inner experience. In this field, however, we cannot devise experiments or tests that prove one concept, derived from that very experience, "wrong" and another "right."

By the way, I think that confusion between these two approaches is also the reason why Jung has so often been called a mystic, while he claimed that he had always been an empiricist. He was indeed an empiricist, but in the latter sense, taking and investigating inner experiences as empirical facts. So, to return to the question: So long as there will be a place for that kind of psychology, there will be a place for Jung.

RH: Can you share some of the background on Jung's Children's Dreams Seminar. For example, were the notes from it hand-written by Jung? What have been some of your challenges in the translation? What are some of the things you have learned about Jung through your work?

EF: Jung did not write his contributions down. Several people who attended the seminars took notes, and the publication is based on these notes. As far as the discussions are concerned, this means that we have no guarantee that this is word for word what Jung and others said, but it should come pretty close. People knew shorthand at the time. Many of the papers on which the discussions are based are extant; where this is not the case, it is noted in the book.

Please bear in mind that I did no original research for this volume. I translated the already existing German edition of those seminars, compiled by the editors at that time. The translation was indeed a challenge. First of all, I am not a native English speaker. Second, I tried to orient myself on the basis of the existing Jung translations. These, however, are often not consistent. So this was a tightrope walk, trying to find a balance between un-English, but "correct" terms, such as "feeling-into," and a translation that does not read like a translation. Third, Jung and others touch on so many fields and topics, using so many terms that cannot be found in any conventional dictionary, so that it took some time to research the correct equivalents in English.

I still vividly recall the passage, for example, in which all the different kinds of gladiators in ancient Rome are listed, fighting with sword, net, armor, etc. Plus all those quotes and crypto-quotes from Goethe to the Bible, from the Tibetan Book of the Dead to the Gilgamesh Epic ... I had three great helps in this project: Tony Woolfson, who helped to render my (I like to think) correct translation into idiomatic English; the Internet, particularly LEO, a professional translators' forum, where colleagues generously contributed; and the support of the Philemon Foundation—the patience of Steve Martin, and the invaluable support of Sonu Shamdasani with anything concerning Jung.

Finally, I would also like to thank Princeton University Press. I have had some 40 books published so far, and rarely was the cooperation so professional, smooth, and friendly. What did I learn about Jung? That he was brilliant and authoritarian, convinced of his views, but also uncertain at times. That I learned more about his ideas in these seminars than, with very few exceptions, in any of his writings. That he could be unforgiving towards people who did not see or were too stupid to understand what he was trying to show.

That he could be generous towards others who came up with ideas, of which he himself had not thought. In other words, that he had a clear agenda in mind of what to teach others, but that he was no fanatic, that he was open to learn more—within his own frame of reference, to be sure. Finally, that he comes through, in these seminars, as a man of flesh and blood, and not as a "Jungian."

RH: When Jung was certain about something he would say he knew and did need to believe, for he felt that believing indicated that he did not know. In your work with these seminars what did you learn about the uncertain Jung?

EF: Jung was absolutely convinced of a few things, the existence of God, for example, or of the collective unconscious. One could not argue with him about those. He was once asked if he believed in God. He answered that this was a rather stupid question. No, he said, he did not believe. If you believe, he continued, you do not know. But if you know, well, you needn't believe. But while never questioning these basic assumptions—or this "knowledge," as he would have put it—he could be quite uncertain about the specific meaning of *knew* to some particular material brought forward by an analysand or a dreamer.

He came well prepared to the seminars, though, having at his fingertips all kinds of possible parallels from literature, mythology, alchemy, religion, history in general, etc., trying to see if they fit this particular material, but always open to change his mind if further information, e.g., further dreams in a dream series, indicated something else. So what these seminars show us is a Jung who is both certain about the basic tenements of his theory, and at times uncertain about how to best apply this theory in a particular case. Once he had become sure, however, of what something meant, he could be quite harsh on participants of the seminar who were unable to see this.

RH: Jung believed that children live the unlived lives of their parents. What would be gained by looking at the dreams of children?

EF: As far as I understand Jung, he did indeed believe that some parents may try, unconsciously, to make their kids live their unlived lives, or to enforce their own problems on them, with sometimes terrible consequences. And he was, together with a few others, a pioneer in thinking so. This may be commonplace knowledge today (or not), just think of so-called relational psychoanalysis or object relations theory, but he was among the first modern psychologists to go that way. (Off topic, by the way, he usually also does not get credit for other notions that are everyday lingo today, such as the midlife crisis.)

But when talking about children's dreams, this was not his top priority. In these seminars, his focus was on so-called big or great dreams, staying in memory for a whole lifetime, on children being so much nearer the collective unconscious, on what we can glean of those dreams and of what this encounter with the collective unconscious may have meant for that particular child. He did, however, try to distinguish very clearly between the collective and personal stuff in those dreams. This approach is also one great difference to Freud, by the way, who found children's dreams quite simple and basically uninteresting. For Freud, young children just dream of what they want (e.g., strawberries).

RH: This book is part of the Philemon Series of the Philemon Foundation. What is your sense of the claims of the Philemon Foundation about the unpublished work of Jung's?

EF: I have been a Freud scholar for some 35 years, and I have had fits about the restrictions the heirs and archives placed on seeing the material. For Freud, although the situation is still not optimal, scholars are now in a very good position. Pretty much of the relevant material is now in print or relatively easily available in archives. This is not so for Jung.

There is an unknown Jung out there (some 30 volumes not contained in his *Collected Works*, plus manuscripts later published in substantially altered form, plus letters), and this is what the Philemon Foundation wants to publish, first of all in English translation. I think it's a no-brainer that the writings and letters of one of the most influential psychologists and psychiatrists of the 20th century be published. Of course Jung is controversial. But how can anybody make an informed judgement about the value of his ideas if half or more of his writings, amongst which absolutely crucial texts, such as the so-called *Red Book*, are not published? And how can anybody make an informed judgement about the development of his theory if many of his works are practically unavailable in their original form, but only in later, heavily altered editions? Or not at all in English?

RH: Ernst, I have enjoyed our time and I have one last question. Besides translating Jung's Children's Dreams Seminar, you have also been working on Freud's letters to his children. As a father, have you learned something from these two brilliant men that has helped you with your own children or with better understanding your own childhood?

EF: Well, Rob, the pleasure was all mine, although you end by asking a very tricky question. In one sense, I have "learned" next to nothing as far as my own children are concerned. I do not think I would have acted very differently if I had never heard of Freud or Jung. As a matter of fact, I feel there should exist a kind of what one could call a psychological incest taboo between parents and children, that is, that we should be most careful not to psychologize and analyze our relationship with them too much. This is not a professional setting, and, after all, many non-psychologists and non-therapists are getting along just fine with their kids, while many shrinks, or even child psychotherapists, are having great problems with their own children. When one of my kids had a nightmare, for instance, I would not have "dreamed" of analyzing it, but rather just tried to soothe them and be a loving and caring father. On the other hand, one cannot study Freud and Jung and escape untouched, or at least I would think so. Reading them, and, even more important, having had the experience of two analyses with a psychoanalyst and an analytical psychologist, has definitely influenced me, and my understanding of my own childhood and development. But I would be unable to pinpoint exactly the quantity and quality of that influence.

FILM REVIEWS

Lars and the Real Girl. Ryan Gosling, Patricia Clarkson, Emily Mortimer, Paul Schneider, Kelli Garner. Screenplay by Nancy Oliver. Directed by Craig Gillespie.

REVIEWED BY VICTORIA C. DRAKE

I say whatever one loves, is. —Sappho

Winter has descended when this postmodern fable begins in a frozen, rural, randomly isolated Minnesota community. Twenty-seven-year-old Lars Lindstrom (Ryan Gosling) is shivering from head to toe, avoiding contact with both his inner and outer landscapes. He is clearly at a crossroads, gripped by a kind of spiritual impasse which is bracketed by two traps: managing the exhausting tension between his self-protective introversion and a basic, yet unrealistic, desire for safe, uncomplicated connection.

Victoria C. Drake is currently working on her Ph.D. in Depth Psychology at Pacifica Graduate Institute in Santa Barbara, California. After attending Harvard University (B.A. 1983), she followed her passion to become a life-long international wildlife conservationist and environmental community justice advocate. Victoria lives in Chicago with her husband, James Evan-Cook (from Kent, UK), their three daughters, Angelica, Isabella, and Lily, and assorted animal companions.

Lars is a wounded exile in more ways than one. He has always been at tenuous odds with his persona and orphaned sense of self since his mother died during his birth, leaving him at the mercy of a distant father and older brother, further alienating the feminine from his early experience. Lars's emotional development is arrested because he cannot allow himself to feel or trust another for fear of losing them as well. The catastrophic absence of what would have been his primary anima figure has crippled his ability to establish relationships with men or women, but more importantly with himself. It has also repressed his capacity for any independent imaginal creativity. In fact, it is all he can do to navigate the necessary coordinates of a lackluster workday for survival, enduring as little human interaction as possible before retreating to the cloistered refuge of a garage (trading one cubicle for another) behind his family childhood home, now occupied by his brother and pregnant sister-in-law. No one understands Lars, least of all his family, despite their repeated attempts to lure him out of his solitude, which they do more from a sense of duty than choice. They are at a loss—no one more than Lars. No one seems to understand Lars, that is, except his patient co-worker, Margo (Kelli Garner).

As if in answer to an unspoken prayer, Lars unexpectedly learns about an intriguing, yet accommodatingly chaste solution to his painful loneliness through a reliable source of magical interventions: the Internet. Within a matter of days, Lars introduces a made-to-order female companion to his family and friends. But, she is not what they expect. Enter "Bianca" with long, raven-colored hair and a half Danish, half Brazilian lineage. She must use a wheelchair (evoking the handicapped feminine motif), ostensibly because she is a life-size, anatomically correct doll with no mobility of her own. The sole purpose of customizing these dolls is typically for sex. But sex is the last thing on Lars's innocent mind or in his naive soul, for that matter. Like Bianca, he is pure, virginal, with only honorable intentions. Nothing messy or awkward will ideally ever come between them. Still, Lars appears to truly invest Bianca with all the other qualities of a real flesh-and-blood girlfriend, the highs and the lows. He even appears to worship her. So, everyone else around him does, too, in kindly respect for this seemingly harmless, even playful phase—a bridge between his conscious and unconscious selves. He begins to relax and thrive in animating both the male and female roles, thus correcting and integrating the disassociated, fragmented feminine affect of his nature that has been buried for so long.

At this point, the alchemy of the film's logic takes hold and buoys the viewer along in its celluloid currents. This is where our story lifts off into an archetypal realm of metaphor, shedding any material grounding. In fact, it doesn't have to be believable to touch a deep inner chord. There is humor here, to be sure, but it is collective, not divisive. This is when the viewer must suspend the criteria for any concrete literal narrative and surrender to the open-ended symbolic realm of dream, mythography, and fairy tale imagination.

The pivotal figure in facilitating this singularly unique community *participation mystique* is Dr. Dagmar (Patricia Clarkson). Initially, Lars consults the doctor on behalf of Bianca and an inferred ailment. Soon, it becomes obvious who really needs therapy. Clarkson's thoughtful performance is beautifully wrought without being maudlin, skillfully nuanced without a hint of cruel sarcasm or humiliating irony. For all we know, the lonely doctor may see more than a bit of herself in the Lars/Bianca dyad, being a trifle touched by the angels as well. She takes a professional risk to protect the integrity of Lars's fantasy by recruiting his family and small community in "playing along" to awaken the collective unconscious. In doing so, she affords Lars the permission to fully tend his fantasy (much like a dream) and do the necessary inner work all by himself, thereby playing it out to the end. Otherwise, Lars may be irretrievably haunted—cocooned in his grief if he is robbed of this opportunity. Her only treatment is offering supportive patience and attentive concern as she senses the serious gravity of the matter at hand—more invisible than visible. She wisely realizes that Bianca is Lars's unorthodox way of healing his own unexcavated source of personal power and gets out of his way. The doctor's gift is that she believes in his redemption before he can believe in himself. And, to everyone's surprise, her gamble pays off.

The astonishing effect of Bianca's incongruous presence is infectious in thawing out not only Lars's eclipsing inhibitions, but also that of others. After all, she is the ideal soulmate: undemanding, unconditionally attentive, refreshingly quiet. You can be your true self with her, the self that maybe no one else knows. Eventually, everyone is willingly under her surreal spell.

Before long, to Lars's bewildered consternation, Bianca starts to "have a life" that doesn't always include or require him. She begins socializing, volunteering at the hospital, sharing secrets, revealing depths within her ageless emptiness, becoming herself (evoking Merleau-Ponty's idea of the body's silent conversation with things). This is definitely not part of Lars's original compensatory plan. He begins to consciously interrogate and revise its merit. Is this an echo of the ruptured unity with his mother, even a betrayal? Bianca's powerful and popular feminine charm grows too real for Lars to remain strategically dormant, unlike Bianca's static lack of choice. Dramatic tension builds as he becomes ready to break through the veil of inner invisibility. Finally, he sees and recognizes the real girl, Margo, by his side, for the first time. It is she who has been stoically waiting for him all along. Margo is his real contemporary witness. Spring arrives with its revived opening for new life, and the film shifts towards the promise of a real love story.

Some of the most interesting images in the film seem to act as allusions to Snow White, Sleeping Beauty, Isis and Osiris (even Pygmalion and Galatea) with a twist. Here, Lars is Bianca's humble prince offering brotherly protection and projection. By bringing her to "life" from her plasticine sleep, he also "rescues" and awakens himself. The fires of true Love (Eros) are kindled and, thereafter, no one's interiority is ever the same again. But, "happily ever after" eludes Lars and Bianca in the traditional fairy tale sense. This knight has other important metaphorical conquests to face and sacrifices to make, the biggest one being fear. As Jung writes:

> In the shape of the goddess, the anima is manifestly projected, but in her proper (psychological) shape she is *introjected;* she is the "anima within".... She is the natural *sponsa* ... whom the endogamous tendency vainly seeks to win in the form of mother or sister. She represents that longing which has always had to be sacrificed. ... Layard speaks very rightly of "internalization through sacrifice."[1]

To paraphrase Michael Meade: The polytheism of Beauty is an antidote to monochromatic fear. It is no accident that Bianca appears as a beautiful maiden in a state of (debatable) compromising distress being confined to a wheelchair. Ruth L. Ozeki says: "We make things because we lose things: memories, people we love and, ultimately, our very selves."[2] Lars is able to vanquish his lifelong fear of abandonment through experiencing himself as the beloved exotic object of a beautiful maiden's scripted affections. In fact, Bianca represents the first rewarding, reciprocal relationship of his life.

Bianca is Lars's idealized mediatrix to love and wholeness, but she is also considerably more than that—more than just a passive doll. She takes on a life of her own in the film and in our collective imagination. We, too, become like Lars in cultivating affection towards her. We are co-creating, co-transferring onto each other. Like Lars, in seeing through her presence, we are mutual transitional objects for the other. As a result, Bianca transcends her inanimate fate to temporarily participate and transform the subtle body of soul as a creative symbolic extension of Lars. But, as Don Fredericksen writes:

> *Symbols cannot be reduced and remain symbols.* We have no recourse but to accept and value their irreducible complexity as the best possible, spontaneous expression of something relatively unknown or ultimately unknowable. ... [Hence] the need to make an interpretive effort .... That interpretive gesture is amplification.[3]

There is one core scene in the middle of the film that wordlessly sums it up best. Lars and Bianca are at a party. While she sits, beer in hand holding court, Lars listens to the music and begins to sway in reverie, captivated, eyes closed. The range of expressions on Lars's tender face is inexplicably holy. Is he finally remembering, perhaps as far back as in the womb before time began, when all was complete? He needs the invitation of this moment more than any other to realize his as-yet-unborn self in all its affective possibilities. Gosling manages to embody Lars with such remarkable grace and sensitivity; the synthesis couldn't be more authentic. With humor and pathos, Lars evokes the unlikely protagonist in a Samuel Beckett play. *Lars and the Real Girl* is a poignant, affecting, restrained study in initiation; from boy to man, orphan to lover, broken to healed, Winter to Spring.

Ralph Waldo Emerson once wrote:

> A nobler want of man is served by nature, namely, the love of Beauty.
>
> The ancient Greeks called the world *kosmos*, beauty. Such is the constitution of all things, or such the plastic power of the

human eye, that the primary forms, as the sky, the mountain, the tree, the animal, give us a delight *in and for themselves*; a pleasure arising from outline, color, motion, and grouping. This seems partly owing to the eye itself. The eye is the best of artists.[4]

NOTES

1. In James Hillman, *Anima: An Anatomy of a Personified Notion* (Woodstock, CT: Spring Publications, 1985), p. 84. See *The Collected Works of C. G. Jung*, trans. R. F. C. Hull (London: Routledge, 1954), Vol. 16 § 438.

2. *Shambhala Sun* (March 2008), p. 75.

3. Don Fredericksen, "Jung/Sign/Symbol/Film," in *Jung & Film: Post-Jungian Takes on the Moving Image*, ed. Christopher Hauke and Ian Alister (East Sussex, UK: Brunner Routledge, 2001), p. 36.

4. Excerpted from "Nature," published as part of *Nature: Addresses and Lectures*.

BOOK REVIEWS

Maria Teresa Savio Hooke and Salman Akhtar (eds.). *The Geography of Meanings: Psychoanalytic Perspectives on Place, Space, Land and Dislocation.* International Psychoanalysis Library, The International Psychoanalytical Association, London, 2007.

REVIEWED BY AMANDA DOWD

THIS WHISPERING IN OUR HEARTS

Co-editor Maria Teresa Savio Hooke writes in her Introduction to this rich and thoughtful collection that the idea for this book came from the Australian Psychoanalytical Society's Conference, "This Whispering in Our Hearts: Intuition in the Service of Psychoanalytic Work in the Australian Milieu," held in Uluru, Central Australia in 2000. Papers have also been included from later conferences, especially: "Unsettling the Settlers: History, Culture, Race and the Australian Self—Psychoanalytic Perspectives," held in Sydney in July 2007.

Amanda Dowd is a Jungian analyst member of the Australian and New Zealand Society of Jungian Analysts (ANZSJA) and of the International Association for Analytical Psychology (IAAP). She lives and works in Sydney, Australia. She has a particular interest in the vicissitudes and mythopoetics of relationship and the formation of self, mind, identity, and cultural identity. Her current work includes an exploration of the traumatic effects of migration for both individual and culture and the interrelationship between psyche and place. Contact details: adowd@aapt.net.au.

The "whispering" that is referred to comes from the title of a book by historian Henry Reynolds and speaks to the unspoken distress and anxiety about the relationships between indigenous first peoples in Australia and the mainly white settlers. Yet, as contributor Craig San Roque (chap. 5) states, the whispering also speaks to the intuition necessary to read the states of our social and political national milieu—in whichever "place" we find ourselves—and, I would add, the states of our interpersonal relationships, wherever they may be, but exemplified, perhaps, in the therapeutic space of the consulting room.

Intuition, the whispering, also requires a receptive mind—a potential space made available for gathering, holding, so that "thoughts" may find a "thinker."

By gathering "thinkers" from the diverse but related domains of history, literature, anthropology, and psychoanalysis, the book itself performs a psychotherapeutic act by providing a "place for gathering, holding and reflection" and, in so doing, it returns to mind what, in post colonial times, so easily "falls" out—is "forgotten"—denied and disavowed: traumatic pasts, deep uncertainties about and hence crises of self, identity and cultural identity, "states" of alienation, traumatic loss. In the final chapter, James Telfer refers to "the condition where there can be no Other" and links this to what Mircea Eliade calls the "terror of history:" where the force and power of the unknowable, the unthinkable, and hence the unspeakable Otherness within and/or Otherness without destructively and repetitively acts out resulting in the collapse of imaginative and hence cultural space with maddening results—for individual, for culture.

This volume is a testament to the courage it takes to return Other to mind: as part of personal identity, as part of cultural identity, Other as Country, Other "Way" of being. It is a recognition of the plurality of the human psyche and the necessity, therefore, of multidisciplinary thinking in the consideration of such complex issues as dispossession, the trauma of dislocation, relationship with country.

The collection presents itself to this reviewer in two ways. Each individual chapter is well written, coherently argued, and any interested reader could profitably dwell in the ideas, language, experience, and specifics of these related themes. In Part 1, Space, Thomas Wolman explores the meaning of "spacial" experience and elaborates around the question of how we locate ourselves in space and hence place. Describing the dynamic relationship between the personal and collective domains, internal and external space, his main point, I think, comes at the end of his chapter: "...the major division," he states, "is between human space—internal or external—and what I call unchartered space or the void." (p. 44)

The naming of the Void—as empty space—a place de-void of personal meaning—sets up the reader for Part 2, Place, Time and Land. Australian novelist Kate Grenville, historian Bain Attwood, psychoanalyst Eve Steel, and psychoanalyst and cultural analyst Craig San Roque have immersed themselves in the "region of [Australian] psychic pain between the Tjukurrpa [indigenous dreaming] and the European dream." These four profoundly moving chapters need to be read together and form the backbone of the collection as a cultural case history, if you will, of the ongoing effects of the "terror of history" as experienced in Australia: the traumatic confrontation with a land devoid of personal meaning, the disavowal of and attempted annihilation of the indigenous Other, and the fear of knowing the truth. Grenville takes up the question of "feeling foreign in one's own place." Attwood explores the writing of "history," the way in which trauma, by collapsing the space between past and present, subverts the project of "distantiation," the implicit modern distancing of the past from the present which renders invisible the voices of Others "below"—in particular, the experiences of loss of indigenous peoples, migrants, women, sexual minorities, slaves. Steele also takes up the theme of the fear of knowing the truth, the silence, as resisting history, and focuses on the forced removal of indigenous children from their homes, what has been called in Australia, the "Stolen Generation." She holds in mind the children "lost between worlds," "hidden from history."

By the time the reader has reached Chapter 5, one might be ready to appreciate the subtlety and complexity of the description of Tjukurrpa—the Other dreaming or Mind in the country—as written by Craig San Roque:

> ... the essence of Tjukurrpa is a multidimensional pattern of connectedness ... somehow very like the neurological systems externalised and set into the geography of the country ... it is a poetic calculus ... organised to sustain life, animal beings, food, knowledge, relationship ... it is psychological. (p.121)

San Roque's detailed description of Tjukurrpa as mental container is instructive, offering insight into the complexities of intercultural communication as it "may involve trying to make links between quite different orders of mental reality and different ways of doing transformation work" (p. 120). One gets a deep sense of what it might be like to lose such a sense of coherence and integrity that participation with Tjukurrpa might bring.

Part 2 concludes with a chapter written jointly by Professor of Psychiatry Stuart Twemlow and his poet son, Nicholas, who explore their Maori heritage and theorize on the formation of identity and cultural identity as a constant negotiation between the "me and not me," leading to the ultimate recognition of the nature of self as a plurality.

In Part 3, Dislocation, co-editor Salman Akhtar and James Telfer address the traumatic experience of dislocation and the clinical implications of working with states of alienation. These multilayered chapters explore the "environmental transference," the importance of the non-human environment in psychic development, and the connection between "spirit of place" and the development of the capacity for symbolic thought.

The second way in which this collection can be read is as the unfolding of an intuitive thread, implicit in the original conference and followed through by editors Hooke and Akhtar: that of the primacy of place. Philosopher Edward Casey, in *Getting Back into Place*, says this:

> ...place serves as the condition of all existing things. This means that, far from being merely locatory or situational, place belongs to the very concept of existence.[1]

It follows, therefore, that to be dis-placed and/or dis-possessed of one's place results in alienation...the uncanny experience of feeling out of contact with human experience.

By listening to the whispering and restoring "place to mind" this volume serves a deep human need. By listening to the whispering of the voices "hidden from history" this collection contributes significantly to breaking the silence that surrounds the "terror of history"—individually and culturally—and serves as a counterbalance to the personal and collective resistance to the recognition of the truths of our individual and cultural identities.

I strongly recommend this rewarding book to clinicians—in whatever place they may practice—and to those who have some familiarity with the experience of feeling "out of place."

NOTES

1. Edward S. Casey, *Getting Back into Place, Toward a Renewed Understanding of the Place-World* (Bloomington, IN: Indiana University Press, 1993), p. 15.

BOOK REVIEWS

CATHERINE ANN JONES. *The Way of Story: The Craft & Soul of Writing.* Studio City, California: Michael Wiese Productions, 2007.

REVIEWED BY HENDRIKA DE VRIES

The subtitle of this rich little book could just as easily have been "The Craft & Soul of Living." Crafting a good story, it appears, is much like crafting a good life. Dedication, discipline, and the will to learn about plot, character, and dialogue are important ingredients, but it is the ability to connect to the meandering depths of soul that make for both the kind of writing and way of living that Catherine Jones poses to her reader. She insists,

Hendrika de Vries has been a licensed depth-oriented Marriage and Family Therapist in private practice in Santa Barbara for over twenty years. Her training in depth psychology and background in theological and mythological studies guide her therapeutic approach. She has been actively involved with Pacifica Graduate Institute since 1986 both as a conference presenter and as adjunct faculty in the Mythological Studies program. Her published articles and public presentations include: "The Chrysalis Experience: A Mythology for Times of Transition," *Depth Psychology: Meditations in the Field,* eds. Dennis P. Slattery and Lionel Corbett (Carpinteria, CA: Daimon Verlag & Pacifica Graduate Institute, 2000), pp. 147-159; "Seeing in the Dark: the Power of Mythic Perception in Troubled Times;" and "Inviting the 13th Fairy: Embodying Soul in our Personal Myths."

The *Way of Story* approach to writing includes the whole of you, not just the rational mind. You must bring all of you to the table: body and guts, feelings, intuition—yes, even your dreams (p.23).

While reviewing this book I was reminded of a dream from many years ago when I was regularly driving the freeway from Santa Barbara to San Francisco to do dream work with an analyst.

In the dream I am driving on the 101 Freeway, but every mile is blocked. Signs mark confusing detours that test my patience. Frustrated and testy I suddenly find myself catapulted, as one does in a dreamscape, onto the California Coast Highway instead. The winding road clings precipitously to the edge of the bluffs that hang above the Pacifica Ocean. Yet as I slowly wend my way up the narrow coastal road every cell in my body begins to relax. Patches of fog demand careful attention and at times the road clings so close to the edge that I say a prayer for the earth to hold. So now and then I pause at one of the rest stops or flat grassy knolls along the way. Refreshed by the pungent scents of sycamores and sea, I notice myself smiling at the barking of the sea lions frolicking in the surf.

When I awoke I knew that the dream was the soul's reminder that its way was not the way of the linear 101 Freeway but more akin to the winding road that clings between land and sea, a slower path that offers breathtaking vistas calling forth spontaneous gratitude, while at the same time demanding the careful attention of mindfulness in the present moment. The dream offered a compass for the shift from the linear demands of my ego to the deeper course of the soul that navigates that winding edge between the oceanic depths and the visible landscape.

The Way of Story offers just such a compass for the writer's journey, whether that writer happens to be a would-be novelist, a playwright, screenwriter, or simply a person setting out to discover the sacred story of his or her own life path. It shows the reader that the process of both writing and living is not the journey of a straight line but more that of a dreamlike meandering path carved between bluffs and wild waves, which is best expressed through myth and poetic metaphor.

Every journey has its own story or stories. Stories are the magic shows, the mirrors that reveal the nuances of the journeys life calls forth from all of us. The beauty of *The Way of Story* is largely due to the careful way in which the author guides the reader into the process of the mythic depths as well as the narrative of story. We are reminded that myth is not narrative. Narrative is easily changed through a conscious shift in point of view, but myth suggests an archetypal depth that challenges us to become aware of the god or goddess that has us in its thrall. It calls for a relationship to the characters in our personal and collective mythology, a wrestling with inner angels or demons in order to find our point of view in their landscape not ours. In this way the process of both writing and living is one in which the soul finds its way towards the stories that want to be expressed and lived through us, not those that the ego insists upon telling.

Being the superb writer that she is, Catherine Jones does not tell us what archetype, what god or goddess holds a writer close. She shows us instead. Through personal anecdotes, intimate glimpses into her personal and professional life, inspirational quotes, and brilliant reviews and analyses of structure, plot, dialogue, and conflicts in stage plays and motion pictures, the author has found a way to pull the reader into the personal mythology of a successful writer. I felt myself at times in the presence of a modern-day Scheherazade. In the vein of that fabled Persian story-telling queen of 1001 Arabian Nights, she seduces the reader with tantalizing tidbits of stories from movies, plays, novels, and her own life encounters as an actor, playwright, and screen writer.

I also heard the deep wisdom of steadfast Hestia, the Greek goddess who guards the sacred fire. Despite the author's reflections on her marriage, motherhood, and her mythic connection to Ariadne, the goddess of Crete who gave up everything for the man she loved, it is not the goddess Hera, Demeter, or even Ariadne that addresses the reader through Catherine's writing. Rather we encounter a Hestia guarding the sacred flame of creativity even when the Muse abandons her and the fire burns too low to inspire or energize her passion. As such *The Way of Story* also reminds the reader of the importance of knowing your personal myth. What mythic tale hinders or supports the crafting of your story?

At times Catherine's personal story may seem a bit daunting to the would-be writer reading this book. Serendipitous events bring her face to face with precisely that one celebrity that wants to read her manuscript and agrees to star in her movie or the exact person she needs to carry her script out into the world, as if in a charmed fairytale. But that is, of course, the point of her approach. She shows through her own examples that serendipities begin to happen when we follow the deep call of soulful passion.

We discover that while this particular author could dream an entire movie before she wrote the screen-play and managed to be in the right places at the right times, she also suffered through years when her writing gift disappeared and all she could do was to turn inward to tend her soul.

Her story reminds us that the story-making journey has a mysterious life of its own. When the outward expression of the creative process appears blocked, willful force may do more harm than good. On one occasion Catherine fell and broke her wrist when she tried to force it. She urges her readers to surrender and change direction, to discover through dream work and inner exploration where they got off track and left their soul behind. The writer who tends the process with this kind of spiritual attention and inner devotion is ready for the moment when serendipity calls and the Muse steps through the door to fan the tiny flame of the imagination into a fiery passion again.

I do not want to suggest that Catherine's book is all about depth, myth, and meaning. Much of the book is a very practical how-to guide that walks the reader through clear, concise steps in developing story structure, writing outlines, creating character and plot, and writing "stunning dialogue." There is a whole chapter on "transcending" writer's block, and most of the chapters are followed by powerful experiential exercises that can help improve technique and integrate it with the process of inner discovery.

This pragmatic soul-centered approach to the difficult task of creating great stories, whether in a novel, screen play, or a personal life, makes this book unique in the plethora of books available to writers and would-be writers wanting to improve their craft. Catherine even offers a model of her own writing workshops for anyone interested in facilitating her approach.

Imagine that the fabled Scheherazade offers to share with you her secrets of story telling. Would you turn that down? Personally I would have found the addition of an index helpful, but then that is the 101 Freeway approach again, and this book is, after all, more about the winding coastal journey where soul and craft meet.

Pay attention with all your senses and enjoy the ride!

New Books by C.G. Jung

The Red Book: by **C.G. Jung**
Expected Publication: **Late 2009**

Children's Dreams: Notes from the Seminar Given in 1936-1940: by **C.G. Jung**
Lorenz Jung, Maria Meyer-Grass (Eds.), Ernst Falzeder, Tony Woolfson (Transl.)
January 2008, ISBN 0691133239, Princeton University Press

The Jung-White Letters: by **C.G.Jung** and **Victor White**
A.C. Lammers and A. Cunningham (Eds.),
Murray Stein (Contr.Ed.)
November 2007, ISBN 1583911944, Routledge

PHILEMON FOUNDATION is pleased to announce the publication of the first two of the estimated 30 volumes of hitherto unpublished original works by C.J. Jung. Within these volumes will be manuscripts, seminars, and correspondence whose historical, clinical, and cultural importance equals, and in some cases surpasses, the importance of Jung's already-published work. The task of bringing these volumes to publication and available to the widest reading public is estimated to require 30 years. The mission of the Philemon Foundation is to complete this work.

A major component of Philemon's mission is to raise the funds necessary for this enormous undertaking. Your support is crucial and important! Tax-deductible donations fuel the combined efforts of the editors, scholars, translators, and publishers to maintain a regular publication schedule through the coming years. The Foundation depends upon and welcomes contributions and gifts-in-kind from the professional and lay community of those who value and appreciate the importance of having a full body of Jung's work available.

Please join us in this effort.
Make your contribution through the Philemon Foundation website,

www.philemonfoundation.org
Learn more about special discounts available to donors as each new volume is published. Read about the editorial process, the relationship to the *Collected Works* begun by the Bollingen Foundation, and the works in progress.
Your generosity is welcomed and deeply appreciated.

119 Coulter Avenue, Suite 202, Ardmore, PA 19003
www.philemonfoundation.org

Evocations of the Unexpressed: Archetypes and Healing

Assisi Institute's 2008 Programs

Founded 1989 by Michael Conforti, Ph.D., Director

Summer Conference in Assisi, Italy

July 8 – 15, 2008

"Healing as Epiphany"

Michael Conforti, Ph.D.
Engaging the Archetype of Healing

Brian Goodwin, Ph.D.
Fields and Archetypes as Agencies of Biological Form

Dennis Patrick Slattery, Ph.D.
Poetic Renderings of Stasis and Transformation

SPECIAL PRESENTATION
with **Jean Houston, Ph.D.**

"Archetypes of Whole System Transition: The Social Artist as Catalyst of Visionary Leadership"

Summer Intensive in Archetypal Pattern Analysis

Brattleboro, Vermont
August 14 – 17, 2008

"Dreams, Symbols, and the Objective Psyche"

Frederick Abraham, Ph.D.
Initial Conditions and Generation of Form

Michael Conforti, Ph.D.
Archetyal Coherence and Pattern Analysis

Pamela Donleavy, J.D.
Archetyal Patterns

David Rottman, M.A.
The Objective Psyche

Beverly Rubik, Ph.D.
Biofields and Healing

Beyond the veil of manifest reality lies the archetypal, silently shaping experience

Archetypal Pattern Analysis Training Program

Michael Conforti, Ph.D., Founder & Director

A Two-Year Interdisciplinary Program in Vermont leading to certification as an Archetypal Pattern Analyst. Open to individuals from all backgrounds.

This unique program combines in-depth exploration of the workings of archetypes with extensive practice in the methodology and application of archetypal pattern analysis. Our trans-disciplinary curriculum is informed by the work of C.G. Jung, M.L. von Franz, discoveries in the new sciences, and the eternal truths of the world's wisdom traditions.

Program Highlights:

- Four weekend seminars and an 18-hour mentorship each year
- Ten teleseminars per year
- Internationally recognized faculty
- Dynamic, creative learning community

2008 - 2009 Program Dates

September 11–14, 2008
An Archetypal Developmental Approach

November 6–9, 2008
Initial Conditions: Theory and Practice

All programs are held in Brattleboro, Vermont. The Assisi Institute employs a rolling admissions policy. Students admitted into the program may begin at any one of the class dates.

For additional information, contact Assisi Institute:
(802) 254-6220, assisi@together.net
or visit www.assisiconferences.com

Assisi Institute
For the Study of Archetypal Pattern Analysis

UNIVERSITY OF
CALIFORNIA PRESS

JOURNALS + DIGITAL PUBLISHING

Psychology

JUNG JOURNAL

EDITOR // Dyane N. Sherwood

Jung Journal: Culture & Psyche is an international quarterly
published by the C.G. Jung Institute of San Francisco, one
of the oldest institutions dedicated to Jungian studies and
analytic training. The journal was founded in 1979 by John
Beebe under the title, The San Francisco Jung Institute
Library Journal. In 2007 the title was changed to reflect its
evolution from a local journal of book and film reviews to
one that attracts readers and contributors from the academy and the arts, in addition to Jungian analyst-scholars.

WWW.UCPRESSJOURNALS.COM

C. G. Jung Foundation of New York
Spring 2008 Programs

FULL-DAY SATURDAY WORKSHOPS

MARCH 8   WORKING WITH PERSONAL MYTHOLOGY, JULIE BONDANZA

APRIL 12   CHARLATANS, HEALERS, VISIONARIES, FALSE PROPHETS: WHAT IS WHAT AND DOES IT MATTER? HEIDI KOLB

MAY 10   ARCHETYPAL UNDERPINNINGS OF THE PROCESS OF CHANGE, KATHERINE OLIVETTI

CONTINUING EDUCATION COURSES

- ZEN GAMES AND DHARMA BATTLES, MORGAN STEBBINS

- BLACK SKINS, WHITE MASKS: AN ARCHETYPAL EXPLORATION OF "RACE," RACISM AND SLAVERY, HARRY W. FOGARTY

- ACTIVE IMAGINATION USING PAINTS, MAXSON J. MCDOWELL

- THE WAY OF COMPLEXES, PART I, SYLVESTER WOJTKOWSKI

- THE ARCHETYPE OF LUCK, DAVID ROTTMAN

- FOR BETTER OR FOR WORSE: ANALYTIC INSIGHTS ON THE TRANSFERENCE BETWEEN CLERGY AND CONGREGATION, DOUGLAS TOMPKINS

- AION: A GUIDE FOR THE PERPLEXED, MORGAN STEBBINS

- PERSONALITY TYPES: JUNG'S MODEL OF TYPOLOGY, JANE SELINSKE

- DREAM ANALYSIS: JUNG'S ROYAL ROAD TO THE UNCONSCIOUS, MAXSON J. MCDOWELL

- THE WAY OF COMPLEXES, PART II, SYLVESTER WOJTKOWSKI

FIRST TUESDAY LUNCH FORUM

TUESDAYS, 12:30 - 1:30 P.M., MARCH 4, APRIL 1, MAY 6

CALL FOR DETAILS AND TO REGISTER, 212-697-6430.
VISIT OUR WEB SITE AT WWW.CGJUNGNY.ORG

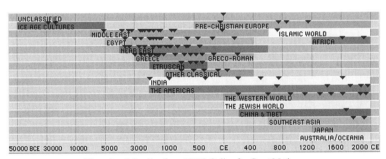

Wisdom of the Psyche:
Depth Psychology after Neuroscience
Ginette Paris, PhD.

Ginette Paris is a psychologist, therapist and writer. She teaches Archetypal and Depth Psychology at Pacifica Graduate Institute in Santa Barbara, California. She is an honorary member of the Jung Society of Montreal, member of the International Association of Jungian Studies, and member of the Board of Directors of the Foundation for Mythological Studies. Her previous books include Pagan Meditations (Spring Publications), and Pagan Grace (Spring Publications).

As a leading scholar and writer in the field of Archetypal Psychology, her latest book Wisdom of the Psyche received the following endorsements:

"Emotionally personal, immediately useful, surprisingly original, beautifully deep, this page-turning read also turns the page into a new century of psychology. What an achievement."
James Hillman, former Director of Studies at the Jung Institute in Zurich

"Once again Ginette Paris demonstrates that she is quite simply the most original and eloquent of all writers on contemporary depth psychology. This book is a brilliant and beautiful account of how a serious accident, a near-fatal brain injury, became not just a trauma but a rare and wonderful opportunity. After the concussion and coma, Paris did not just regain consciousness. She experienced a life-altering transformation that led her to delve below all the gray matter of the current, trendy fascination with neuroscience to explore the "deep psyche." In this book Paris invents an entirely new genre of psychological writing, one that combines intimately personal autobiography, humanely inspirational stories from patients, and radically imaginative theoretical proposals for the future of depth psychology."
Michael Vannoy Adams, Jungian Psychoanalyst

"Wisdom of the Psyche is the bright book of the future for everyone involved with depth psychology and its creative transformation of the arts and sciences. Ginette Paris's stunning achievement is to combine autobiography, history of ideas, clinical originality, psychological theory and philosophical sophistication with the arts of a poet and novelist. Her book is at once lucid, erudite, a delightful companion, and a serious challenge to the academy and the consulting room. Paris gently and powerfully embeds depth psychology in the humanities, making Wisdom of the Psyche essential reading for the twenty-first century. We are all the richer for it."
Susan Rowland, Reader in English and Jungian Studies, University of Greenwich, UK

For more information on the work of Ginette Paris please visit:
The Foundation for Mythological Studies
www.mythology.org

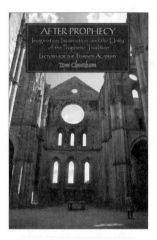

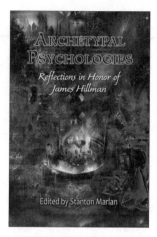